Saving
Big Blue

Saving
Big Blue

PART VIII
On the Future   267

Contents

Saving Big Blue

---

*Leadership Lessons and Turnaround
Tactics of IBM's Lou Gerstner*

ROBERT SLATER

McGraw-Hill

New York   San Francisco   Washington, D.C.   Auckland   Bogotá
Caracas   Lisbon   London   Madrid   Mexico City   Milan
Montreal   New Delhi   San Juan   Singapore
Sidney   Tokyo   Toronto

Library of Congress Cataloging-in-Publication Data

Slater, Robert
Saving Big Blue : leadership lessons and turnaround tactics
    of IBM's Lou Gerstner / by Robert Slater.
New York : McGraw Hill, 1999.
p.   cm.
HD9696.2.U64I257   1999
004/.068 21
0071342117
Includes bibliographical references and index.
International Business Machines Corporation.
Gerstner, Louis V.
Computer industry—United States.
99019749

McGraw-Hill

A Division of The McGraw·Hill Companies

1 2 3 4 5 6 7 8 9 0 DOC/DOC 9 0 3 2 1 0 9 8

ISBN 0-07-134211-7

Printed and bound by R. R. Donnelley & Sons Company.

McGraw-Hill books are available at special quantity discounts to use as premiums and sales promotions, or for use in corporate training programs. For more information, please write to the Director of Special Sales, McGraw-Hill, 11 West 19th Street, New York, NY 10011. Or contact your local bookstore.

This book is printed on recycled, acid-free paper containing a minimum of 50% recycled de-inked fiber.

Deep Blue to Mr. Kasparov: Checkmate!

"A defining moment"

WEDNESDAY, MAY 7, 1997: Equitable Center in New York City, thirty-five stories above the cacophony of midtown Manhattan. Lou Gerstner struts into the Deep Blue war room. Ordinarily the arrival of the CEO would turn heads—but not now. Though these are corporate offices, the scene that lies before Gerstner seems more like something from a science fiction thriller. In place of traditional mahogany desks and swivel-backed chairs, there is a chessboard, with several people hovering over it. Others gaze intently at a video screen across the room that displays the coded thoughts of a super-computer affectionately known as Deep Blue. A second screen shows Gary Kasparov, dressed in a blue jacket and gray trousers, pacing behind a chessboard in the next room.

The war room is ordinarily a television studio. With all the lights and switches and panels, it looks more like a spaceship, but no one in the room has spaceships in mind today. They are too busy watching history in the making. This may seem like an ordinary chess game, but nothing is further from the truth: this is the ultimate contest of man versus machine. A computer is playing a game of chess with a human being.

That's not such a remarkable occurrence in and of itself, but Gary Kasparov is no ordinary chess player; he's the greatest chess player in the world. If Deep Blue wins, it will be the first time a machine has defeated a reigning world chess champion in tournament play.

Computer scientists have wondered for years whether a computer could defeat a human being in a chess game. The reverse has always been considered humdrum, and indeed Kasparov defeated a similar supercomputer two years earlier. But for a computer to win—ah, that would be awesome! That would make history.

The World Is Watching

So nerves are frayed among the IBM research team who built Deep Blue for a mere $2 million. They know that this is Deep Blue's big chance. For some time, the supercomputer has been performing mundane chores that the public seemed to take for granted: running airline reservation systems, simulating nuclear explosions, designing new drugs. Few had paid attention to Deep Blue—until now. But this time the world is watching, and if Deep Blue is able to defeat Gary Kasparov, the world may finally give credence to Lou Gerstner's battle cry ever since he took over IBM: mainframes must remain a key factor in the computer industry.

With Deep Blue and Gary Kasparov still plotting their moves, no one in the room wants to engage Lou Gerstner in long conversation, even though he is their boss and you don't look away when the CEO wants to chat. The team grudgingly exchanges greetings with Gerstner. They are not awed by his presence. They have heard all the horror stories about Gerstner's intimidating nature, but they feel no trepidation. They have a job to do and are glad to see that the boss doesn't plan to stay long. He is here to congratulate them for teaching a computer to play chess at championship level, and while they appreciate the visit— well, sort of—they are far too involved in the match to figure out the real reason for it. If Deep Blue wins, Gerstner wants to make sure he is on hand to relish the historic occasion, because if it wins, this one-ton piece of iron will shine the kind of favorable spotlight on IBM that Gerstner has craved for years.

Rooting for Deep Blue

But there are no guarantees. For IBM to benefit from this event, the Big Guy must perform like no other computer ever has, and that will not be easy. Gary Kasparov is chess's greatest living grand master—many even say the best ever. He can evaluate two moves a second—an impressive speed for a human being. But compared to a computer, it's a turtle's pace. How fast can Deep Blue process moves? Two *million* moves a second—fast enough to put Gary Kasparov's gray matter to shame. Such breathless speed does not automatically mean that the Deep Blue machine can defeat Kasparov in a chess game; it just means the machine can "think" far more quickly. It has always been assumed that for a computer to defeat a human in a chess game, it would need that most human quality, intuition, a quality that no computer ever built appeared to possess.

Despite the long odds, Lou Gerstner finds that he is rooting for Deep Blue, as a father might root for his son competing in a Little League game—with one major difference: this "son" just might make history. With so much riding on the outcome, the IBM chief is starting to feel the pressure. He wants so much to show everyone that what he's been doing at IBM is solid, serious, long-term. The supercomputer in the next room looks like his best bet to convince others that he has done more than turn the company around; that, in fact, he has begun a process that will make IBM the most respected business entity in the United States.

It has been just over four years since Gerstner took over IBM. When he assumed command in April 1993, as shocking as it sounds, the company appeared to be going through its death throes, losing billions of dollars each year with no hope of recovery in sight. Few expected him to be able to perform a miracle—the company was simply too far gone for that. But in the last four years, Gerstner has proved his detractors wrong by performing one miracle after another: rightsizing the bloated bureaucracy, finding all sorts of ways to cut costs, and bringing the company's expenses in line. Sooner than anyone thought possible, he turned losses into profits and lived up to his reputation as one of the greatest turnaround artists in American business.

As he takes in the incongruous scene before him, he knows better than anyone else that IBM can command respect. He knows that the

Wall Street analysts still regard him as a lightweight, as someone who can improve IBM's bottom line, but is incapable of making the company grow and returning it to its former glory. So he wants to give the outside world something to latch on to, something that will signify that IBM is truly back. That is why the events playing out in this tiny room are so important to him today. In an era when the media is infatuated with the software king out in Redmond, Washington, when Wall Street analysts are intoxicated from the heady air of the Internet start-ups, when so many computer companies are growing faster than IBM, a victory by Deep Blue just might make the world sit up and take notice of IBM's recovery, and give Lou Gerstner his rightful due.

Kasparov and Deep Blue are well into the fourth of their six-game match. Thus far, man and machine are dead even: each side has one victory and there have been two draws. The final two games will be played on Saturday and Sunday.

As Lou Gerstner arrives, the game has taken a turn for the worse for IBM's contestant. Kasparov has just taken the initiative with a bold pawn sacrifice. The atmosphere becomes tense. Over the next few hours the two players make a total of fifty-six moves. Neither side gains an edge. The game ends in a draw. The Deep Blue team is worried. Very worried.

Cheering the Team

To dispel the gloom, Gerstner gives his team a pep talk. "It's great what you've done," he says enthusiastically, thinking of all the positive publicity that IBM is reaping from this spectacular match. Gerstner loves what is happening, naturally. The media is exalting him and his company. (On other occasions, in other contexts—when the articles seem not so favorable—Lou Gerstner will turn against the media.)

On one day alone during game 3 earlier that week, the Kasparov–Deep Blue Web site receives 22 million hits. The match also has the effect of bringing all 300,000 IBM employees together in a united cause. No longer merely workers, but now hard-core fans, they gather around television screens at IBM offices to watch thirty-minute highlights of each match; the scene seems more like Monday Night Football than a game of chess.

The historic chess match finally comes to an end on Sunday, May 11. After eight days of back-and-forth drama, a winner emerges; much to the shock of everyone, it is Deep Blue. Gerstner is thrilled. The computer's triumph will set off much debate over how a machine could defeat a human being in chess. Some will argue that the computer's speed in processing information is the secret, while others will credit the computer with the ability to think. But the debate doesn't matter to Gerstner. What really excites him is that many people will be talking about what Deep Blue's victory means for the whole field of information technology.

Had Deep Blue lost its match to Gary Kasparov, Lou Gerstner would not have despaired. Even without the massive publicity that victory brings to IBM, he is confident that he made the right decisions: to get behind mainframes and to promote them as one of IBM's principal product lines. But now, flush with victory, Gerstner is confident that the business world, which had questioned whether he could turn IBM around, will finally stand up and applaud him. Now he feels vindicated.

Deep Blue's victory is a defining moment, a watershed of sorts in computing history. It opens up all sorts of possibilities, some positive and exciting, some decidedly negative and frightening, but all suggesting that one day computers will act like human beings. If the event is a defining moment, however, it will take years to sort out. Meanwhile, the victory showers much attention, all of it positive, on Lou Gerstner and IBM. It helps to erase a lot of the agony and frustration Gerstner has felt during the past four years. It helps to make people forget that a mere four years earlier IBM was at death's door.

On the Road to Collapse

A world without IBM? It sounded preposterous—like a world without television, or automobiles, or baseball. IBM had been one of America's great institutions, one of its most powerful. Wall Street didn't call IBM stock "blue-chip" for nothing. For decades, IBM was the most successful corporation in history. Stripped to the basics, the company made computers, but to call IBM a mere computer maker was to miss the pervasive and all-encompassing nature of the enterprise. This was an institution that had changed the face of corporate America, the way

Americans worked and thought. It was the company that a driven self-starter named Thomas Watson Sr. had built, an organization that had the same solidity, the same durability, as the federal government. The company was known as "Big Blue," after the color of its heavy-duty mainframe computers. The phrase suggested not merely immense size but greatness, not just products but the best products, not just surviving but prospering.

Yet, as the giant computer maker moved through the early 1990s, the enterprise had been brought to its knees and seemed headed for collapse. IBM's founders would have been horrified. After all, they had built the company into a corporate powerhouse through keen business insight. Since its early days in the 1920s, Thomas Watson Sr.'s company had read the business landscape amazingly well. At no time was this more true than during the early 1950s when IBM's leadership began sensing a shift in consumer tastes from one kind of technology to another, from electronic calculators to the dazzling new world of computers. Suddenly, companies choosing to integrate the new mainframe technology into their data processing efforts discovered whole new possibilities for corporate growth. And IBM practically had the field to itself; it was the dominant force throughout the 1950s, 1960s, and 1970s. Indeed, the words "IBM" and "computer" seemed synonymous. In 1964, when IBM moved into its sprawling corporate headquarters atop a hill in Armonk, New York, the company not only dominated the computer industry but stood as the model American corporation of its day.

The decade of the 1980s appeared to be yet another period of splendid IBM success. Certainly the company's financial record was impressive. IBM made more money after taxes—$51 billion—from 1980 to 1989 than any other company in the world. Its market capitalization reached a high of $106 billion in 1987. Three years later, it was the most profitable company on the *Fortune* 500 ($5.987 billion) and its revenue that year reached $69 billion.

In the late 1980s, however, IBM fell on hard times as its arrogant executives stuck to their long-term game plan, endorsing mainframes over the newly emergent personal computers. Earlier in that decade, the company had failed to adapt to the next big change in the world of information technology, personal computers. In 1982, IBM weighed in with its own personal computer. It was small enough and cheap enough to enable people from all walks of life to own a computer, something that until then had been out of the question. For some time, IBM dominated the PC industry, but smaller, more market-savvy competitors gradually ate into IBM's market share. In 1994, Compaq Computer replaced IBM as the top PC maker. IBM missed the boat on other aspects of the technology revolution as well, and that would cost it dearly in the future.

The more the business environment changed, the more market share they forfeited to competing start-ups, the more IBM executives stuck their heads in the sand. Inevitably, as their market share declined, the company hemorrhaged money. By late 1992, the company was out of cash. By 1993, IBM—by now dubbed the dinosaur of the computer industry—seemed on the verge of falling apart. It was suffering the worst year in its history. Though its 1992 revenues were an impressive $64.5 billion, the company had lost money for the second straight year—this time, a whopping $4.97 billion! As a result, over 117,000 employees lost their jobs and the company was forced to write off more than $28 billion in restructuring charges.

Worst of all, while corporate re-engineering would have improved IBM's income statement, few of its executives had the heart to drive a knife through the "job-for-life" policy that had been a cornerstone of the IBM culture. The only solution, however paradoxical, was to dismember the mighty corporate behemoth, to split the whole into a series of smaller, independent parts. The only way for the patient to survive was to sever the body, limb by limb. Was this really the best way to save Big Blue? By January 1993, though the plan to split the company up was going forward, the IBM board decided it was time to make a change at the top. Although the board wasn't convinced that an IBM turnaround was even possible, John Akers, the current chairman and chief executive, had to go. The company was losing billions and billions of dollars under his leadership.

Does Anybody Want This Job?

IBM's financial woes were hardly a secret, so finding someone to take on such a tough assignment would not be easy. At first, the board had hoped to entice one of the great captains of industry to take over the IBM helm. Leaders with impressive track records in the technology field were given preference. The argument went that only one of those leaders could steer IBM out of its rut. Some of the top CEOs in the United States were sounded out. All of them were flattered, but none would touch the job with the proverbial ten-foot pole. They had read all the somber news stories, and they did not want to sully their hard-won reputations by attempting to run a company that seemed beyond repair.

The board grew desperate. If the original criterion—finding someone with years of hands-on experience in running a technology company—had seemed important at first, it fell by the wayside as the rejections piled up. The board had no other choice but to lower its standards. The new CEO need not have technology experience, but preferably, he or she would have experience in turning large companies around. Some board members began focusing on a man who had been running a huge snack food and cigarette company, RJR Nabisco (of *Barbarians at the Gate* fame). Lou Gerstner had been chairman and CEO of RJR Nabisco for four years, and had spent the previous eleven years as a top executive at American Express. He had acquired a wonderful reputation for turning around companies in trouble. The problem was that he had no direct experience in running a technology company. Some board members were disturbed by that, but the more the board focused on Louis V. Gerstner Jr., the more they thought he was the right choice.

In April 1993, Gerstner took over as chairman and CEO of IBM. For the first time in the company's history IBM had found a leader from outside its ranks. Few gave him much chance of reviving IBM; most thought Thomas Watson's firm would slowly wither away. Gerstner's task was monumental—nothing less than the toughest managerial job in corporate America. The challenge was to keep this once-legendary icon alive, and, once survival was assured, get the patient out of intensive care. No one expected Gerstner to return IBM to its earlier heyday. That seemed out of the question.

Today, six years later, Lou Gerstner has turned IBM around and once again established it as the world's greatest computer maker. No one in American business can quite believe it. But no one denies that Gerstner has performed the miracle that everyone thought was impossible. Taking over a company that was stagnating, Gerstner presided over an IBM in 1998 that had record revenues of $81.7 billion, a 4 percent increase over the previous year ($78.5 billion, then the sixth highest revenue rate of American corporations). Reversing a trend that saw

IBM lose money for three straight years—1991, 1992, and 1993—
Gerstner turned the company around so that in 1998 it had a profit of
$6.3 billion—up $200 million over the previous year. The Gerstner
miracle has been forged through the kind of corporate re-engineering
that had been unacceptable to previous IBM leaders. Gerstner examined every nook and cranny of IBM with the fresh, bottom-line perspective of an outsider. And then he made his moves, rebuilding a new,
more competitive IBM, more customer-oriented, more conscious of
the ever-changing business environment.

In making IBM profitable once again, Gerstner still struggles with
the age-old question of how to make a company the size of IBM grow
steadily and consistently. IBM's strength—and its weakness—is that it
remains a hardware-oriented company. Today, $34.7 billion of its total
1998 revenues come from hardware sales. Yet, those hardware sales have
been essentially flat since 1995. Moreover, IBM ended 1998 with about
half—$40 billion—of its businesses down. Overall, IBM was not grow-
ing very much at all (only 4 percent in 1998 and 3.4 percent in 1997,
down from 5.6 percent in 1996; and quite a way off the 12 percent
growth of 1995).

The lack of meaningful growth is strong evidence that the Gerstner miracle is not complete. He has made IBM profitable again. But he
has done so by relying upon a set of business techniques that have little or nothing to do with spurring the company's growth. That has
been Lou Gerstner's dilemma. As he struggles to achieve a complete
turnaround at IBM, or more accurately perhaps, because of his strug-
gle, Gerstner and IBM constitute one of the most intriguing business
stories of our era.

How did Lou Gerstner achieve the turnaround at IBM? What has
he succeeded in doing? And where has he failed? Answering those two
questions will form the main theme of this book. We will use Gerstner's
management secrets and business strategies as the organizing principle
for this work and show the reader how those secrets and strategies provided the linchpin for IBM's recovery. But we will also examine the
shortcomings of Gerstner's strategies and explain how they have kept
IBM from becoming the growth company that it once was.

I

The Death Spiral and the Savior

———◆———

"The fact that we're losing share
makes me goddamn mad. . . .
Everyone is too comfortable at
a time when the business
is in crisis."
(John Akers)

———◆———

Chapter 1

———◆———

Don't Take Success
for Granted

**"We've gone from being perhaps too invincible to
perhaps having more problems than people expected."**

*F*OR DECADES, it seemed routine to think of IBM
as the most successful company on the planet. No other company
enjoyed so dominant a position in corporate life; was so well managed;
and was such a trendsetter. The company was founded by a New York
farm boy named Thomas J. Watson Sr. Prior to his days at IBM, he had
been a traveling organ salesman, a sewing machine salesman, and a
peddler of phony building company stock (although he did not know
they were phony at the time). Around 1900 he began working for the
National Cash Register Company in Dayton, Ohio, and became its best
salesman. In 1912, indicted along with owner John Patterson and
twenty-seven other NCR officials for antitrust violations (including
sabotaging competitor's machines), he was convicted and sentenced to
a year in jail, but he won a retrial on appeal. The trial never took place
because when a flood hit Dayton, NCR's officials, including Watson,
acted heroically in the disaster relief effort; no one wanted to prosecute
the case further and Watson served no jail time.

After John Patterson fired Watson over a minor dispute about sales strategies, Tom took over the Computer Tabulating Recording Company, forerunner to IBM, in 1914. It had been marketing an electrical punch-card accounting system developed for the 1890 census; it also sold adding machines, scales, and meat slicers. Watson was a genius of a salesman and doubled sales to $10 million by the early 1920s. In 1924, Watson changed the name of his business to International Business Machines Corporation, conveying the scope he envisioned for his fledgling company.

Because of the Depression in the 1930s, Watson's efforts to push tabulating machines and time clocks were greeted with little success. By 1939 IBM had sales of only $39.5 million a year. Nevertheless the company managed to grow while the rest of the American economy was in a tailspin. Always interested in creating loyalty, IBM was one of the first firms to provide group life insurance (1934), survivor benefits (1935), and paid vacations (1936) to its employees. In a historic and mountain-sized gamble, Watson ignored the weak demand for new machines and kept his factories humming. Two events occurred that provided IBM with a big boost. One was the Social Security Act of 1935; the other was the Wages-Hours Act of 1937. Both pieces of legislation required businesses to record the wages paid, hours worked, and overtime earned for America's 26 million workers; the legislation brought to life virtually overnight the market for tabulating machines and time clocks.

Because it had continued to manufacture products during the Depression, IBM was positioned to lead the new industry. Orders from other American government departments soon followed. IBM was on its way and Thomas Watson never looked back. From that time on, IBM dominated its markets, always setting the standard, always out front. In the early 1950s, in one of the most important steps in American business history, IBM produced the computers that transformed the way people worked. For years, IBM *was* the computer industry!

IBM went from strength to strength after World War II. In 1946, its revenues reached $119.4 million, with $18.8 million in profits. Four years later, the company controlled nearly 95 percent of the punch-card machine business. That supremacy gave IBM tremendous advantages when it entered the computer market in 1952. Although rival Remington Rand was first out with its Univac, Thomas Watson launched an all-out drive and built a better electronic computer, called the 701; it was designed primarily for scientific calculations and performed 21,000 calculations a second. The 701 was widely considered far superior to Univac; as a result, IBM felt free to charge whatever it liked for its new product. Twenty 701s were produced, leased at the extraordinary price of $24,000 a month. Known also as the Defense Calculator, the 701 launched IBM as a real computer firm.

In 1956, IBM's revenues had grown to $734.5 million, with profits of $68.6 million. IBM clinched its lead in the computer industry by designing, building, marketing, and servicing the System 360, the first real general-purpose mainframe computer, which it introduced in April 1964. The 360 rapidly swept up 70 percent of the computer market. By 1965, IBM's revenues had mushroomed to $2.4 billion, with $333 million in profits. That same year, IBM controlled 65.3 percent of the computer industry's market. (Sperry Rand, its next closest rival, controlled only 12.1 percent.) In 1979, IBM's revenues had grown to $9.4 billion with a spectacular bottom line of $3 billion, an unheard of feat in today's business world, where competition and costs keep profits in check.

IBM's muscular showing in the 1950s and 1960s was due to a number of factors. Its management was among the best in the country. Its products were always at the cutting edge of technology and they were user-friendly. (Because IBM equipment was rented, not purchased, it was easy to upgrade both hardware and software.) And the company was not afraid to invest heavily in its future, allocating huge amounts to research and development. Its research unit had division status and was second to none.

But the key to IBM's success was its finely tuned corporate culture, which prized excellence above all else. But it was a culture that reflected Watson's maniacal ego and encouraged almost blind obedience to his sometimes quirky convictions. Other business leaders encouraged corporate cultures that followed along strictly business lines, but with Watson, the emphasis was always on the personal. Other CEOs offered vague hints that employees should dress in a businesslike manner. Nothing in the Watson dress code was left to chance; every article of clothing fit Watson's image of the professional businessman. With its insistence on dark suits, dark ties, white shirts, starched collars, garters, and fedoras, Watson's dress code was supposed to make the

IBM employee always look presentable, but he also hoped to engender fierce company loyalty, which he believed was a vital ingredient in the IBM success formula. His bizarre approach to the culture may seem extreme, but IBM did dominate the computer industry for decades, so it's hard to fault Watson's peculiar style. Nevertheless, while corporate pride may have been his goal, what he really created was the kind of rigidity and uniformity that one might expect to find among obedient soldiers serving under some Patton-like general.

Early-Morning Frank Sinatras

The IBM culture regulated almost all aspects of an employee's life, from the way he dressed to the way he thought. To encourage employees to take more time in deliberating the best business move, Watson placed THINK signs on office walls. As part of that "Isn't IBM just great?" theme, no form of behavior, however unbusiness-like, was off limits. He even encouraged employees to belt out company songs, turning them into early-morning Frank Sinatras. (One lyric went: "Our voices swell in admiration; / Of T. J. Watson proudly sing; / He'll ever be our inspiration; / To him our voices loudly ring.") Not only was the employee expected to love the company; he had to lead an impeccable personal life, as defined by Thomas Watson Sr. Divorce was frowned upon, and so was drinking during office hours. If you took a drink during lunch, you were expected to go straight home and not return to work that day. Whatever might prove embarrassing to the company was to be eschewed. When one executive hired *Playboy* bunnies to appear at a sales meeting, he was promptly fired.

In return for doing their jobs well, and to strengthen loyalty even more, IBM employees were promised something that would be unthinkable in today's business environment: a job for life. Short of hiring *Playboy* bunnies for a sales meeting, you were assured of never being fired. Those found wanting received more training or were given less demanding work. One former employee recalled the company's "rarefied WASP world with few hospitable gates but lots of banners, company songs, Mao-like photos and mottoes.... For generations, IBM was run like a benevolent Jesuit order. You donned a blue suit and white shirt and never touched alcohol in public places. A more straitlaced attitude toward social behavior would be hard to find short of a seminary for prepubescent girls in 19th-century France." Because of the banners, the songs, the Mao-like photos—or perhaps despite them—IBM flourished.

But the Watsons—Thomas Watson Sr., and then Thomas Watson Jr.—did not think they were running IBM like a "benevolent religious order." They preferred to think of the company as their extended family. Watson Sr. insisted that employees try their best, but like a parent who would never expel a child from a family, Watson wanted his workers to feel that they had a permanent home at IBM. Maintaining the theme that "We're all one big happy family," Watson made sure to bestow gifts on special occasions: a silver spoon for a worker's newborn baby, a watch when an employee retired. The gifts carried a subtle message: We are promising you a job for life. In return, we expect you to work hard at your job, follow a few simple rules, and remain fiercely loyal to IBM. Working hard at the job did not mean, however, spending 24 hours a day in the office. Accordingly, for the princely sum of $1 a year, Watson arranged for IBM country club memberships. The employee always came first.

Infected with Blinding Hubris

To work for IBM was to be a member of a special elite. The selection process was rigorous, the pay was great, and the job security was the best. Big Blue's employees were the crème de la crème, and they had no real incentive to look for other work. Why should they? Whenever they arrived at a cocktail party, people acted as if a movie celebrity had suddenly entered their circle. Whenever IBM salespeople showed up at a business, little time was wasted before they were ushered to the corner office. After all, although the company did not sell directly to consumers, it possessed one of the best-known brand-names in the world. An aura of glamour and success surrounded the IBM sales representative.

Feeling a culture-induced pride in the company, feeling that one had the best (or at least the most secure) job in the world, IBM employees produced state-of-the-art products, and then marketed those products with stunning effectiveness. No product illustrated IBM's grip on the market better than its System 360 mainframe, introduced in April 1964. Its six models, launched at the same time, incorporated radically advanced software that worked on large and small computers alike. Soon, the 360 owned 70 percent of the computer market. Thanks to the

360, IBM became the standard in computers at hundreds of American corporations and the undisputed industry leader.

The IBM success story persisted through the 1970s and even into the 1980s. The company seemed invincible. Even when the federal government sought to defang IBM in the late 1960s, charging it with monopolistic practices, the company eventually triumphed: Soon after taking office in 1981, Ronald Reagan decided that the government had no case against Big Blue. In the early 1980s, when the United States was in the midst of a recession, IBM practically doubled its operating income, to $11.2 billion in 1984. As long as the profit margins remained high, as long as revenues continued to grow, the Best Way was the IBM Way. When *Fortune* magazine began publishing its list of Most Admired Corporations in 1982, IBM ranked number one for the first four years. Everyone expected it to remain there forever, especially since it had the best bottom line. From 1980 to 1989, IBM made more money after taxes ($51 billion) than any other company in the world. Throughout the 1980s, it was the most valuable U.S. company; its market capitalization soared to $62.4 billion by 1990, more than double the value of General Motors. It certainly seemed that IBM had figured out the best way to make and price a product, the best way to send a sales force into the field, and the best way to run a company. Customers were in awe of IBM technology, and the word at most corporations was that no one would get fired for purchasing IBM equipment. After all, you don't punish someone for buying the best.

On the surface, the high-flying company was riding the greatest wave of prosperity in its history. Until the late 1970s, IBM had been renting its mainframes rather than selling them outright; but then it joined the rest of the industry and began selling computers to customers directly. That shift sparked unprecedented mainframe sales and it appeared that IBM had figured out how to print money.

But hard as it may seem to believe, in the midst of all its stunning success, IBM was a company with deep, potentially fatal flaws. For no one wanted to ask the right questions, and no one had the temerity to argue for change. Why sound ornery and cynical about a company that seemed almost too good to be true?

Although executives refused to acknowledge it, their very success contained seeds of the hubris that would hasten their downfall. The problem started when they began to believe in the company's invincibility. They had become infected with a blind arrogance that would send the company into a near-death tailspin. So confident was IBM back in 1981 that its mainframe-driven business had only one way to go—up—that its executives set a goal of expanding revenue from $40 billion to $100 billion by 1990.

Unfortunately, that smugness had the effect of keeping IBM from recognizing the massive changes taking place in the computer industry. The personal computer revolution was in full swing, but you wouldn't have known that at IBM. Lucy Baney began working at IBM in 1973 as a programmer and at one time was assistant to chairman John Akers; later she was director of service marketing before she left the company in 1992 and became president and CEO of Access Technologies Group in Norwalk, Connecticut. She attributed IBM's shortsightedness to an all-pervasive conservatism that allowed its leadership to dismiss the new reality without a second thought: "IBM executives were not allowed to talk to the press without a whole cadre of people around them. IBM didn't court the press. IBM didn't court people, which amazed me because the world was changing. They had always done things one way and that was the way they were gong to do it. They didn't entertain new ways of doing things. Consequently, they were very isolated from what was going on in the rest of the world. They still possessed that mainframe mentality despite the fact that the PC revolution had taken place in the early 1980s. It still hadn't hit home that the world was changing and IBM simply could not maintain its huge investment in mainframes."

Overlooking Bill Gates

So anchored were the company's business strategies on the mainframe, so flush was IBM from its huge profits, that it would adopt any measure, however wrongheaded, to assure that mainframe sales were not affected. It was a case of "if it ain't broke, don't fix it." At one stage, the company undertook research to replace traditional mainframe processors with new low-cost microchips called CMOS—complementary metal-oxide semiconductors. But IBM's management dismissed CMOS technology, unrealistically confident that rivals would not adopt the technology and thus force Big Blue into doing the same. At another stage, IBM failed to exploit a new technology called RISC, which stood for "reduced instruction-set computing." The irony was that IBM had invented the RISC microprocessor in 1974; it understood better than others that the new technology would mean simplified and faster computing, and would be well suited to the newly popular mini-computers. But none of this mattered when weighed against IBM's commitment to the mainframe. Nothing would eat into Big Blue's mainframe profits. As a result, RISC lacked a champion inside IBM. It remained on the company shelf while its rivals, free to pursue new technologies, plunged ahead with its development.

By staying so narrowly focused on mainframes, IBM missed opportunities to grow. Back in the 1980s, when Microsoft and Intel were mere mortals in the computer industry, IBM might have tried to acquire them, but being acquisitive was not a part of Big Blue's culture. Rather than try to buy out Bill Gates, IBM permitted him to grab the license to the operating system for IBM personal computers. It also failed to capitalize on business that was well within its reach, such as developing relational databases. It sat back as computer mogul Larry Ellison took the idea and built Oracle into a software powerhouse. Retrospectively, IBM cannot bring itself to look at the disastrous 1980s with any degree of frankness. The company history that appears on its Web site acknowledges that IBM struggled and was thrown into turmoil by the PC revolution; and then by the client-server revolution, which linked PCs (the clients) with larger computers (the servers). It also acknowledges that the shift toward PCs deprived IBM of its traditional "solutions" business: "Both revolutions transformed the way customers viewed, used and bought technology. And both fundamentally rocked IBM. Businesses' purchasing decisions were put in the hands of individuals and departments—not the places where IBM had long-standing customer relationships. Piece-part technologies took precedence over integrated solutions. The focus was on the desktop and personal productivity, not on business applications across the enterprise." What the company history leaves out is the crucial role that hubris and arrogance, exhibited at the highest levels of the company, played in causing IBM to miss and dismiss the obvious changes that were occurring within its midst.

A Moment of Panic?

For someone who took the time to probe the company, it was not that hard to figure out what was happening to IBM. Even as the handwriting was on the wall, as personal computers became the hot, new product of the 1980s, IBM stubbornly clung to the past. When it came to mainframes, IBM had figured out that the wisest course was to control all profit sources by manufacturing everything: hardware, software, and semiconductors. But when it came to producing its own personal computer, which went to market in 1982, IBM seemed to have suffered from a memory lapse, forgetting the strategy that had served them well for so many decades; rather than produce their own equipment, IBM looked to Microsoft to supply the operating system software and to Intel to supply the chips. Other companies were also sought out: most of the disk drives came from Tandon, SCI Systems made the circuit boards, and Epson manufactured the printer. Moreover, IBM refused to use its own innovative chip technology; if it had done so, it could have eliminated the need to turn to rivals Microsoft and Intel.

It should be pointed out that IBM was powerful enough in those days to dominate the personal computer industry. For example, it would not have been too difficult for the company to have bought out the two enterprises that are major factors in the personal computer industry today, namely, Microsoft and Intel. But instead, IBM inadvertently turned those two companies into its chief rivals. To some IBM analysts, the decision to outsource parts of the IBM personal computer was a dramatic turning point in the company's slide. Some saw it as a moment of panic, a time when IBM was so desperate to get product out into the market that it abandoned its long and successful policy of manufacturing all parts of a product itself. Had it chosen to do otherwise, it would have reaped all the profits that instead went to Microsoft and Intel, and it might have enjoyed the same lock on the personal computer industry that it held on the mainframe field.

For all the misjudgments it had made, IBM was pleased to watch its PC unit grow into a $5 billion business within two years. The early success, however, would not last: IBM's overheads were too steep; and by creating an "open" system for its PC, IBM allowed a myriad of clones to grab market share. Newcomers selling personal computers grew into industry giants at vertiginous speed: Apple Computer reached the *Fortune* 500 list in only five years, a record that lasted only until Compaq, founded in 1983, accomplished the same deed in only three. The victory of the clones should logically have been IBM's loss, but the company's executives did not feel demoralized. Still convinced that IBM's main business was in mainframes, IBM executives remained dismissive about the whole new field of personal computers; if their own product, the IBM PC, was losing ground to other PC rivals, so be it. At least it was proving no competition to the company's mainframe business. By 1988, IBM's share of the personal computer field had dropped to 16 percent. Compaq, leader of the clones, had twice IBM's market share. Ironically, for all of IBM's efforts to keep its mainframe business from sliding, that market share had atrophied from 70 percent to only 53 percent.

While any other business leader would have insisted that IBM diversify, that it build up other product lines besides its mainframes, nothing would budge John Akers and his colleagues. Though Bill Gates, the chairman and CEO of Microsoft, understood from the start that the real growth business of the 1980s and 1990s would be software, not personal computers, IBM's leadership clung to the view that it was hardware—read mainframes—that would drive any computer business. "Software," noted Sam Albert, the veteran IBM watcher who worked at the company from 1959 to 1989, "was looked upon as the stuff that had to run on hardware. The IBM salesman got a commission for selling hardware. He didn't get a commission for selling service, or software."

Swimming through Peanut Butter

Though IBM appeared to be doing well financially during the decade of the 1980s, fissures appeared, dispelling that notion. For instance, in 1985 and 1986, IBM's profits dropped for the first time since the 1930s. In 1986, revenues (then around the $50 billion mark) were flat, marking the first time the company had not grown in forty years. That same year, IBM's market value fell by $22 billion during one seven-month period and the company's return on equity fell by 6 percent. Still, it was hard to find too much fault at IBM, since the company's profits (nearly $5 billion) topped all other corporations.

The public seemed to be growing weary of IBM. Of the 300 companies ranked in *Fortune* magazine's Most Admired Companies list for 1986, IBM ranked second in financial soundness but fifth in its ability to attract people, eighth in long-term investment value, ninth in the quality of its management, and tenth in the use of corporate assets. In 1985, it had been first in all those categories. Worst of all, IBM was no longer the most admired company in America. It had fallen to seventh place. When he learned of the latest list, John Akers offered this vague, indeed lame, explanation: "We've gone from being perhaps too invincible to perhaps having more problems than people expected." One indication of how desperate the company seemed: It announced that 1987 would be "The Year of the Customer" and everyone at IBM was told to put the customer at the top of their priorities—as if customers didn't head that list at all times.

By putting all its eggs in the mainframe basket, IBM was forced to spend huge amounts of money on that aspect of the business. If anything happened to that business, the company would be left with all those expenses and no revenues to show for them. The logical conclusion was to cut expenses as quickly as possible. The trouble was that IBM kept its collective head in the sand throughout the 1980s and into the early 1990s, and it was slow, terribly slow, in coming to a decision that the costs associated with the mainframe business were way too high.

The biggest costs came from its bloated bureaucracy. The excessive fat had its genesis in the development of the System/360 in the mid-1960s. Manufacturing the then new family of System/360 computers required the building of five factories. This was too complex a task for the company, and chaos ensued. To end the chaos, IBM added one employee after another, and the bureaucracy mushroomed. Between 1963 and 1966, while sales in constant dollars were rising about 97 percent, IBM's head count went up almost 130 percent, from 87,000 to 198,000. Over the next twenty years employee rolls mounted slowly but surely, to a peak of 407,000 in 1986. All those people. All those salaries. The costs were enormous.

Philip Baker spent many years working for IBM's telecommunications unit. He was managing a group of engineers in the late 1980s, "and it just so happened that our management was meeting in Tampa. They would meet for several days and I would take my whole department to Tampa, all expenses paid, for two to three days. It was certainly a very expensive proposition. And it wasn't unique to us."

IBM was becoming bloated. Just as an overweight boxer finds it difficult to bounce around the ring, IBM's top-heavy bureaucracy had problems making quick moves in the increasingly competitive computer field. Trying to get action out of IBM personnel, suggested one irate customer, was like swimming through "giant pools of peanut butter."

While customers were swimming through peanut butter, insiders at IBM were running up against a mixture of Byzantine politics and nasty little fiefdoms that anesthetized the entrepreneurial spirit which had made IBM famous. Ideas to save money, however good, however useful to the company, had little chance of being implemented. The decision-making process was simply too long, too complex, too off-putting. "It seemed like you had to run it up the management chain," said one former midlevel executive. "Everyone had to get a shot at it. What mattered the most were the personalities and politics involved. Who was going to be inconvenienced? Whose ox would be gored in the process? Whose budget would it come out of?"

Attacking without a Machete

Whatever IBM tried in the 1980s seemed a case of too little, too late. Even when it embarked on a program to reduce the size of its bureaucracy, the old corporate culture that centered on the job-for-life outlook kept IBM's leadership from making much headway. From 1986 to 1991, IBM decreased its workforce by 21,000 employees and closed nineteen American factories, but costs were not reduced quickly or extensively enough since IBM refused to violate its long-standing no-layoff policy. No one was fired. John Akers simply pared payrolls through normal attrition and highly attractive early-retirement packages. Employees working in plants that were to be closed were simply transferred to other IBM plants. It was as if Tom Watson Sr. had reappeared, shaking a finger of warning at John Akers, insisting that he honor Watson's most important business precept: respect for the individual. Sam Albert recalled the pressures on Akers: "It was sacrosanct not to fire somebody or to lay somebody off. It was called respect for the individual—taken to the extreme. A person's job counted more than the balance sheet of the company. In fact, IBM's executives couldn't even bring themselves to call what they were doing 'layoffs.' How could they fire people who had been their friends for years. They called it 'surplussing action.' You were 'surplussed.' The job simply went away. That policy of not firing people accounted for 80 percent of the debt that IBM accumulated in the early 1990s."

From 1986 through 1992, IBM claimed to have reduced its workforce by over 80,000 employees, but that figure is deceptive. It *did* reduce the workforce, but it did so largely through attrition. The actions that John Akers took, while seemingly prudent, were all illusion: Big Blue stayed big—too big. As a result, IBM could never get its costs down to where it could compete in the emerging markets of PCs and workstations. Even when earnings began to fall, it was difficult for IBM to cut back. In an ideal world, the boss would have seen what needed to be done and given orders to dismiss people. But John Akers was far too much of an IBM insider to turn on his own friends. According to Dan Mandresh, who worked for IBM from 1957 to 1967, and then as a senior analyst of the computer industry with Merrill Lynch from 1975 to 1998: "Akers recognized that the problem was, where you have a history and ties to the past, every time you aim at the target, it moves; Akers was prepared to change things, but he was part of the very culture that he wanted to change. He attacked it but without a machete."

Rather than help IBM recuperate, Akers' fictitious pruning had serious negative effects. Concerned that they would soon be "surplussed," IBM employees became apprehensive about everything they did, more cautious, more conservative, more inclined to toe the line. By the early 1990s the concern had turned into raw fear. If the company that would never fire anyone had come around to "surplussing" people, if hardworking, competent IBM employees near the end of their careers were encouraged to leave, the next step could well be outright dismissals of recently recruited employees. And so the fear spread, creating an environment where people kept their heads down and thought less and less about what was good for the business. Meetings went on endlessly without seeming purpose and new ideas were anathema. No one wanted to take the risk of suggesting an idea that others would veto. "You didn't innovate," said one executive who was eventually let go. "You didn't want to do anything that would give you a high profile unless you could find something that was really great."

At the outset of the 1980s IBM's executives, intoxicated by the heady air of high profits, sensing that the company had no place to go but up, were optimistically predicting that Big Blue would be a $100 billion business in ten years. And at first blush, there seemed no reason to question their forecasts. What they could not see—what they simply *refused* to see—were the warning signs bubbling just under the surface.

The out-of-control costs that made it impossible to be profitable. A love affair with mainframes that blinded everyone to the new realities of the marketplace. A conviction that what had worked for IBM so well in the past would automatically work in the future. The warning signs should have caused executives to take IBM down new paths, should have forced them to place their resources and their inventories in fresh product lines. But the blindness to reality that had dictated IBM's course of action in the 1980s would wash away the hoped-for growth. By 1990 the company had revenues of only $68 billion, far short of the $100 billion figure that IBM leaders had so naively predicted. But far worse than the diminished revenues was the sense that the once-vaunted leader of the computer industry was edging toward a precipice and would soon fall over, plunging to disaster.

Chapter 2

———◆———

Arrogance Can Be Fatal

**"A company that was once in control of the industry
had lost control of the industry in every respect."**
(Laura Conigliaro)

*W*HAT HAD BROUGHT IBM to its knees? Most argued that a noxious arrogance had infected the company, an arrogance based on the conviction that IBM's historic achievements gave its employees the right to believe that the company had all the answers. It knew what products to bring to market better than anyone else; it knew how to market them better; and it knew how to get the most out of its employees. When a reporter asked IBM chairman and CEO John Akers in 1988 whether it wouldn't be wise for the company to bring in outside managers who might have new perspectives and new ideas, Akers seemed shocked, even offended at the suggestion. IBM, he insisted, had the best recruitment system anywhere and spent more than anyone on training. No doubt it might make sense to seek outsiders with unusual skills, he acknowledged, but the company already employed the best people in the world. In short, IBM had *all* the answers.

John Akers was the quintessential IBM leader: direct and decisive, charming and self-confident. He was said to have sound instincts and a firm grasp of the big picture. He was so self-disciplined that, according to a former college roommate, he even scheduled time to play cards.

His workday ended at 5:30 P.M. sharp and he never worked weekends, reserving that time for playing golf or bridge.

John Akers was born on December 28, 1934, in Boston. After graduating from Yale University, he served as a carrier pilot in the U.S. Navy until he was discharged in 1960. Soon after, he joined IBM as a sales trainee in San Francisco and rose quickly through the marketing ranks—the traditional path to senior posts at IBM. In 1976, he was appointed vice president; six years later, he was named senior vice president. He was elected IBM president in 1983, CEO in February 1985, and chairman of the board sixteen months later, in June 1986.

Because Akers and his colleagues had come up through the company's marketing ranks, they believed that IBM must keep growing. They were cautious men as well, and accordingly they came to rely on the old standby, the mainframes, for that growth. The risks in successfully steering new products to market seemed unreasonably high. Big Iron (the phrase used to describe mainframes) had been good to them over the years, and they were going to stick to their mainframes come hell or high water.

IBM's institutional arrogance ran deep. Arrogance kept senior executives from asking some key questions: Does relying on hardware make sense in the new business environment? Shouldn't IBM move heavily into the service dimension, given consumers' need for help with their computers? No one at the top was prepared to argue that IBM ought to give more weight to other product lines, or focus more on the needs of computer consumers. No senior executive had the foresight to propose that IBM move into the service field with full force. At times, John Akers appeared to catch on; he suggested that IBM would soon go through a paradigm shift, that the company would move beyond selling only large computer systems, that it would get into software systems and consulting services. But that was all lip service. Nothing changed.

It was not as if everyone was blind to the company's problems. Those closer to the customer—at the lower and middle levels—sensed that the company had to shift gears. But their superiors had no interest in such heretical talk. "The senior people knew what was going on but they were insulated and inward-looking," observed Gideon Gartner, who has been a top IBM watcher for several decades: "There were people who had some sense, who did read the outside press, who had tracked what people were saying—and who knew of all the criticism of

IBM. IBM had weathered the minicomputers as an alternative to mainframes in the 1970s, but the minis had not had as much impact on mainframes then as PCs would have. By the early 1980s, when personal computers came along, IBM's leaders simply grew too confident."

No More Foils, Please!

Making matters worse, IBM's ultraconservative culture militated against change, dampening all entrepreneurial initiatives. It was as if the spirit of Thomas Watson Sr. was greeting every IBM employee each morning with these words: "We've done things this way for a long time, and it's worked. Don't rock the boat!" Executives were rewarded less for coming up with ideas than for making classy presentations at meetings. One middle-level executive from that period recalled "this unreasonable anxiety about whether your foils were going to be aesthetically adequate. If not, you'd get criticized, maybe more so than for the ideas and content. It got to be so crazy that our group executive told us: 'Stop this. I don't want to see all these multicolored foils [or overheads, in today's vernacular] and expensive presentations.' But it didn't stop. It was a sign of the times that it didn't stop."

Here and there some senior IBM executives tried to speak out in favor of change, but they were almost entirely ignored. Carl Conti began at IBM as a junior engineer in 1959. Before leaving the company at the end of 1991, he had risen to become senior vice president and general manager of IBM's enterprise systems, of which the mainframe division is a major part. He had always felt that IBM was not doing as badly as others had suggested; it had good products and it knew how to sell those products. But he acknowledged that a certain malaise had set in. "It troubled me greatly. Frequently in the press the mainframe business was blamed. But exactly the opposite was the case. The mainframe business was successful and profitable. I always talked about the need for other kinds of computing and tying them all together. Tying them together was IBM's unique capability because IBM could play in every arena. Frankly, we didn't execute well. For example, it took IBM forever to get a competitive workstation."

Why was there a lack of execution? "Corporate welfare was a heck of a problem," he recalled. "The tendency was to tolerate a different set of standards for new, emerging businesses than the company was accustomed to in existing businesses. We [in the mainframe business] were making money hand over fist. I can certainly understand when the people who ran IBM wanted to use highly profitable existing businesses [like the mainframe division] to fund new businesses. But they should have been tough and hard-nosed with the new businesses. So we didn't move rapidly and precisely as we should have."

Like Carl Conti, many other IBM employees understood the new reality: They knew that IBM's sales force had become lazy, spending less and less time where it counted—in the field, holding the customer's hand. (One IBM-sponsored survey revealed that company sales reps had been devoting only 30 percent of their work time to customers.) But no one thought it necessary to light a fire under the sales force, or to ask why the company had grown so indifferent. The answer was all too apparent. By the 1960s and 1970s, when it seemed that IBM's supremacy would last forever, the incentive to work hard had declined. If senior executives were indifferent to the growing ennui at the lower levels, IBM's customers most decidedly were not, often complaining that it was becoming too burdensome to work with IBM employees.

On the Verge of Collapse

For years, the name IBM had been sufficient to woo customers in large numbers to the company's mainframes. It was assumed—incorrectly, as it turned out—that the same would hold true for its PCs. IBM salespeople simply took for granted that customers would eat up whatever the company rolled out of its factories. But the 1980s were not the 1970s; there were many more products from which to choose, and that forced the consumer to shop for the best value. With so many attractive options, they no longer had to buy whatever salespeople recommended, which, in the past, had usually been IBM. Customers were discovering better values in the personal computer market, so increasingly they opted for personal computers from companies like Dell, Compaq, Radio Shack, Kaypro, and Apple. As IBM's market share in personal computers dropped, John Akers and his team, ignoring the realities, pointed the finger of blame at anyone and anything but IBM. It was the fault of the American economy, or the turmoil in Europe. It was never IBM's fault. It simply could not be.

———

By the 1980s IBM seemed to be spinning out of control. Respect for John Akers' leadership was steadily diminishing. When he made corporatewide pronouncements over the company's video network, IBM-ers breezed past the screen, rarely stopping to watch the boss. They were disdainful of the "Akers Network," as they called it derisively, because the boss appeared more eager to grab the limelight than to communicate any meaningful message. The sad image of John Akers issuing pep talks over a video network that no one watched seemed an apt symbol of the company's decline. As Laura Conigliaro, a managing director in the Investment Research Department at Goldman, Sachs, saw it: "IBM was on the verge of collapse, definitely, but not in the traditional sense of a financial collapse leading to bankruptcy or something like that. But it was no less calamitous. A company that was once in control of the industry had lost control in every respect. It was being pulled and tugged by other smaller companies. Not only did IBM have no direction, but the actions it took within the company were making things worse. It employed Band-Aid approaches to problems. Management rarely gave the impression that it was stepping back and making a strategic assessment. Management was very impressionable. They were getting advice from every direction. The last advice was the advice they took. There was a serious absence of forceful leadership."

Goddamn Mad

John Akers kept struggling, hoping to find a way to resurrect IBM, but getting angrier and more frustrated at every turn. In June 1991, he commented in uncharacteristically harsh tones, "The fact that we're losing share makes me goddamn mad.... Everyone is too comfortable at a time when the business is in crisis." Akers offered these frustrated comments to an internal IBM management class of some fifty people, a class he assumed had been closed to the media. One manager from Canada, Brent Anderson, thought that the entire company should know what their boss had just said, so he fired off an e-mail to all 300,000 IBM employees, recounting the episode. Peter Thonis was a member of IBM's public relations staff during the late 1980s and early 1990s. He recalled the impact of Akers' words, especially the "goddamn mad" phrase. It hurt the employees enormously to hear Akers blame them

when they felt they were working hard. But what really got their attention was the language the chairman had employed to get his message
across. Never before had any senior executive uttered such earthy and
inflammatory language in what amounted to a public setting. Thomas
Watson would have been appalled. It was simply not part of the nearly
puritanical corporate culture. The employees could draw only one conclusion: When the boss starts cursing in anger, things must really be
bad. To Thonis, Akers' speech was a defining moment for IBM, for it
marked the first time that many at IBM felt that the company was in a
death spiral. If John Akers was "goddamn mad"—not just upset, not just
angry—then IBM must be in a lot of trouble.

The chairman's remarks were a journalist's gold mine. IBM had
always enjoyed a wholesome, do-no-wrong image in the media; its
executives never raised their voices, never swore, never admitted to
any uncertainty or frailty within the company. "IBM had the image of
motherhood and apple pie," Peter Thonis remembered. "Everyone
loved each other. There could be no contention within. Certainly the
chairman would never curse his employees." But that was precisely
what was happening, and the press got all over the story. Thonis's
phone began ringing off the hook. Hoping to quell naysayers, the public relations man urged Akers to join in the fray and reply to the e-mail
(perhaps using more delicate language), and then release the electronic statement to the press. He proposed that Akers use more upbeat
language: "Look, I hear you. I want to put what I said in perspective.
The point I wanted to make was that I love this company. But I just
wanted to get people charged up. I know you're working extremely
hard." But once Akers realized that the media had learned of his can-
did comments, he had no desire to address IBM's problems in public.
There would be no e-mail response, and to journalists who asked for
Akers' precise remarks to the management class, Peter Thonis was
authorized only to issue what amounted to a vague, unresponsive, and
at times misleading reply: the talk had taken place, it had been tough,
and it had been well-received by management. "I didn't acknowledge
the curses," the public relations man later said. Akers, for his part,
wouldn't budge. "He stayed in his bunker," recalled Thonis. "He listened to his human resources people, and they all said it would go
away." It didn't go away. *Business Week* ran a cover story pegged to the
Akers speech. It was not the kind of coverage IBM cherished. Now the

whole world had picked up on what was really happening inside IBM, making matters a million times worse. "It wouldn't go away," said Peter Thonis. "This was the beginning of the end."

Singing the Baby Blues

But Akers was not ready to give up without a fight. On December 5, 1991, he announced a drastic program aimed at turning the company around. He planned to break IBM into smaller units (dubbed by wags the Baby Blues). He promised—as he had seemingly countless times before—that the new step would fundamentally redefine the company, making it more responsive to customers and markets. He announced a series of new companies and business units. One of the new businesses, Pennant Systems Company, would be responsible for the development and manufacture of IBM's worldwide advanced-function printers and related software and for advanced printing services (a $2 billion IBM business). The new Storage Products line of business would be responsible for the development and manufacture of IBM's disk, tape, and optical storage products and related software (an $11 billion IBM business). "We expect," said Akers, "these more independent businesses will make better investment decisions because they are more agile, faster and closer to the markets they choose to serve."

But weeks later when IBM announced its third-quarter "earnings" for 1991 (a loss of $2.77 billion; revenue was $14.7 billion), it seemed that no revolution could help the company. In response to the dismal numbers, Akers announced new cuts and a $3.3 billion third-quarter writedown. IBM's stock plunged to a ten-year low of 52.

A Disastrous 1992

By year's end, IBM was on a collision course with disaster. In the last six years IBM's market share had dropped from 30 to 19 percent; each percentage point represented $3 billion in annual revenues. With its stock hovering around $100, it had recently lost $18 billion in market capitalization. Although revenues had climbed over the past five years, the company was growing at the paltry annual rate of 6.6 percent. IBM's global market share had fallen by a third, from 30 percent to 21 percent. Its profits, though still the largest of any company's in the world, were slipping. In 1990, the company had earned $5.9 billion on $68.9 billion in revenue. But that $5.9 billion figure was deceptive: it was 10 percent less than IBM had made in 1984 on only $46 billion in revenue. Its return on equity in 1984 had been 24.9 percent; six years later it was only 14.8 percent. Few were impressed with these figures. In the latest *Fortune* magazine list of most-admired American companies, IBM had slipped to number 32. While it had $64.7 billion in revenues in 1991, it had lost $2.86 billion that year.

Despite IBM's attempts to bring costs in line and restructure the company, 1992 turned out to be one more disastrous period for the computer giant. The company had revenues of $64.5 billion, but losses that amounted to $4.97 billion, the largest net loss in American corporate history. Its fourth-quarter loss of $5.4 billion was far worse than its fourth-quarter loss of $1.46 billion in 1991. Its share price plunged 50 percent, hitting an eighteen-year low of 41⅛. John Akers and his senior colleagues were forced to take 40 percent pay cuts. Most troubling was the fact that IBM's mainframe processors and storage systems business, a $50 billion world industry that it had dominated for decades, was faring poorly. Somehow, IBM would have to replace these diminishing revenues, which had accounted for 50 percent of the company's revenues and as much as 60 percent of its profits. But, IBM's sales of that equipment grew by only 2 percent in 1992. Revenue from IBM's mainframe processors dropped 10 to 15 percent in 1992, to about $7.5 billion. Other mainframe companies, meanwhile, were posting impressive revenue gains.

To get Wall Street on his side, an increasingly difficult task, Akers suggested to analysts and reporters that he had a plan that would redefine IBM. He intended to dismiss 25,000 workers, cut $1 billion from the company's product development budgets, slice $1 billion from administrative expenses, and take a $6 billion charge against 1992 fourth-quarter earnings to cover terminations and asset sales. Akers' announcements gave rise to a certain optimism if only because the IBM chairman finally appeared to be coming to grips with the changing business environment. Most dismissals were to come in IBM's mainframe units.

However much John Akers struggled to straighten IBM out, hope was fading. It all seemed so astonishing: the company that had been the computer industry was now in a life-and-death fight for its very survival. And, worst of all, no one seemed to have any easy answers.

Chapter 3

———◆———

Outsiders Know More Than You Think

"Watch the turtle. He only moves forward by sticking his neck out."

THE 59-YEAR-OLD John Akers did not want to quit. He knew that a year down the line, when he turned 60, he would be forced to retire. Retiring at 60 was customary for all IBM executives—no shame in that. He just didn't want to be hounded out of office. He desperately wanted to hang on for another year. Yet his eight years of leadership, dating back to 1985, had proven disastrous. An empire was crumbling, and the IBM board had to serve up a scapegoat to increasingly furious shareholders.

Now, as business magazines called for his resignation, as board members squirmed in discomfort, Akers winced at the mounting tide favoring his departure. He hoped for a reprieve, but was all too aware that the board was increasingly distraught at the constant hemorrhaging of money. It was all so frustrating. He had tried time after time to make changes, to create a new IBM, but each time he had failed. Things seemed to get worse, not better. He knew that as long as the IBM stock kept sliding, there would be no reprieve.

A Black January

It all fell apart in January 1993, unquestionably the worst month in the company's history. Sales had continued to decline both in mainframes and minicomputers. The blackest day for Akers came on January 19, when it was announced that IBM had suffered a staggering $4.97 billion loss for 1992, the largest in American corporate history. Revenues were down slightly to $64.5 billion. IBM's losses in 1992 were nearly double what they had been the year before ($2.86 billion). Five days later, the stock, which had reached a high of $175 in 1987, had plunged to a mere $49 a share; the previous summer of 1992, it had been at the $100 mark. IBM seemed to be in a death spiral and no one seemed to know how to stop it. The only point on which board members could unite was that John Akers had to go. When he finally acceded to the board's wishes and stepped down as chairman and CEO, there was the distinct feeling of a ship sinking in a stormy sea.

On January 26, IBM announced that it was beginning a search to replace Akers. The board gave itself three months to find a successor, appointing a committee of seven outside directors, headed by James E. Burke, the retired chairman of Johnson & Johnson, to find the new chief executive. (At the same time, underscoring how dire its financial position was, the board cut its quarterly dividend payment to shareholders for the first time—from $1.21 to 54 cents.)

The board's challenge was staggering. It would have to find someone willing to take the post at a time when the company was in the worst imaginable straits, someone with a strong enough reputation to command the respect of the employees. The task would be daunting as few employees were going to welcome a new boss who would almost certainly put the company through its most devastating period of austerity ever. Under ordinary circumstances, the selection committee would have probed within the IBM ranks for Akers' replacement. Never before had the board reached beyond the company for a new leader. For nearly eighty years, IBM had prided itself on its uniqueness and its stunning record of achievement, and it was always taken for granted that only someone who knew the company inside out could run it.

These were not ordinary circumstances, of course. Beyond that, IBM offered few top-notch candidates from which to choose. All of them seemed tainted by having played a major supporting role in the bleak Akers era. None of them seemed to possess the credentials to lead IBM to recovery. Among the insiders most often cited as candidates for the top job were Robert J. LaBant, the 47-year-old marketing chief, and James A. Cannavino, who at 48, headed the personal computer and workstation operations. But the board showed little enthusiasm for either of these two men.

Salvation, if it was to come, would have to reside in the form of an outsider, preferably someone who had exhibited great success in running a major American corporation. Still, the very idea that IBM acknowledged it was looking to the outside seemed odd. "It's fair to say some new blood would be better," observed Microsoft chairman Bill Gates at the time. "But I will be surprised if they pick somebody outside. It's so non-IBM."

While the selection committee did its work, the IBM board busied itself with asking more than a hundred industry executives for advice on a cure for the ailing computer firm. One of those asked was Microsoft chairman Bill Gates, one of IBM's chief rivals. Gates's advice certainly had a self-serving ring to it: He thought IBM should sharpen its focus by building up its mainframe business. As the king of software, he certainly had no interest in IBM becoming a major software rival to Microsoft; better for it to stick to mainframes. He argued that mainframes would become even more important to the future computer industry and advised IBM to sell off its unprofitable personal computer business as well as the profitable AS 400 minicomputer line.

A Used Car That No One Wanted

Pressure on the selection committee was constant and intense. The business media pursued the IBM succession story aggressively, reporting every tiny bit of speculation about who would be given the toughest job in America. Much to its chagrin, the committee, which had hoped to conduct its search in secret, found a bright media spotlight focused on each of the rumored candidates.

According to media reports, the committee short list was a veritable who's who of American business leaders: AT&T executive Robert M. Kavner, Compaq Computer chairman Ben Rosen, General Electric's Jack Welch, Microsoft's Bill Gates, Motorola's George Fisher, former Hewlett Packard president John A. Young, former presidential candidate Ross Perot, Apple Computer's John Sculley, and Morton Meyer-son, the CEO of Perot Systems. In fact, the committee never seriously imagined that it could lure Bill Gates to IBM. Why would the most successful business leader of the computer industry want to abandon Microsoft and take over a crumbling company? Moreover, it is widely believed that the committee was less keen on John Sculley getting the IBM job than Sculley himself was.

Some candidates did, however, get serious consideration from the committee. One such person was AlliedSignal's Lawrence Bossidy. In February, when rumors flew that he was in the running to replace Akers, Bossidy told a group of his AlliedSignal staffers that Big Blue needed someone who "is 35 years old, knows computers, and can clone himself 25 times." In other words, someone other than the 58-year-old Bossidy. Undoubtedly, Bossidy could have had the IBM job, but he had just completed a successful restructuring at AlliedSignal and was about to launch a major effort to spark growth. Leaving Allied would have meant sacrificing $23 million in restricted stock and options as well. By March 10, he declined the offer.

A few days later, John Young denied that he wanted to be considered for the IBM post. Next it was George Fisher's turn to deny any interest. John Sculley insisted to his board that he had no intention of leaving Apple Computer even though it was not at all clear that anyone at IBM was pushing for him that hard. Still, reporters, investors, and employees urged Sculley to change his mind. He acknowledged that he found the pressure unbearable—but he did not recant.

The board was clearly disappointed at the lack of interest among the top business figures in the country, and for that matter, among second-rung executives as well. It seemed that IBM, once the most prestigious company in the world, had trouble luring even B-list players to Armonk. It was as if IBM were a used car that no one wanted to buy.

There was no end in sight to the media buzz, and James Burke divulged no details of the job search. The mystery deepened. The press loved the story. An American icon was crumbling. The man at the top had been unceremoniously dismissed. No other business offered such a challenge to the person in charge, and yet no one seemed to want the job. For all those reasons, reporters churned out their speculation, adding pressure to the board, which was fast approaching its self-imposed deadline of April 30. Most thought a decision was imminent if only because the company's annual meeting was set for April 26. Surely IBM would want to announce a successor by then.

Let's Call "Abel"

One business figure the selection committee had in mind was Louis V. Gerstner Jr., the chairman and CEO of RJR Nabisco. He was certainly not in the same league as Jack Welch or Bill Gates, but he had an impressive record turning around companies that had fallen on bad times. For that reason alone, the committee turned its attention to Gerstner. To preserve the secrecy of its list of 125 candidates, the board issued code names. Gerstner was "Abel." He was the first person James Burke turned to in January, but at that time Gerstner seemed uninterested. To Burke he said politely, "That's not for me. I'm happy where I am." Burke did not give up. He pursued other candidates, but when the top choices fell by the wayside, Gerstner looked better and better.

Gerard R. Roche, chairman of the executive search firm Heidrick & Struggles, tried his luck with Gerstner. By now, Gerstner had thought more about the IBM job, especially about the challenge of running such a large company. He told friends privately that perhaps he had one more big job in him, running a corporation the size of a General Motors or IBM. But when Roche phoned him, Gerstner sounded indifferent, or at best ambiguous: "Don't bother me now. I'm busy," he said, hinting that he could only meet him on non-RJR time. Roche picked up the signal. Gerstner had an open mind about the job. He was no longer turning it down outright; he just didn't want to hold negotiations while sitting at his desk at RJR Nabisco!

Hanging up the phone with Roche, Gerstner's enthusiasm mounted. The thought of running a once-mighty company in such desperate straits as IBM would give him the chance to employ the turnaround tactics he had learned and honed in previous years. He reveled in crisis management, in making tough decisions, in tackling complex business operations. He would have all of that at IBM. Moreover, he was being considered for the IBM job at an ideal time for him. As of March 10, Gerstner could exercise all the stock options he had received in 1989 when he joined RJR Nabisco. Though RJR's stock had not yet skyrocketed, Gerstner could leave the firm with $22.5 million. Finally, IBM was not exactly alien territory to him. His 54-year-old brother Richard had spent his career at Big Blue, running IBM's Asia operations and then the Personal Systems division, which makes PCs and workstations.

The selection committee was eager to find out whether Gerstner could be enticed, so it brought out its big guns. In early March, Gerstner held a secret 3½-hour meeting in a Washington hotel room with a senior IBM executive, a get-together arranged by James Burke. The meeting was arranged for Washington not only because Gerstner was attending a meeting in that city but because the nation's capital was considered a "safe" location—well away from IBM's headquarters at Armonk. After slipping out of his meeting, Gerstner met with the IBM executive and fired off question after question; the executive responded to each one frankly and added that IBM needed a technocrat now, not a technician. It needed a manager, a change agent. All of this was what Gerstner wanted to hear. The session, Gerstner later remarked, "convinced me that a great deal of what needed to be done would fall into the 'managing change' category." It was familiar territory for him.

Some IBM board members had expressed concern that Gerstner lacked the technological knowledge to run the giant computer maker. But Burke had supreme confidence in Gerstner's ability to handle the job: "Lou was tougher than nails. Hard things needed to be done, and I knew he could do them. We needed somebody who was by instinct, training, and interest very strategic in his thinking. Everybody knew that was one of Lou's hallmarks. He thinks strategically about everything. I once asked him if he thought strategically about his dog."

The Cookies and Tobacco Man

By the third week of March, the media was touting Gerstner as the leading candidate for the IBM position. He remained silent. Some still believed the board would not choose someone lacking in computer industry experience. To get him acquainted with what the job entailed, Burke supplied Gerstner with all sorts of documents, some written by IBM employees, some by outsiders, leading Lou to crack, "Apparently, IBM gets a lot of free advice." When he sat down with Burke, Gerstner recalled: "He began to convince me that it was important to the country and the economy that IBM be restored to the force that it once was." By now, Gerstner found the job nearly irresistible. But he still needed time before making such a monumental move After all, this was unquestionably the most important decision of his business life. He had already proven his mettle both at American Express and RJR Nabisco, but he could fall on his face at IBM. Was that the way he wanted to end his business career?

While Gerstner played hard to get, more and more board members grew comfortable with the thought of him running IBM. They liked his record of turning around major corporations. They liked that he had a solid knowledge of technology's role in corporate life. They particularly liked the fact that he was an outsider. That alone would gain him immediate respect at IBM. He was also appreciated for his fiery determination and ability to size up solutions to complicated business problems quickly. Senior IBM executives warmed to Gerstner as well. Jim Cannavino doubted that IBM needed "a technical genius to run the place. I didn't think Sculley or Gates could or would want to do the job. Bill had too much disdain for other computer models. Apple never made it into the business community, so choosing Sculley wouldn't give customer confidence. But, Lou Gerstner, with his American Express experience, more than his cookies and tobacco experience, had showed us that customer services model."

Meanwhile, Gerstner was awfully close to making a decision. He read a book called *Computer Wars*. He took long walks on the beach outside his vacation home in southern Florida. A favorite phrase of his came to mind as he took those walks: "Watch the turtle. He only moves forward by sticking his neck out." It was the turtle's behavior that finally brought Gerstner to a decision. He liked the challenge. He liked the risk. He admitted to himself that he didn't mind sticking his neck out. "I've never been a person who plays it safe," he suggested soon after letting the board know that he would take the job.

As the chief executive of RJR Nabisco, Lou Gerstner presided over the Nabisco Dinah Shore Ladies' Professional Golf Association tournament every year. It was at this tournament that Gerstner let the three partners at Kohlberg Kravis Roberts, RJR's largest shareholder, in on his plan to step down as head of RJR Nabisco. The three partners—Henry R. Kravis, George R. Roberts, and Paul E. Raether—used all their talents of persuasion to change Gerstner's mind, but his mind was made up.

On March 24, the *Wall Street Journal* reported that IBM planned to appoint Gerstner as John Akers' successor. The secret was out. "Abel" had the job.

Chapter 4

———◆———

I Love Beating
Competitors

"It was the supremacy of the idea
that was important."

THE MAN WHO would take over IBM in 1993 was no stranger to the computer industry. His critics would try to portray him as an outsider, and even his allies would worry that he was too removed from the industry to preside over the world's most important computer maker effectively. But Lou Gerstner seemed to be preparing for the IBM job almost from the start.

Lou Gerstner was born on March 1, 1942, in Mineola, New York, on Long Island. He grew up in comfortable circumstances, as his father was a traffic manager for the F & M Schaefer Corporation brewery. The second of four boys, young Lou faced enormous pressure from his parents to achieve. His brother Dick, two years older, recalled how his parents pushed the boys to excel: "From the first time we got report cards, the question was: Why not all A's? It started with me as the oldest. If they were letter grades, they were to be all A's; if number grades, 90 or above."

Chaminade High School, where Lou attended, was as demanding as Lou's parents, and less forgiving. Teachers returned marked tests, making sure to shout out the test scores. Discipline was severe, and students knew that repeated offenses could lead to expulsion from the school. Teachers sometimes slapped students.

Lou enrolled in Dartmouth in 1959 and graduated *magna cum laude* in 1963 with a degree in engineering. That degree would serve him well when he became the head of IBM as he had something in common with tens of thousands of IBM employees. At school on a scholarship, Lou was bright and highly focused. A classmate recalled that he did not tolerate fools. If someone displayed weakness, Lou would say, "That's not very smart." When anyone issued an unsupported claim, Lou would retort, "Back it up." Hardly surprising, then, that Lou became so competitive later on.

The *Wunderkind* Consultant

In 1963 Gerstner enrolled in the Harvard Business School and graduated two years later, taking a job with the well-known New York management consulting firm of McKinsey & Company. At age 23, he was the youngest M.B.A. ever hired by the firm. His most notable accomplishment was in building up the firm's financial-strategy practice. The McKinsey experience planted the seeds for some of Gerstner's most important business strategies. As he observed:

> **McKinsey had a culture that fostered rigorous debate over the right answer without that debate resulting in personal criticism. It was the supremacy of the idea that was important, whether it came from the youngest associate or the most senior partner. The task was to come up with the right answer.**

Something of a *wunderkind*, after only four years—rather than the usual six—Gerstner was offered a partnership. In 1968, he married Elizabeth Robins Link from Danville, Virginia. (They have two children, Louis III and Elizabeth.) At age 33 Gerstner became one of McKinsey's youngest directors. He distinguished himself by overhauling the bankrupt Penn Central Railway. J. McLain "Mac" Stewart, a senior partner, groomed Gerstner to take over McKinsey's vaunted American Express account and, starting in 1970, to act as adviser to James D. Robinson III, Amex's new chairman and CEO. Gerstner and Robinson got on well, and Gerstner helped plot the company's diversification into Wall Street.

But eventually he grew bored. He felt too removed from the marketplace. "I love beating competitors," he told an interviewer in 1985. "I love the thrill of winning in the marketplace." On January 1, 1978, Gerstner left the consulting firm to become an executive vice president and head up the credit card division of American Express. Since Amex had been one of his major corporate clients for the past five years, he was quite familiar with the company's business operations and its problems. He knew all too well that its familiar green card, long dominant in the marketplace, was facing tough competition from aggressive upstarts such as Visa and MasterCard, and that its Travel-Related Services (TRS) division was losing money. He overhauled the entire credit card franchise.

In September 1979, Gerstner was appointed executive vice president of American Express and president of its TRS division. He focused on developing services for a global marketplace and on catering to the needs of those affluent customers to whom the American Express card had traditionally appealed. Thanks to him, American Express's TRS division emerged as one of the company's best performers in the 1980s.

At first, Amex colleagues viewed Gerstner as a brazen know-it-all and were cool to him. But when his business talents became apparent, the coolness turned into respect. He believed in brainstorming sessions, and he believed in targeting specific goals, sometimes as many as ten or fifteen at a time. He viewed his task as making sure that colleagues knew how much further they had to go to meet those goals. He made sure that no one got a free card, or a discounted one. If someone suggested offering a free card or tried to make some other exception, he would say, "This is a violation of the brand, and we're not doing it." Thus did one of his business techniques emerge: Once someone sets a strategy, never violate it.

Profits at TRS increased 18 percent annually, and Gerstner won credit for developing new products such as the platinum and Optima cards and steering the company's high-brow advertising.

I Know What Computers Are!

Later, when Gerstner took over at IBM, some accused him of being an outsider, of not knowing computers well enough. The accusation was not really accurate—he was quite familiar with information technology. In 1980, he even had a personal computer on his desk, making him one of the first American executives to use the new gadget. (It was not, however, an IBM PC, which only came on the market two years later.) He became a big advocate of using the latest computer technology to build competitive advantage. He monitored the growth of the company's First Data Resources unit, which became the fifth largest provider of computer services in the United States. And he personally helped to mastermind the overhaul of a $250 million computer system that gave the company a leg up in providing billing information to merchants and cardholders. In the process, Gerstner became one of IBM's more savvy customers.

In 1985 he was named president of American Express, placing him second in command to CEO Jim Robinson and his likely successor. Gerstner's track record was certainly impressive: He had doubled the number of currencies in which the American Express credit card was issued, he had quadrupled the number of cardholders, sales of travelers checks had doubled, and he had turned Travel-Related Services into the company's most profitable division. During his tenure, TRS achieved an average compound annual earnings growth of 18 percent and an average return on equity of over 25 percent. As president over the next four years he increased corporate net income by 66 percent.

Despite all that success, or perhaps because of it, by 1987 Lou Gerstner was searching for his own business to run. He had the chance when United Airlines sought him to become its CEO, but he turned the job down for several undisclosed reasons.

Two years later, when a recruiter for the Wall Street investment firm of Kohlberg Kravis Roberts sounded him out to head a recently acquired company (the food and tobacco enterprise, the former RJR Nabisco), Gerstner expressed interest. In January 1989 Gerstner invited KKR partners Henry Kravis and Paul Raether over to his Greenwich, Connecticut, home. He was ready to take the job, but he warned them: "If you're looking for a liquidator, I'm not your guy. I'm a builder." Kravis and Raether assured him that they wanted Gerstner to make the company grow.

With that assurance, Gerstner agreed to become chief executive officer of the former RJR Nabisco. His appointment aroused huge interest in corporate America. Everyone had been curious to know who would replace outgoing CEO F. Ross Johnson, who was as greedy as he was capricious and larger-than-life. Johnson had been the key player in the corporate saga detailed in the best-selling book, *Barbarians at the Gate,* later an HBO docudrama starring James Garner as Johnson. The KKR takeover of the former RJR was one of the largest and most controversial leveraged buyouts in corporate history. As a result of the takeover, the former RJR was saddled with a massive $25 billion debt, and with annual interest costs of $3 billion. Gerstner lamented, perhaps a bit hyperbolically, that he was taking the "hardest job in America."

I came on board a $17 billion company where, in effect, there were no rules anymore. Instinctively, and maybe even dangerously, I imposed my view of how a modern corporation should be run.

Where Are We Going Long-Term?

In his first 100 days running the former RJR Nabisco, Gerstner was incredibly quick and forceful in making decisions. At IBM, he would hone such behavior into a full-fledged strategy: "Communicate self-confidence. Demonstrate leadership." He brought in a new executive team with new titles and set up new compensation systems and new rules for capital spending. During his first year at RJR, Gerstner traveled 150,000 miles to twenty plants worldwide, visiting supermarkets and putting tough questions to employees, all to learn how the food and tobacco businesses functioned. He seemed like a workaholic, but what really distinguished his performance from that of other executives was an ability to size up problems rapidly and figure out what decisions had to be made.

Gerstner and his management team attended frenzied full-day meetings monthly at each of three divisional offices. Gerstner routinely asked the pivotal questions: "Where are you going long-term?" and "Should you be in this business?" These were the vital questions— Gerstner knew that, but they had apparently not been asked before, or at least not with such clarity. Always, he pushed RJR Nabisco's employees to adopt a long-term strategy:

This was a company that performed very well as a tactician in the marketplace. . . . It had strong marketing skills, strong sales skills.

But the organization needed to confront the question: "Where are we going long-term?"

He was convinced that profitability depended upon brand strength, so he got rid of such lackluster items as Chun King Chinese food and Baby Ruth and Butterfinger candies; marketing dollars were spent on such cash cows as Winston and Camel cigarettes. Determined to find and exploit synergies within the company, he wanted the food and tobacco divisions to work together to make joint calls on customers and engage in cooperative marketing promotions, and research.

When I got here, there was absolutely zero flow between the divisions. Mine was the voice crying in the wilderness, insisting that cooperation could be constructive.

Even before taking over at IBM, Gerstner possessed a management style that grated on people. They found him an intimidating presence. As such, they were not going to exhibit great loyalty to him automatically. Gerstner sensed the coolness of his colleagues and he went out of his way to be less intimidating and win employees over. To win that support he knew he had to proceed cautiously. Workers would not simply embrace him and his strategies because he was the boss. He made efforts to deflate suspicions and fears by, among other steps, seeking out employees in their offices rather than calling them in for meetings.

Practicing the turnaround tactics that he would become known for at IBM, he managed to cut costs by eliminating the much-in-demand fleet of corporate jets, got rid of the company's fancy headquarters, and reduced that gigantic debt to $14 billion. He also pushed for new products, worked on new marketing initiatives, and sold $6 billion in assets, mostly food businesses. Trimming 3,000 jobs out of a total of 60,000, he saved $550 million in yearly costs. Most important, he achieved a $1.4 billion swing in net income, from a net loss of $1.1 billion in 1989 to net income of $299 million in 1992.

The Wizard of Turnarounds

Accordingly, Gerstner not only rescued the company from the deep financial hole it had been in, but also turned it into a premium company. He was fast becoming the Wizard of Business Turnarounds, a title he did not necessarily relish; he much preferred to be known as a CEO who knew how to develop companies. Still, in his four years at RJR, he received high marks for crisis management and for providing stability and focus—in sharp contrast to his freewheeling, free-spending predecessor, F. Ross Johnson. Gerstner was not afraid of tough decisions as long as he felt it was the right thing to do for the business. He avoided micromanaging. Once he and his senior executives agreed on the company's goals, short-term and long-term, he adopted a hands-off policy in the expectation that his subordinates would execute plans and programs without coming back to him for more and more clarification.

Both before and after he was selected to run IBM, Gerstner was haunted by skeptics who derogated him as an outsider, as someone who didn't really know the computer business. Yet, his RJR experience had at least supplied him with credentials that showed he knew how to run a large-sized company. More than that, thanks to his RJR days, he was quite familiar with the kind of computer technology IBM sold. As a longtime IBM customer, he enjoyed a special vantage point that even insiders at Big Blue could not replicate. He had a pretty good idea what IBM's customers wanted in the way of computer technology. But his greatest asset was something else: He was one of the great fix-it men of American business who had spent decades perfecting the fine art of turning ailing businesses around. As it happened, those skills were exactly what IBM needed at the moment: the skills of a technocrat, not a technician.

Part

II

Reviving a Troubled Company

———◆———

"We will build on [IBM's]
traditions, but we will not
hesitate to make every change
necessary to meet the challenges
of a very rapidly adjusting
marketplace."

———◆———

Chapter 5

———◆———

Let the Triage Begin

"We will build on [IBM's] traditions, but we will not hesitate to make every change necessary...."

ON MARCH 26, 1993, IBM announced that Lou Gerstner would become its new chairman and CEO. "The most avidly watched talent search in the history of American business" was over. Gerstner would be extremely well compensated for taking the job. He would receive a $2 million salary for 1993; an annual incentive of $1.5 million, tied to IBM's business performance; a long-term incentive opportunity of $500,000, linked to IBM's business performance during the next three years; options on 500,000 IBM shares at the average market price on the date of the grant; and a one-time transition payment of $5 million, intended to offset the value of certain income and benefits Gerstner forfeited by leaving RJR Nabisco. (Gerstner's base salary of $2 million a year was more than twice the $925,000 base salary John Akers received in 1992).

Investors showed little reaction one way or the other to the Gerstner appointment as IBM's stock rose 87.5 cents to $51.37 on the New York Stock Exchange (half the price of nine months earlier; and far less than its $176 high in 1987). One Gerstner friend said the new IBM chief felt "a certain amount of fear and trepidation" at taking over the job. And why not? A *National Public Radio* reporter that day said the IBM post "may be the toughest job in American business." Few challenged the assertion, recalling as they did that the once-mighty IBM, for so long a corporate dynamo, for so long the most respected company in America, had been losing billions of dollars for the past two years. Gerstner seemed to understand how daunting his task truly was.

> **The challenge they've laid out is immense. I don't underestimate its magnitude, but I take up that challenge with a great determination to succeed. We will build on [IBM's] traditions, but we will not hesitate to make every change necessary to meet the challenges of a very rapidly adjusting marketplace.**

Let Me Have a Honeymoon—At Least!

To many, Gerstner's task seemed even more daunting than that of General Motors' new CEO, John F. Smith Jr. At least GM knew what business it was in—making cars. It just had to figure out how to make them better and cheaper. IBM, on the other hand, watching the steep decline of its mainframe business and pondering how to win back some of that lost market share in the personal computer area, could not say for sure what business it was in, what kind of computers it was selling. Some were willing to give Gerstner the benefit of the doubt, or at least a honeymoon period. Others were even predicting that Gerstner, if he turned IBM around, would become a new business hero. "He is," wrote *Fortune* magazine in its April 19, 1993, edition, "a sharp, even brilliant, energetic man who thrives on overhauling corporate cultures."

Many observers forgave his lack of experience in the computer industry, and thought the selection committee had been wise to choose a business strategist not afraid to take risks rather than an out-and-out technology person. To James Burke, the man who conducted the job search, Gerstner's greatest business trait was his belief in decentralizing management—in making sure that those closest to customers make the decisions.

Others, though, were dismayed by the Gerstner selection. When *Computerworld* magazine surveyed the 100 largest IBM customers, it found that 51 percent wanted someone with a technical background to run Big Blue; 36 percent thought a technical background was not essential to the job; and 13 percent had no opinion. Taking the side of those who favored an insider for the job, William J. Milton Jr., computer analyst at Brown Brothers Harriman, observed, "I think it's risky to bring someone in from outside the industry. If a computer firm takes a wrong strategic direction in terms of product, the firm may never recover." Even IBM employees at the lower levels aired their apprehension. Philip Van Itallie, a manufacturing systems engineer at IBM's East Fishkill, New York, plant, had little good to say about Gerstner: "People here were hoping they'd find a computer-literate person, instead of someone with financial concerns only. It would be good if there was someone who knew about computers and could lead IBM out of this mess. But that is wishful thinking."

The editors of *Business Week* were pleased with the Gerstner appointment, but for reasons that had nothing to do with whether he was a good choice. When the editors learned from several sources on Wednesday, March 24, that he would be appointed, they ripped up their planned front cover and substituted a photograph of Gerstner with the headline "IBM's New Boss." The magazine was forced to go to press Wednesday evening so it pointed out that Gerstner's selection was pending.

The company remained in peril. It was deep in red ink and sinking, having posted a $4.96 billion loss on $64.5 billion in revenues in 1992. In contrast to its long-gone glory days, the company had lost a staggering and unprecedented $15.4 billion from 1991 to 1993. Between 1990 and 1993, some $14 billion in hardware profits were erased. Sales of mainframes dropped 50 percent between 1991 and 1993, to about $6.6 billion. IBM was selling $12 billion worth of personal computers, but incredibly was making no profit on them; in fact, they were losing a fortune.

No one seemed to know what the problem was—only that there was a serious problem, and it was getting worse. No one seemed to know how to fix it. The company's expenses were growing and it was losing money. IBM had too many people, and its efforts to cut staff had been so marginal as to be almost inconsequential. Always a hardware company, it was driven by its mainframe business. Yet there was a false sense—as it turned out—that the mainframe business was about to disappear. Even if did not disappear, there seemed little hope that mainframes would spawn large profits, as had been the case in the past. Indeed, mainframe sales for the early months of 1993 were down as much as 50 percent, and analysts were increasing their estimates of IBM's first-quarter loss to more than $300 million (compared to a

$2.5 billion profit in the first quarter of 1992). Few gave IBM much chance to survive, at least as the mighty entity it had been for six decades.

But now it had a new boss. His arrival alone offered hope that a miracle could be performed. He was known for turning other businesses around. Could he do the same at IBM? All eyes were on Lou Gerstner, who personally held the fate of the world's most famous computer company in his hands. It would be up to him whether IBM rose or fell. Within hours of the announcement, Gerstner told *The New York Times* not to expect a quick fix at IBM. "This is going to take time," he asserted. It would take him a few months, he suggested, just to get to know the company.

First Day in Office

As he prepared for his first day in office on April 1, one question troubled him more than any other: Where to begin? What problem would he tackle first? How would he keep morale from slipping even further once he introduced new austerity measures. IBM was in a state of chaos—how could it have been otherwise?—having posted such poor figures for 1992 and gone through the anguishing process of finding a new leader. How could Lou Gerstner end the chaos? Although so much needed to be tackled, Gerstner moved at a measured pace. He had learned such caution at McKinsey. The decisions he would make during this early phrase of his tenure would have an impact on the company for the next three to five years at least. He wanted to make sure to do his homework before making sweeping decisions. It was foolish to come in like a whirlwind with all sorts of pronouncements, all sorts of changes. The analysts were looking for quick answers, and so was the media, but IBM was too big and too complex for someone to make vast changes overnight. It had too much history, its culture was too deeply ingrained in the mind of every employee. Gerstner was not afraid to take decisions. He would move, but he wanted to make sure that when he did, he was making the *right* move.

Meanwhile, as he surveyed the landscape at IBM, he began to realize just how menacing and how widespread the company's problems were. There were, to be sure, a few bright spots on the horizon. IBM was still dominant in such areas as storage technology, disk drives, and hard drives. But Gerstner's real challenge would come in figuring out how to manage the decline of IBM's once-huge mainframe business. And he would have to make decisions within the next few months. If the company was to grow, IBM would have to get stronger in software and services. Those divisions would require Gerstner's full attention.

But before thinking about which businesses to promote and where to spend IBM's investment dollars, Gerstner would have to decide how to bring the company's huge expenses in line. IBM's rivals such as Apple and Compaq were producing revenues per employee nearly three times that of IBM's. Further staff cuts seemed inevitable. The program to cut 25,000 employees in 1993 remained in force. He would not touch that, of course. With those cuts, some 100,000 IBM staffers would be gone and 300,000 would remain. How many more jobs would have to be cut? Some thought the situation was so desperate that Gerstner would actually have to make one more incredible cost-cutting move and slash another 100,000 jobs from the IBM payroll.

An Open Mind

While he pondered these tough decisions, Gerstner would have to give his attention to the most perplexing issue of all: what to do about John Akers' plan to divide IBM into a series of autonomous businesses, a plan that essentially called for the company's dismemberment. Breaking up IBM would almost certainly end the company's chance to return to its former glory. But it seemed to many the most sensible course to follow. As radical as it seemed, and as destructive, the plan actually had quite a few supporters, people who believed that IBM would benefit enormously from having its divisions compete with one another. Some even believed that Gerstner had been specifically chosen to head IBM for the sole purpose of carving the company up into those independent entities. Such conjecture was simply wrong. It presumed that Gerstner had already made up his mind—that he favored splitting IBM up. In truth, he hadn't even begun to study the matter. He had no opinion as of yet. He decided to defer that decision until he had a better sense of how the entire company worked.

Lou Gerstner understood that he had to jolt Big Blue out of its complacency. But he knew that he could not act decisively on the first day, or even the first month; he knew he had to be cautious, to learn the business first. In his first few months running IBM, Gerstner spent more than half his time on the road, visiting company sites. Often he spoke with employees, a hundred at a time. He also met with customers and competitors. In his first few months on the job, Gerstner chalked up twenty-five visits to IBM facilities in North America; he spent a week in Europe and a week in Japan; he sat down with the heads of IBM's Latin American operations. Rather than take his usual two-week vacation in August, he chose to tour IBM research facilities. Weekends provided no respite for Gerstner or his subordinates. On Fridays he typically took three briefcases of work home. On Sunday afternoons he phoned subordinates with his thoughts on what he had read that weekend. All of this studying made senior executives nervous. "There was a lot of suspicion, of course," recalled Lucy Baney. "People were concerned for their jobs. They thought that IBM would lose its heritage and culture. It was clear that Gerstner planned to sit back and observe, so there was suspicion simply because of his lack of activity."

For all of his early caution, Gerstner did make some important changes at the outset—changes that gave senior executives their first peak at the new man's rough-and-tumble management style. Used to the gentlemanly, polite, "Thanks very much" way of doing business that characterized the John Akers era, these executives suddenly confronted a chief executive who couldn't have cared less about being polite or gentlemanly. He wanted results. That was all that mattered. He wouldn't tolerate anything that would get in his way. Lulled into feeling that long meetings were good, that deadlines didn't really matter all that much, the executives suddenly found themselves with marching orders from Lou Gerstner that would force them to produce—or else. Not surprisingly, the Lou Gerstner management style seemed intimidating. No on had ever talked to these executives with quite the same degree of seriousness or toughness as he did, making the new man seem all the more of a martinet. Few IBM executives would ever admit it in public, but most acknowledged privately that in those first few days they had plenty of anxious moments—and they would have plenty more in the future. During those early days, he summoned the top dozen IBM managers to the boardroom at Armonk and gave them an assignment: Write a concise, honest appraisal of their businesses. But this report would be different from what they were used to handing in: There was to be no more whitewashing of the truth. The executives could no longer hide behind their foils and charts. They would have to speak the truth—or someone else would soon be speaking it for them. He asked his managers to write a report of about five pages that answered the following questions:

What business are you in?
Who are your customers?
What's your marketplace?
What are your strengths and weaknesses?
Who are your main competitors?

Gerstner also explained to them that he was going to change the nature of IBM's business meetings in a revolutionary way. Meetings would not run on endlessly anymore. They would be short and to the point—and only those with a clear-cut reason to attend the meeting would be invited. The rest would not.

This was all new to IBM, and quite a shock to the old, sedentary culture. In the past, IBM chiefs had not expected their senior executives to brief them in detail about their respective businesses. Someone like John Akers felt that he knew the mainframe business backward and forward. All he needed from the head of that business was an update every once in a while. But that wasn't good enough for Lou Gerstner. He wanted to think about his business continuously, and even more important, he wanted his senior executives to think about their businesses, not every once in a while, but at *all* times.

An Emotional Memo

Gerstner knew what issue burned in the minds of IBM's employees: Would they still be working at the company in a month? In six months? In a year? In the job only five days, Gerstner sought to assure employees that while some would inevitably suffer as a result of his turnaround program, he would do his best to ease the pain as much as possible. He knew this was what every CEO said in getting ready to lower the ax, but he seemed sincere when he issued a memo on April 6 that included the following:

Some of you were hurt and angered by being declared "surplus" after years of loyalty, and by some reports in the press about per-

formance ratings. I am acutely aware that I arrived at a painful time when there is a lot of downsizing. I know it is painful for everyone, but we all know too that it is necessary. I can only assure you that I will do everything I can to get this painful period behind us as quickly as possible, so that we can begin looking to our future and to building our businesses.

He sent the memo via e-mail to all IBM employees. This was an extraordinary departure from the way IBM leaders had communicated to their employees. Gone were the formal television broadcasts of John Akers which employees had figured out how to ignore. Here, for the first time, was an IBM chief executive sending an e-mail companywide. It was informal, it was personal, it was unheard of—and, it was hard to avoid. How could anyone not open an e-mail written by the company's new CEO? From the start, Gerstner was trying to break with tradition, to show that IBM need not be so crusty, that informality was fine too.

Few IBM staffers would be totally salved by hearing Gerstner's words. But he knew that he had no real choice. As he put it,

The message of the nineties is that no company in any region of the world can guarantee full employment. It's an empty promise.

Still, he knew that he had to open lines of communication with the staff. He hoped that most would appreciate his frankness—yes, there would be more cutbacks—but he also hoped that employees who survived those cutbacks would begin to feel that a corner had been turned. For he was making a promise to them that once these cutbacks were over, there would be no more. The survivors would be able to feel that their jobs were secure for a good long time. They could get back to work without suspicion or worry. How soon would he act? At this juncture, he didn't know. But he was determined that after the one-shot downsizing he would inevitably have to put through, "we can say to customers, employees, and shareholders that we're not just salami slicing here. We're going to get that behind us."

Chapter 6

———◆———

Ending the Chinese Water Torture

"We must focus on customers and not on our internal procedures and wrangling."

*I*N HIS FIRST few weeks on the job, Gerstner scooped up information about the company from his senior executives, product people, and financial analysts. The financial analysts naturally wanted to find out whether Gerstner planned to split up IBM. That was the hottest news item on their agendas, and now they had a chance to ask the man directly. But Gerstner's poker face never betrayed him. Instead, he berated some of those he talked to for focusing too much on what he called IBM's "internal plumbing." They should worry less about restructuring and more about the company's performance. When, inevitably, he was asked what kind of a strategic vision he had for IBM, he remained vague; his only vision, he insisted, was to make IBM consistently profitable.

Sam Albert worked for IBM from 1959 to 1989; for eighteen of those years he was the industry manager and director of what he calls the "leverage" industries: consulting, CPAs, legal professions, and the computer services industry. In more recent years, he had been an information technology industry analyst and management consultant.

On his first visit to Gerstner, Albert was seated in one of the two adjacent love seats at the front of Gerstner's large office. Gerstner sat at the other end of the love seat, facing Albert. "He just went right into his questions," Albert recalled. "Gerstner took five pages of notes—I know that because I counted him turning the paper. He was the best listener I have ever seen." Gerstner was eager to learn whether Albert felt IBM would be able to maintain a strong mainframe business. Was the System 390, IBM's most powerful mainframe computer, now obsolete and heading for a museum? he asked Albert. No, he replied, it was declining in revenue, but people were not discarding their mainframes at the curb. Gerstner then said to Albert, "In what I have read, you never say anything about our products. What do you think about IBM's products?" Albert said customers care about solutions. They are not interested in "reads, feeds, or speeds." Gerstner smiled and said he felt the same way about customer needs. Solutions were what customers wanted.

When Merrill Lynch analyst Steve Milunovich held his first meeting with Gerstner, the IBM chief hinted that he had every intention of keeping the company intact. "Being the six-hundred-pound gorilla has its advantages," Gerstner told the analyst. "IBM's global reach and product breadth are tremendous positives."

He tried to read as much about IBM as possible. At night he looked at the day's e-mails, as they poured in by the thousands in those first few weeks. He didn't encourage IBM employees to send in their thoughts. He didn't need to—IBM employees had a great deal on their minds. Most offered encouraging words to the new chief, and many gave specific suggestions: break up the company, keep it together, acquire this company or that. Sandwiched in between the advice and opinions was one common suggestion: Act quickly. IBM had been through too many "adjustments." That simply could not go on. Swift action was required—now, not later.

Figures for 1993's first quarter showed that IBM had lost $285 million; the company's mainframe revenues continued to slide, while cost-cutting efforts did little to help. Total revenues fell 7 percent, to $13.1 billion; equipment sales alone dropped 19.4 percent, to $5.7 billion. The personal computer business, which had lost an estimated $1 billion in 1992, was profitable in the first quarter. The best news was that IBM's service business had grown an impressive 48 percent, to $1.9 billion.

A Stock That Hastens Old Age

Gerstner was only twenty-six days into the job when the annual IBM shareholders meeting was held in Tampa, Florida. Still enjoying his honeymoon period, Gerstner could not be expected to accept responsibility or blame for IBM's continuing troubles, and therefore the 2,300 people who attended the session fired no barbs at the new CEO. Instead, they directed their harsh words at the board, which was castigated for the 50 percent drop in IBM's stock from the previous summer. The stock closed at just above $48 a share that day (six years earlier it had traded at $175). The steep dividend cut from the previous January was just as painful to attendees. "IBM stock no longer provides for your old age," said shareholder Bill Steiner, who held 1,000 shares. "But it certainly hastens its arrival." That quick-witted remark generated explosive laughter throughout the crowd. Avoiding specifics, Gerstner retorted: "You can't expect quick fixes." He could only promise that new austerity measures, when they came, would offer strong medicine. "The steps we will take will not be pussyfooting, but bold strides.... We will try as hard as we can to get this company right-sized for the competitive industry we are in.... I want to get it behind us so we can say to the remaining IBM-ers, 'You're the team. Now let's go.' " He noted how much the shareholders had suffered because of IBM's problems. "And now, as chairman, I am part of it—and I mean to do something about it." He then set forth four objectives he planned to pursue for 1993:

- Paring IBM to a more efficient size
- Developing a strategy that would make clear which businesses the company would focus on
- Decentralizing decision making
- Taking more care with IBM's customers

Gerstner seemed to be leaning toward keeping the company whole despite the strong urgings of shareholders and the advice he was getting from financial analysts and the media. At the Tampa meeting, Ralph Whitworth, president of the United Shareholders of America, observed: "There are two or three $10 billion or $12 billion companies slopping around in there that don't necessarily have to be under one tent." Gerstner responded that it made little sense to him to "toss a fragmentation grenade" into the company and "atomize" it.

By early July Gerstner had shed little light on what he planned to do to reshape IBM. The buyout program initiated by John Akers was winding down, and estimates were that some 50,000 IBM staffers had opted to take the severance package. Wall Street exhibited patience, recognizing that Gerstner had much to learn before imposing his own programs on the company. The stock remained in the high 40s. Nearly everyone predicted a new round of cuts, especially for the company's mainframe facilities. Gerstner's most decisive action in those early days had been to assemble a new management team loaded with both talent and hands-on experience. No appointment was as important as that of making Jerome B. York chief financial officer; he had come from Chrysler Corporation where he had held that same post and helped restructure the auto manufacturer. Like Gerstner, York had a forceful personality, and when it came time to pare IBM's payroll, he played the pivotal role in making sure the downsizing went off without a hitch. It was sometimes said that Gerstner owed a good deal of his success to the hard work of Jerry York.

To develop loyalty among the 1,200 employees just below the top management tier, Gerstner worked out a new stock option plan, which permitted them to purchase shares at a predetermined price even if the market price rose; under the new plan, the senior managers could replace their old options exercisable at the higher prices of $89 to $169 a share (now worthless owing to the drop in the stock's value) with the new ones exercisable at the lower price of $47.88. Enthusiastic about the prospect of being able to keep employees around, Gerstner talked at length about the new scheme:

> **Competitors are coming after my high-talent people right now. We know it. Some of them have lists of our key people. They're being picked off. I wasn't here when the stock dropped from whatever to 45, but my job for the shareholders is to make it go the other way. I have to deal with what I've got, and what I've got is an employee group with absolutely no incentive to stay here because every one of their options is under water. The new program is very unusual. I know of no other like it. You do not get a 1-for-1 swap. On average, you've got to turn in 2½ old options to get one new one.**

IBM-ers will have to turn in ten of the oldest options to get one new one. These options will have different vesting schedules from previous IBM options. An employee will have to stay two years before any of the new options vest and four years for them to vest completely.

In other words, I'm putting handcuffs on you to be part of the new team. Also, the stock must increase 50% from the April 23 [1993] price and stay there for 30 days before the options become vested. The shareholders have to see some significant uptick in price before you get any vesting.

No More Slice by Slice

By the summer of 1993, Lou Gerstner had completed his examination of the company and was ready to set in action his first major steps at reorganizing IBM. Computer pundits and large investors had been trying to discern what Gerstner was up to, but none ever cracked the code. Gerstner's ambiguous and vague statements only piqued their interest. It seemed as if the whole world was tuned in to the Lou Gerstner story, and everyone wanted a peak at the script.

Finally, by the end of July, Gerstner acted. On July 27, IBM announced that it would cut another 35,000 jobs in what it hoped would be a final effort to trim its worldwide payroll. Most of the cuts would be outside the United States. Gerstner made the announcement in a live broadcast over the in-house television system at 10 A.M. that day; an hour later he held a news conference in New York City that was also broadcast live to employees. IBMers praised him for informing them first of the new austerity moves; under previous regimes, workers seemed to be the last to hear. "The employees of this company have borne an unbelievable burden in the last few years," observed Gerstner. "But we need to get behind us this Chinese water torture we have been going through." In a memo to employees on the same day, he noted with a sense of pride the way the decision was taken: "Making reductions slice by slice, quarter by quarter, as we have over the past couple of years is unfair and debilitating. It creates anxiety for you and uncertainty among our customers." In a rare personal note, Gerstner admitted that the actions he had just taken "certainly have kept me awake at night."

The downsizing was designed, he wrote in that July 27 memo, to make IBM more profitable. "We are not generating any profits to reinvest in the future of our business. And that's critical because without funds to invest—in technology, in people, in new markets—there is no future for any of us at IBM. Profitability brings stability; stability brings growth; and growth brings the security and well-being we want for all of us." His goal, he added, was to make IBM "the most successful company in the world. It was once and I am convinced it will be again."

From that memo, one can discern what Gerstner had learned from the numerous conversations he had had in the previous four months— that he felt there was a lot more right with IBM than wrong; that the company's weaknesses could be overcome by its strengths; and specifically, that its size and global reach gave IBM a competitive advantage second to none. He knew precisely what he had to do: "We need to get the problems behind us and start focusing on growing again."

Echoing these sentiments, Jim Cannavino, who was IBM's senior vice president for strategy and development until 1995, noted that "IBM had taken 80 percent of its resources out before Gerstner got there; but it had been more of a Chinese torture than a sweeping move. He got it over quickly. He got it done. When the cuts were over, he told employees: 'Now your job depends on your performance.' "

In retrospect, Gerstner would have liked to have moved faster. He never, however, had second thoughts about the austerity measures: "We were having serious financial problems. In fact, financially it was the worst year in our proud history. No one suffered more than our employees, who were stunned. For everyone else—customers, shareholders, suppliers, analysts—it was red alert."

From a peak of 406,000 in 1986, IBM's employee population was down to 301,000 in January 1993, with the expectation that it would drop another 25 percent, to 255,000 by the end of 1993 and 225,000 by the end of 1994. At the same time, IBM announced further bad news in its earnings picture—an incredible $8 billion loss in the second quarter of 1993—linked to its massive $8.9 billion restructuring charge to pay for employee buyouts and office space reductions. It was the largest financial charge in corporate history. Without the restructuring charge, IBM reported a second-quarter loss of $40 million on revenues of $15.5 billion. In the same quarter in 1992, IBM reported profits of $734 million on revenues of $16.2 billion. (The layoffs and related plant closings led to an $8.1 billion loss for 1993, the largest in IBM's history.)

Wall Street Applauds

Wall Street applauded the cost-cutting moves and IBM stock closed on July 28 at $45.62, an increase of over $3. It fell back to $44.50 by week's end, and two weeks later it hit an all-time low of $40⅝. (As recently as 1991, IBM's stock had sold for over $135.) Wall Street liked the fact that Gerstner had boldly pressed ahead with a one-time financial house-cleaning, allowing him to move on to the required rebuilding process swiftly. For too long, analysts suggested, IBM had been taking charges quarter after quarter, year after year, reacting to shifts in the market-place rather than mastering those shifts.

The same financial analysts, however, were concerned that Gerstner could not complete the turnaround of IBM simply by cutting costs; he would have to figure out not just how to cut expenses (and thus boost earnings) but how to make the company grow. So when analysts met with Gerstner that afternoon, they pressed him for answers, but he was still reluctant to go into specifics. At a press conference, he sounded aggressive and upbeat and tried to put down the notion that he could provide an answer to all of IBM's problems in one simple package.

There have been a lot of questions as to when I'm going to deliver a vision for IBM, and I would like to say that the last thing IBM needs is a vision. What it needs is very tough-minded, highly effective . . . strategies for each of its businesses.

His goal at the moment, he argued, was to staunch the company's losses, restore company morale, and revive IBM's reputation with customers—and to introduce aggressive pricing in personal computers and mainframes.

At the time, Gerstner's assertion that IBM did not need a vision irked financial analysts, who thought that a clear vision was *precisely* what the company needed. They were searching for signs that IBM was now in the hands of a strong and decisive leader; instead, Gerstner came off as weak and indecisive.

For the past four months, these analysts had given Gerstner the benefit of the doubt. They had waited patiently for him to craft his plans for the company's recovery, and cost-cutting measures only went so far. They wanted to know how he planned to rebuild the company. Up to this point, he had let them down.

Forging a Less Bureaucratic IBM

Six weeks later, on September 13, Gerstner officially declared what had pretty much been company policy since he took over in April: he was keeping IBM intact and scrapping John Akers' program to break up the company into independent units. He announced his decision in a three-page letter to IBM employees that began "Dear Colleague."

> **I have reached the firm conclusion that decentralization vs. centralization is not our most important organizational dilemma. Rather, it is the working relationship across our operating units.**

It was unquestionably Gerstner's most important, and most controversial, step in the reinventing of IBM. Many IBM watchers were convinced that Akers had been on the right track, that it had made sense for IBM to function as a whole when its main business was mainframes, with its slower cycle times and steadier customer base; but now that personal computers reigned supreme and the shelf life of computers could be measured in months or even weeks, where competition was fierce for the many products the industry was now making, it made much more sense for IBM's units to compete against one another.

In that same letter, he began to lay the groundwork for IBM's renewed emphasis on customers. What the company needed to do, he wrote, was "to focus on customers and not on our internal procedures and wrangling, including and especially getting our products to market faster." It also needed

> **to create a new attitude in which customers come first, IBM second and the individual businesses third."**

He had held numerous conversations with IBM customers during the past few months, and more than one had impressed upon him a desire to deal with one IBM salesperson rather than a whole slew of them. Gerstner took that suggestion and many others to heart. Tom Watson Sr. had given priority to the customer. For that reason, Gerstner truly believed that he was not putting the company through a revolution; he was simply following in the footsteps of its founder.

To improve working relationships across IBM's operating units, he announced the creation of the Corporate Executive Committee, made up of ten senior company executives and himself. The aim of the new committee was to reduce redundancy and bureaucracy. The committee would form a corporate office and each of the ten executives would have as a principal focus overall corporate results—not individual unit performance. It did not escape the attention of IBM watchers that eight members of the new committee were veteran IBM executives, rather than outsiders. The executives would receive their bonuses based not on their individual performances but on IBM's overall results. He formed another new group, the worldwide Management Council, which consisted of thirty-five executives from various elements of IBM who would meet for two-day sessions four or five times a year to discuss companywide initiatives.

Gerstner wanted to assure everyone that he was not adding to the bureaucracy. The new corporate executive committee would not be another layer of operating management: budgets and strategic plans would be handled at the operating unit level. Nor would it function as an operation review committee: operating performance would remain the main responsibility of IBM's product and marketing units. "The focus will only be on policy issues that cut across multiple units," Gerstner wrote.

The changes he outlined in the September 13 memo aimed, he wrote, at

maintaining responsive, decentralized business units while at the same time coordinating critical resources and customer solutions across units. I believe these changes will, over time, streamline our decision-making, speed our responsiveness to the marketplace and, perhaps most importantly, enhance our customer relationships.

The media and financial analysts were still pressing hard to get a glimpse of Lou Gerstner's grand vision. How did he see the giant computer maker in the long run? What products would it emphasize? Would it remain a major manufacturer of hardware, especially mainframes? Or would it deemphasize mainframes? (IBM had never pondered getting rid of mainframes entirely.) Would Gerstner give special emphasis to personal computers and attendant software, thus trying to go head to head with the IBM clones which had sprung to life in the 1980s? Or might he take the company down the road of services and solutions, giving the actual production of computers a backseat to an approach that other companies were beginning to follow? Such questions went almost entirely unanswered in those final months of 1993, although few doubted that Gerstner planned to answer these questions sooner rather than later.

Chapter 7

———◆———

The Game Plan
Looks Good

**"The question about IBM is no longer one of survival.
The question now is can IBM grow."**

SIX MONTHS INTO the job, Lou Gerstner
remained Mr. Conservative. With Wall Street hounding him for a quick
fix, he knew the most that he could expect to do in his first year in office
was to run IBM better—to manage the place so that it ran more efficiently while keeping costs in line. He could not be expected to have
IBM's various divisions grow overnight; the product line changes that
he planned would take two to three years to kick in before solid results
could be achieved. But the financial analysts on Wall Street were growing impatient. They had watched IBM deteriorate over the past decade,
and they assumed the hiring of Lou Gerstner meant there would be a
quick turnaround. They were wrong, of course, but they still formed an
unpleasant pressure group that never let up on Gerstner.

Meanwhile, every three months IBM had to roll out its financials,
and in late October 1993 it was ready to announce its third-quarter
results. Wall Street always hotly anticipated the IBM results, and even
more so this time around. After all, Gerstner had been at the job for half
a year, and the figures might give some clue as to how he was doing.

Analysts expected IBM's losses to remain high. To nearly everyone's surprise, the company reported a modest loss of "only" $48 million, less than one third of the $160 million the analysts had predicted. Adding the $22 million it paid out to preferred shareholders, the company's loss came to $70 million. The analysts also believed that IBM's quarterly revenues would fall, but they remained steady at $14.7 billion, slightly higher than the quarter a year earlier. On the strength of that "good" news, IBM's stock rose $1.37, to $46.25. IBM's leaders knew it was far too early to celebrate. All Gerstner would say was that the company appeared to be "on the right track." Jerry York, the CFO, was equally cautious: "One quarter does not make a turnaround," he intoned, "but at least some things are moving in the right direction."

Once again, the shining star was IBM's service business, which rose 27 percent in the third quarter for revenues of $2.3 billion. While personal computers sales remained strong, their low margins kept IBM from racking up larger profits. Hardware revenue declined, as did software.

While he had promised to keep IBM whole, Gerstner did not exclude the prospect of spinning off certain businesses that did not fit with his cost-cutting strategy. Many federal jobs were awarded on a "cost-plus" basis, whereby a firm collected a predetermined, fixed amount of profit that was based on a percentage of costs. No matter how much costs were cut, profits would not increase, as the government set a ceiling on profits. So it was no surprise to learn that in early November IBM was thinking of selling its entire federal contracting division, which sells computers and electronic components to military and civilian agencies of the federal government. Based in Bethesda, Maryland, the operation had sales of $2.2 billion in 1992. The sale made sense if only because of cutbacks in federal spending with the end of the cold war. It was assumed that IBM would reap between $750 million to $1 billion in the sale. Some analysts wondered why Gerstner would want to divest one of IBM's few profitable businesses. In 1993 it contributed $153 million to IBM's bottom line.

Then on December 13, it was announced that IBM would indeed sell the Federal Systems division to a fast-growing New York–based defense firm named Loral for $1.575 billion in cash. To Gerstner, such re-engineering was almost the easiest part of what he had to do.

Our first task was to attack the critical problems: our uncompetitive cost structure; inefficiencies and unconsummated strategies that were destroying profits; and products that were not competitive. Frankly, deciding to fix these problems wasn't hard. It was very clear what had to be done.

There Goes the Art Collection

The sale of Federal Systems marked Gerstner's first major effort to get rid of unprofitable assets, but it was by no means his last. He was determined to sell anything and everything that did not contribute to the bottom line, including 350 paintings from the $25 million art collection started by founder Thomas Watson Sr. in 1937. He also sold off IBM's forty-three-story skyscraper at 57th Street in midtown Manhattan for $200 million (IBM retained rented offices in the building), as well as its 556-acre complex in Boca Raton, Florida (the birthplace of the IBM personal computer), for $48 million.

Over a four-year period—from 1993 to 1997—Gerstner unloaded 25.3 million square feet that had been used for manufacturing, warehouses, and offices: an area more than six times the space of one of the two towers at the New York City World Trade Center.

During his early years at the company, Gerstner took other bold steps to improve the company's bottom line. He had no choice: Wall Street would not tolerate a stagnant IBM. To that end, he engaged in a two-pronged effort: lowering the amount of taxes IBM had to pay the federal government and repurchasing IBM stock.

IBM's effective income tax rate had been 41.5 percent in 1994 and 47 percent in 1995. He brought it down to 37.7 percent in 1995; 35 percent; and 1997, 32.5 percent. This financial reengineering was accomplished as the company expanded into markets with lower effective tax rates. Other major corporations had tax rates in the low to mid-30s.

To improve the bottom line, Gerstner made another shrewd reengineering move. Beginning in 1995, he initiated an aggressive IBM stock buyback program (the figure would reach $20 billion by 1998). He preferred to use the company's free cash to repurchase stock rather than make acquisitions; not only were acquisitions unpopular at IBM, but Gerstner knew the risks involved in buying up companies.

While he was definitely putting the company on the right path, it would take a while before Lou Gerstner's cost-cutting drive showed up on IBM's bottom line. By the end of 1993, the company's income statement still looked dismal. Revenues were down to $62.7 billion, $1.8 billion less than the year before and $6.2 billion less than the 1990 figure. But the real disaster had to do with the company's profitability—or lack of it. Never had IBM turned in a worse figure—$8.1 billion in losses. It was a sad day for the company, but for Gerstner the figures had a silver lining. He felt that the company had undeniably hit rock bottom; at least he hoped it wouldn't get any worse. He took comfort in the knowledge that, in undertaking his new austerity program he himself had made IBM's figures look worse, a temporary phenomenon he hoped to correct as quickly as possible.

The Funeral Dirge Is Over

The first concrete signs of the Gerstner turnaround came in April 1994 when the company announced its first-quarter results. Though IBM's mainframe sales slipped an additional 12 percent in the first quarter (after dropping 32 percent in 1993), net income was once again on the plus side, coming in at $392 million, in contrast to the $399 million loss the company had suffered in the first quarter a year earlier. Dan Mandresh, the Merrill Lynch analyst, called it "a blowout quarter, really on track or ahead of the game in every respect." Despite the improvement, Jerry York was not crowing: Given that sales were $13.3 billion that quarter, he felt that the profit level was "nothing to write home about." He was satisfied with profitability in only a few of IBM's major businesses, including minicomputer hardware and software and maintenance. (The first-quarter profits were inflated owing to a one-time gain of $248 million from IBM's sale of the Federal Systems division.)

Those $13.3 billion in revenues represented an increase of 2 percent over the first quarter in 1993. Improvement was shown in the overall sales of hardware, which rose 9 percent to $6.3 billion, higher than analysts had predicted.

Lou Gerstner never sounded so upbeat as when he appeared before IBM shareholders at the annual meeting on April 25 in Toronto. "Barring the unforeseen, we are planning on being profitable in 1994," Gerstner predicted. Quite a statement since it would mark the first time since 1990 that IBM had been in the black. "It's not time to blow our horn and declare victory," Gerstner said with cautious reserve in his voice. "But the time for the funeral dirge is over."

The shareholders felt better when IBM's stock rose that week to $58.25 on the strength of the solid first-quarter results. Toward the end of June, *The New York Times* asserted: "So far, the Gerstner game plan is looking pretty good," though the IBM chief executive himself held back from pronouncing the turnaround a done deed. "Look, this is a three-steps-forward and one-step-back kind of process," he insisted. "And we certainly can't declare victory yet, but I think it's starting."

In the third week of July, IBM announced second-quarter results that far exceeded Wall Street's expectations for the second straight period. Its net income had reached $689 million this quarter. Analysts agreed that the issue was no longer whether Lou Gerstner would turn IBM around, but how far and how fast he would be able to move the company in the next year or two. With Gerstner's efforts impacting the bottom line, analysts concluded that IBM's biggest challenge was to improve revenues. There was some good news on that front as well. Sales of IBM's computer equipment—which included not only its high-profit mainframes, but its low-profit personal computers— accounted for the largest share of quarterly sales at $7.7 billion, an increase of 3 percent over the 1993 quarter.

Once more, in late October, IBM reported solid quarterly figures. Only the personal computer division continued to defy the Gerstner magic with sales up only slightly at 3 percent over the previous quarter. Profits amounted to $710 million in the third quarter on revenues of $15.4 billion; in the same quarter a year earlier IBM lost $87 million. Hardware sales in the third quarter rose by 13 percent. IBM's stock continued to rise and was now hovering around $75 a share. One of the key drivers of the stock price increase was Gerstner's ability to cut $5.6 billion in costs, half of that staggering figure in 1994 alone; the company hoped to pare a total of $8 billion by 1996. IBM had shrunk—from 302,000 employees at the end of 1992 to 232,000 in the fall of 1994— although the rate was slower than expected owing to renewed demand for IBM products.

So 1994 was a watershed year for IBM. It was during that year that IBM earned $3 billion—its first profitable year since 1990—enough to make the company the ninth most profitable company of the *Fortune*

500. But Gerstner's achievement was even more remarkable, for the company's earnings had gone from an $8 billion loss in 1993 to a $3 billion gain in 1994—in short, a profit swing of $11 billion! In 1994, IBM had also achieved its first year of revenue growth since 1990 as total revenue grew to $64 billion, up 6 percent from the year before. His drastic cost-cutting program was now in full gear: he had cut $3.5 billion in 1993 and another $2.8 billion in 1994. IBM finished 1994 with more than $10 billion in cash. And it reduced its core debt—debt in support of operations—by $3.3 billion, to $2.9 billion.

Gerstner was genuinely pleased with the turnaround thus far. "I think it's fair to say . . . that the question about IBM is no longer one of survival. We've stabilized the company financially and beyond that, strengthened it. IBM is back, and we're here to stay. The question now is, can IBM grow? I believe it can and that it will."

Part III

Building a New Corporate Culture

———◆———

"You need to change the way
you think and act, every hour
of every day for the rest of your
IBM career."

———◆———

———◆———

Chapter 8

Don't Liquidate: Splitting Up Is Hard to Do

"Keep IBM together and make the breadth of its products, services and skills its most potent competitive advantage."

THEY WERE DUBBED the Baby Blues. They were to make up the brave new world of IBM, a new federation of businesses to salvage the moribund company. Under the Akers plan, Armonk would be little more than a holding company, managing a portfolio of distinct businesses. Akers had made the bold decision in late 1991, believing that the parts of IBM outweighed the sum, that it was better for each of these units to pursue its own destiny. He knew that some or even all of the units might be spun off entirely and with each spin-off IBM would surrender more and more of its once-vaunted corporate identity. But Akers felt he had little choice. To sit on his hands and do nothing seemed a sure prescription for disaster.

The individual units were given separate names, anticipating their eventual independence. Adstar was the name assigned to the storage business. The high-speed printer business was designated Pennant; the low-end printer and printer supplies business was spun off to became Lexmark International Group. Each business had its own public relations staffs as well.

On the surface, splitting IBM up made sense if only because each newly created independent unit would have a better chance to compete with its rivals. Wall Street had routinely applauded the spinning off of parts of a larger company, convinced that the sum of a company's parts would be worth more than the existing whole. The feeling was that IBM's split-off units could get closer to their markets. They would no longer face the overheads that were eating into their profits, and they could raise morale by providing certain perks to senior executives such as stock options.

However popular the idea was on Wall Street, John Akers faced a great deal of opposition within his own IBM ranks. All of the strengths that IBM had derived from being a single corporate entity—presenting one face to the customer, economies of scale, synergies among IBM businesses—would be lost, certain executives argued. Had the company been functioning better, Akers might have listened more carefully to their arguments, but he was a desperate man. He knew that the company was headed for a year that would show several billions of dollars in losses, with the prospect of even larger losses down the road. He simply had to do something, and initiating his breakup plan seemed like the most prudent course of action.

Gerstner's Most Difficult Decision

When the IBM board chose Gerstner, it appeared to favor the Akers plan, but Gerstner was not forced to commit himself one way or the other. Still, senior IBM executives assumed that the new boss would be keen to implement Akers' dismemberment plan. It enjoyed widespread popularity within the company, and many believed, incorrectly, that Gerstner had been handpicked for the job in order to carry out the breakup.

When he took over as the head of IBM in April 1993, Lou Gerstner faced one of the most difficult decisions a CEO could face: Should he keep the company intact, or should he allow the Akers plan to go forward? Gerstner was confident about how to tackle IBM's most critical short-range problems—its uncompetitive cost structure, its inefficiencies, its bloated bureaucracy—but

what wasn't clear was what kind of company IBM was going to be. We had a couple of choices. We could have adopted a model that worked for other companies—break IBM into a collection of businesses. This would have left the pieces competing out there on their own, with the other 60,000 niche players in this industry. The company was on that path when I came on board. The alternative was to keep IBM together and to make the breadth of our products, services and skills our most potent competitive advantage.

Those who believed that Gerstner would plunge the stake into IBM's heart were mistaken. What they failed to understand was that Lou Gerstner wanted to help companies grow, not preside over their destruction. Gerstner's management philosophy of keeping IBM one integrated business had deep roots. As he had told the men who had wanted him to take over RJR Nabisco back in January 1989, "If you're looking for a liquidator, I'm not your guy. I'm a builder." Gerstner prided himself on being a turnaround artist, and it was fundamental to the thinking of turnaround artists that the company they are running must remain united and whole. "I love to build companies more than anything else," Gerstner said in 1989, implying that he had no desire to break them up. Gerstner knew what the pro-federation people were saying, that autonomous businesses would move faster in the marketplace. But he dismissed that notion as "just a theory," one that he obviously didn't share.

No one would have blamed Lou Gerstner for carrying through with John Akers' breakup plan. But the new IBM chairman and CEO had other thoughts, as spelled out in an interview with *The Economist:*

When I agreed to take this job, I started reading up about the company. I remember reading—and I hate to say this, but I do believe it was *The Economist*—a very, very awful piece, but troublesome to me. It said that the industry was breaking up into horizontal pieces. There were these layers and the real way to compete was around these layers and that IBM was the old example. And I said, that's interesting, but it doesn't register with me as a customer.

> The idea that this very hard, very complicated technology, very-difficult-to-integrate technology, was going to be bought by the customer in this model didn't make any sense to me.

As with most of the major decisions he made after becoming the head of IBM, Gerstner took his time. But, two months into the job, he gave a hint of which way he was leaning:

> I don't think getting the economics right in a business is necessarily the same thing as decentralization. There is a misconception that small is always more beautiful than big. Just fragmenting an organization does not create conditions sufficient for success. Given a black-and-white choice between centralization and decentralization, I am a dyed-in-the-wool decentralist. But I don't want to be forced into that binary choice. The job of corporate in IBM is to try to decentralize the responsibility to serve customers, to get as close to the customer as we can. Our second job is to figure out how to bring the power of the entire company to those decentralized units with a minimum of bureaucracy. I don't know yet what the balance should be between the two.

Keeping IBM Intact

He dropped another significant hint that he planned to keep IBM intact in his memo of July 27, 1993, to employees when he said: "You and I want to make IBM the most successful company in the world. It was once and I am convinced it will be again." Had he been thinking of dismemberment, he might not have spoken so warmly of IBM as a corporate whole.

By September 1993, Gerstner had made up his mind: he would not break up IBM. No decision that he would make in the early phase would loom larger than scrapping the Akers plan. There was never any formal announcement, just a series of pronouncements that let employees know that the Akers plan had been quietly discarded. As his September 13 memo to IBM employees shows clearly, his goal was to keep IBM intact and to derive the greatest possible synergies across the businesses. To that end, he created the Corporate Executive Committee to "lead the implementation of corporate-wide integration initiatives across the company and to advise on broad issues of corporate strategy." This new committee was being put in place not to destroy IBM but to keep its various parts functioning as a team. As Gerstner wrote near the end of that memo,

> In summary, the changes outlined above are aimed squarely at one objective: maintaining responsive, decentralized business units while at the same time coordinating critical resources and customer solutions across units.

Gerstner came to his decision to keep the company intact after listening to customers who wasted little time in conveying their wishes. "We want solutions to the increasingly complex information systems problems out there—and we want one-stop shopping." In other words, customers wanted a company like IBM to take over *all* of its computer needs, to supply the necessary equipment and to provide the requisite computer service. A dismembered IBM could not have offered the kind of integrated approach customers were looking for. Only a single, unified company, showing one face to the customer, could do that. Gerstner understood that IBM had a competitive advantage as long as it remained whole. "Our ability to integrate is a unique asset of this company," he explained.

Wall Street applauded the Gerstner plan. As a Lehman Brothers report noted: "Gerstner put an end to the breakup of IBM under the assumption that if any company could provide end-to-end computing solutions, in an ever more complex market place, customers would find this valuable. IBM was, and is, uniquely positioned to deliver this type of structure owing to its huge size and market share in the computer industry."

Not Satisfied with Only the Louvre

In some quarters, however, Gerstner was assailed for countermanding the Akers plan. Most derisive were the comments that came from veteran IBM analyst Robert Djurdjevic, who argued that Gerstner's decision to keep the company intact was little more than a maneuver to burnish his personal image. "Perhaps," the analyst wrote in a newsletter, "the key, and yet the unspoken, reason why IBM's CEO is so vehemently opposed to a breakup of the company is that such an IBM would not need an Armonk! It would not need a hands-on 'CEO-king,' just a good bookkeeper. That's because it would have several competent 'CEO-kings' running the spun-off units. But such an IBM would need a leader with a vision, who would put the shareholders' pocketbooks ahead of his ego. Evidently, Gerstner is not it. On the contrary. Just as Louis XIV, for example, was not satisfied with only a Louvre, and had to built a Versailles, so has IBM's Louis XIX already announced plans to build Armonk II. Students of history may recall what eventually happened to the former residents of the Louvre and Versailles. 'Those who don't learn from history are doomed to repeat it,' goes the old saw. The IBM chairman would do well to heed it."

Needless to say, Lou Gerstner did not enjoy being compared to Louis XIX. But he could take comfort from the fact that large segments of the financial community praised him warmly for keeping IBM united and whole. For example, J. Gerald Simmons, the president of Handy HRM Corp. of New York City and a former IBM executive, penned a letter to *Fortune* magazine that was published in its January 24, 1994, edition: "I have followed the company closely for the past several years, particularly since Lou Gerstner took charge. In our role as management consultants, we work extensively with information officers in major organizations, and I assure you that they are more interested in a vendor who possesses the best solutions than in one who has the fastest computer speeds." And Gerstner was absolutely right when he said, 'Of the thousands of customers I have talked to, no one has argued that they want IBM to be broken up in little pieces.' "

In effect, Gerstner was laying down a bet that a *whole* IBM would be worth more than the sum of its parts. He wanted to enhance shareholder value—one of his primary goals—and that could only come from a single, unified IBM. So he sent a message to the business community: he was going to do his best to make sure that IBM survived—and flourished.

In an interview with *Software* magazine, he reiterated why he had been inclined to keep IBM together:

When I arrived in the spring of 1993, the company had a big decision to make. We had to decide whether IBM was going to become some loose confederation of niche companies, competing

at the piece-parts level of our industry, or whether we were going to hold IBM together and make the depth and breadth of our products, services and skills a competitive advantage. Frankly, coming to IBM as a customer of this industry, I had a very strong opinion that there was a need for someone to play the role of integrator—to do more than deliver neat technology—to bring that technology to customers as an integrated solution to a business issue.

Gerstner had come to believe that information technology was not meant simply to enhance the productivity of an employee. Rather, information technology had become basic to how a firm functioned. Accordingly, CEOs would have to think of information technology as critical to their business strategies. And if they did, their companies would gain a competitive advantage over others less interested in information technology. To be in a position to offer these companies the widest array of information technology, to package it in "solutions," to provide the service that had become a key ingredient of the computer technology of the 1990s, would require IBM staying together.

It was not easy for customers to deal with a computer industry that seemed to be disintegrating before their eyes. Everything was terribly confusing. The way to deal with the confusion was for a company like IBM to take different parts of the computer industry and integrate them, to link applications together into a network arrangement. Individual companies that sold only one product line would have a much harder time satisfying their customers' complex demands.

In making a strategic decision to keep IBM intact, Gerstner knew that the strategy would only work if he could get the best out of his employees. By July 1997 he could say with confidence that he had made the right decision.

The decision meant we had a lot of work to do because the strategy would only work if each of our offerings could stand and compete on its own merits. We had to restore the competitiveness of our product lines, move more aggressively into services, and build a solutions business that begins with an understanding of the customer's core business issues—speed, competitiveness, global expansion, customer satisfaction. . . .

> We believed the decision to hold IBM together was right at
> the time. Today, with the industry shifting to a computing model
> based around global networks, our customers are placing an even
> greater premium on integration. Look at what many of our com-
> petitors are doing—buying each other, striking deals and alliances
> so they can offer more pieces of the solution. In many ways,
> they're trying to cobble together a lot of what IBM already has.

Despite Gerstner's eventual success, proving it was shrewd to keep
IBM intact, some IBM employees were not that impressed with the
Gerstner years, and were upset that he had not implemented the Akers
breakup plan. One such executive from the 1960s and 1970s recalled in
the summer of 1998: "When I joined IBM, I was so proud.... It was the
best company in the world. Today it's just another company.... Gerstner's made it a pedestrian company. The pride, the culture he's effectively destroyed. You could argue that if he hadn't kept IBM intact, the
company would have been destroyed. My sense is that Gerstner inher-
ited something that was about to hit a wall. The way he went about
doing it from a Wall Street perspective was very successful. But from
the perspective of someone who knew how special this company was, it
was a tragedy. I would have liked to see the company broken up. There
is no entrepreneurial spirit any more. A lot of people are going through
the motions. This is no longer a lifestyle company. Gerstner is running
it as just another financial institution. So what bothers me is that they
had something so precious. My sense is that as smaller entities they
could have maintained some of the culture they created, some of the
entrepreneurial spirit. That's lost now. I remember the way it was."

Pundits would argue the pros and cons of keeping the company
together and it certainly appeared that advocates of a united IBM had
the better part of the argument. But just as importantly, Gerstner's
decision not to break up IBM provided him with the opportunity to
become a major figure in the business world. Gerstner had to factor that
in when he made his decision. Had he allowed the dismemberment of
IBM, there would have been no corporate giant to turn around, and
Lou Gerstner would have become yesterday's news very quickly.

Chapter 9

—◆—

Live and Preach
the Culture, or It Just
Won't Happen

**"If the CEO isn't living and preaching the culture and
isn't doing it consistently, then it just doesn't happen."**

NOTHING STOOD IN the way of Lou Gerstner's
plan to reorganize IBM as much as its corporate culture. Thomas Watson Sr., the founder of the company, was long gone, and so was his son,
but their influence, especially that of the elder Watson, remained as
strong as ever. The corporate culture that these two men had created
and shaped had been the backbone of IBM in its glory days; and it was
the corporate culture—a twisted, warped version of the original—that
had been pulling the company down in recent years. Gerstner knew
that changing the culture would be no easy task because it was the glue
that held the company together. But he also knew that IBM desperately
needed a new corporate culture if it was to recover.

Thomas Watson Sr. had built a company that had no rival. And he
established a corporate culture that was paternalistic and, by today's
standards, outmoded. Yet, as IBM's spectacular growth and earnings
proved, the culture turned the company's men and women into a highly

trained, highly motivated army of workers. Watson's aim was to create a family atmosphere in which employees felt comfortable and secure, to make sure that people worked hard but had time to relax as well. In much the same way that members of a family know their place—and know the rules—IBM staff had no trouble discerning what was acceptable behavior and what was not.

The main anchor of IBM's corporate culture, the anchor that would make every IBM employee feel secure, was the no-layoff policy. In this respect, IBM was no different from many other companies that put the needs of their employees above those of the bottom line. Not only did Watson offer life-long security; he also wanted employees to feel they were part of one big, happy, productive family. As head of the "family," Watson assumed responsibility for the comfort and serenity of the workers, especially outside IBM's corridors. IBM went to great lengths to care for the various needs of employees and their families: the company found them homes, located work for their spouses, and provided employees with privileges at private country clubs. In short, Watson wanted to make sure that the IBM employee had few worries on the home front and thus could be free to focus on company business.

I Sing of Thee, Thomas Watson

The corporate culture was not simply patriarchal. It sent messages, subtle and otherwise, that employees were expected to show intense loyalty to IBM. Such devotion would presumably make workers more productive. Just as a football coach tries to get the team revved up for the next game, Watson encouraged his managers to hold daily pep talks with employees—to get them "up" for their next round of sales calls. Employees were expected to express the same kind of loyalty to IBM that family members demonstrated toward their families. Often, however, loyalty to IBM and to Thomas Watson Sr. became confused, or at least thrown together, as when the founder commissioned a company songbook with titles like "Ever Onward" and "Hail to the IBM," and with lyrics like these:

> Our voices well in admiration;
> Of T. J. Watson proudly sing.
> He'll be ever our inspiration.
> To him our voices loudly ring.

If the company songs were meant to inspire workers, a whole series of slogans, appearing in offices, washrooms, even closets, was designed to make employees work harder. The slogans were vague, but compelling:

THINK
Make Things Happen
Ever Onward
Beat Your Best

Watson the elitist created a mystique about IBM, implying that its employees were a breed apart from the rest of the corporate world. So that employees would not embarrass themselves—or, more importantly, IBM—through indecent behavior as defined by Watson the conservative, he established firm rules governing what was permissible and what was not. The result was the creation of the quintessential "IBM-er," where every employee was interchangeable with every other employee. Starting with the dress code, the IBM lifestyle was heavily conservative, in keeping with the values of Thomas Watson Sr. An almost Puritanical cast pervaded the corridors; smoking and drinking were forbidden on company premises. Employees who took a drink at lunch were barred from returning to the office. Drinking at home was allowed in moderation, but the shades should be drawn; excessive drinking could slow down promotion. Divorce—indeed anything that might bring embarrassment to the company—was frowned upon as well.

Thomas Watson Sr. was not the least bit bothered by outsiders who railed at IBM or ridiculed the company for such behavior. He watched the company grow in leaps and bounds and took great pride in having created the most successful corporation in America. The corporate culture was effective—that was all that mattered.

This Must Be the IBM Building

The same obsessive culture that fostered new standards of excellence in product development and employee performance also encouraged an unhealthy mixture of complacency and arrogance which sapped IBM employees of their once-vaunted energy and enthusiasm. All that uniformity, which for decades had produced the "model employee," had led to rigidity at IBM. Just how rigid is best exemplified by a clever joke that made the rounds of the computer industry: It involved the pilot of a small airplane who had lost his way in the fog over Atlanta. His radio was knocked out by lightning. Groping through the fog, the pilot finally saw a man standing in the window of a tall building.

"Where am I?" the pilot shouted.

The man replied, "You're in an airplane."

Banking his plane, the pilot soon landed at the airport.

One passenger observed, "It's miraculous that you landed us here safely, but how in the world did that man in the window help you?"

"Oh, that's easy," the pilot replied with a smile. "What he had said was completely correct and totally irrelevant to my problem, so I knew it had to be the IBM building."

Who could blame IBM for being so rigid? It had reached a level of success unprecedented in the annals of American corporate life. It had come to dominate its markets to such a degree that the effect was intoxicating. Rigidity seemed a blessing under such circumstances. Jim Cannavino, who until 1995 had been IBM's senior vice president for strategy and development, recalled that back in the late 1950s IBM had placed a $5 billion bet on its new System 360 mainframe computer. "We were a billion-dollar company and IBM bet five times its revenue stream—$5 billion was the amount of research and development money put into the project. And IBM wound up with control of the market. It also had pricing control. Keep in mind that the 360 had very high margins. Once you get on that heroin, you get less and less competitive. The heroin was your ability to keep moving the prices up," instead of cutting costs and becoming more efficient. In short, IBM began to feel invincible.

We Know You Tried Your Best

Out of that new rigidity came unpleasant by-products. Once, the culture had encouraged consensus, but that had not impeded the decision-making process. Now, consensus had become so much of a company watchword that it took forever to make decisions. "Our culture," said one senior IBM executive, "was very congenial, so congenial you never knew where you stood. Meetings would always go fine. You'd go in, and everything would be very proper and well-dressed, and a bunch of people would sit around and have a nice chat. The results might be good, and people would say, 'Thank you very much.' Or the results might be awful, and it would still be, 'Thank you very much; we know you tried your best.' " Consensus was eating away at IBM's capacity to function productively.

The need for consensus, in its worst forms, led to a companywide insularity. If IBM had once been the standard by which all others in the computer industry were judged, as time passed, its employees seemed further and further removed from the new mainstream that was developing around them. Nothing so typified that insularity as the IBM-specific language used to describe computer products—a language that was totally out of synch with the one employed by the rest of the industry. IBM staffers called disk drives "hard files." Circuit boards were "planar boards." Personal computers and workstations were called "clients." Mainframes became "servers."

To turn IBM around, Lou Gerstner would not only have to wrestle with the existing culture, he would have to create a new culture within the organization. The task was daunting—not only because IBM's culture was so deeply embedded, not only because hundreds of thousands of employees knew of no other way to behave, but also because he was the new kid on the block and would therefore be regarded with suspicion and distrust.

Gerstner knew how difficult it was to effect cultural change in large organizations.

The process is highly personal, in the sense that I am unable to articulate it completely. I can say what I want done, but I can't articulate how to do it. I can't do it for other people. I can't say, "Now look, I want you to be entrepreneurial. Here is what you are going to do; now read this book." My big challenge is how to maintain our momentum while the organization grows, without spending all my energies in the process.

Gerstner concluded from his previous leadership experiences that, in a large corporation, a very small window of opportunity existed to implement change. At the start, employees allowed the new boss a kind of a honeymoon period: the new CEO could try to develop major strategies and could deal with those strategies in a direct, hands-on way. But once that window of opportunity started to close, the hands-on approach gave way to a more distant kind of managing. The lesson Gerstner brought with him to IBM was this: if you want to make changes, do it quickly.

> You look at the creative input to any problem-solving, the real insights and important issues are set in the early stages of problem-solving, in the phrasing of the problem, in the assumptions you choose to make, in the research methodology you pick. In the early stages, problem-solving contains enormous potential to create insight. As you move on, all you get served up are two or three options. The real range of options has been largely filtered out months earlier.

Gerstner remembered how hard it had been for him to make changes at American Express. When he sought to overhaul the company's culture, he discovered that culture focused on many things, but not the one thing he had in mind—performance.

> In one of the divisions [of American Express], longevity had previously been important; in another the politics of being on the right team was. There was a value placed on moving quickly through jobs. "How quickly can I get to the next job?" When I arrived the average time in a job was sometimes less than a year. If you were going to be in a job for only a year, how could you possibly show performance? How could you possibly develop subordinates? How could you possibly develop a sense of how you could do this job better than anyone else?

From his experience at American Express, Gerstner was all too familiar with corporate cultures that were way out of synch with the business environment; with companies whose executives spent more energy fighting one another than trying to understand the business environment; with stubborn executives who thought their way was the best way—the only way. Recalling American Express's rigid organizational structure, the high degree of internal competition among operating units, the internal rivalry between new and old product lines, he noted that, even worse than these defects, was the resistance to the idea that the world could change. It was, he noted, very much an attitude of "We have done it this way for years and have been successful. Don't talk to us about new competitors."

> In our strategic planning, we identified competitors, but we didn't always reach an internalized sense of what was going on outside that told us what we should do inside. Perhaps this phenomenon was related to the great—almost unique—success the company had enjoyed over the years.

Painfully aware that he was likely to revisit some of these same problems as he took over at IBM, Lou Gerstner understood that a national treasure, an icon like IBM, would be very resistant to change. For decades it had nurtured a culture that set norms and patterns of behavior for hundreds of thousands of employees. Change was anathema. Change was counterculture. Change was the enemy. Yet, to truly correct IBM, Lou Gerstner had to tackle that culture, to make sure that the sweeping changes he planned would be accepted by IBM's employees. In some ways it would be his greatest challenge, one that was made even more difficult because IBM had started to fragment itself into thirteen autonomous businesses.

Gerstner knew there was only one way to change the culture, and that was for him to lead the fight as if he were a general going to war.

> If the CEO isn't living and preaching the culture and isn't doing it consistently, then it just doesn't happen. This is a *sine qua non*— this is not a sufficient condition, but a necessary one.

But, he suffered no illusions that it would be easy to enact change in company culture.

> It finally became clear to me after a year or two in American Express that changing the organization was a lot harder to do than I had thought. My view had been that it would take me a year to get the basic elements in place and be ready to go. In fact it took four years. Early on it became clear to me that creating an environment in which change could occur fairly rapidly was very important.

What did Lou Gerstner think of the old IBM culture? First of all, he recognized that the culture had done quite a lot of good for IBM. But he was well aware of its shortcomings as well.

> **I'm almost not trying to understand IBM's culture. In a sense I may be disrespectful. Parts of that culture are very important, and I'm trying to reinforce those like crazy: a high degree of attention to the customer, sensitivity to the individual inside the company, dedication to quality. Those values have been part of cultures I've created elsewhere. But I'm not interested in the part of the culture that defines processes as opposed to values. I don't want anybody to tell me about the processes.**

He felt strongly about this point. During his first few months at IBM, Gerstner gained the impression that past company leaders had meddled far too much in the day-to-day operations instead of just letting the place run under a set of clearly stated operating principles.

> **I do not think we can or should be a procedurally driven company. That doesn't mean we don't have processes. Effective processes that serve the customer are important. But we have more procedures in this company than I have ever seen in my life. We tell people how to behave, what to do, how to do it—everything. We have to stop. We have to be a company that bases its decisions on some very fundamental operating principles. If we all understand those principles, and we all work by them, then we will transform IBM into a leader and a winner.**

Two months into the job, he was not prepared to utter a blanket disapproval of IBM's culture.

> **I haven't reached a conclusion about whether there is or isn't complacency. All I know is that we're going to figure out some things that have to get done and then we're going to do them very fast. Look, I refuse to say, "Let's go back and decide all the things that are wrong with IBM. What did we do wrong?" I have not uttered those words since I've been at IBM. I am not interested in our putting on a bunch of hair shirts.**

"We have been too bureaucratic and too preoccupied with our own view of the world," he wrote, noting that the company had earned a reputation for arrogance, "but it's not going to happen on my watch."

Unquestionably, Lou Gerstner planned to change the IBM culture. He knew it needed changing, though he didn't want to dwell on all the reasons why. That was the past, and he was only interested in the present and the near future. Making the cultural change that was vital would be problematic—he knew that. He knew that he had little time to put his changes into practice, and that the best way to manage change was to give as much decision-making power to the people under him as possible. Despite such truths, he would not let himself feel constrained. He planned to be an activist CEO, and he had no intention of letting IBM's eighty-year-old corporate culture get in his way.

Chapter 10

Sweep Aside the
Old Corporate Culture
If Necessary,
But Do It Quickly

*"I'm looking for people with the guts to go above,
below, around or through internal hurdles."*

THOUGH HE WAS determined to have a major
impact on IBM, Lou Gerstner faced a certain dilemma: Much of what
founder Thomas Watson Sr. had instilled in the company Gerstner
found useful and important. He liked to say that in many ways the IBM
he envisioned was actually a return to the old IBM. By that he meant
the Watson Sr. era, not what came later—not the IBM that took so long
to make decisions or that was complacent to the point of paralysis.

**I'm talking about the *old* old IBM, the company that was cus-
tomer-obsessed. That didn't start by asking, 'What technology do
you want?' but 'What are the key business issues you need to
solve?,' the IBM that consistently led the way, and led this indus-**

try. The IBM that bet the company on a vision—the System/360—and won, big. The IBM that defined excellence for business organizations and that over and over again invented the future.

I haven't talked much about this, because it's been important to focus on other, more urgent things: survival, and then growth, and then establishing our relevance to a new computing era. Also, frankly, many people here looked at the company's past with an unproductive nostalgia. We had turned aspects of the past into icons, and we sat around worshipping them, rather than reacting to the world around us and how it was changing. That's something that neither T. J. Watson Sr. nor Jr. ever did. But now I think we're ready to fulfill our destiny—and that goes back to a lot of the things this company has always stood for.

In trying to change IBM's corporate culture, Gerstner was careful to note that he did not want to destroy IBM's core strengths, its technology, its bright people. He did not want to throw the baby out with the bath water. But he did want to change the culture.

[The problem] was more the attitudes, the kind of management structures and the management behavior that got built up in the face of success. I call it the curse of success.

In trying to change the way people at IBM behaved, Gerstner had no interest in tinkering with the corporate structure.

We have a geographic reach that others would kill for. Everybody's talking about the age of Asia. Look at the size of IBM's Asian operations and how long they've been there. And Latin America. We had all these great skills and, despite that, we managed to screw up. So that gets to behavioral issues. I've been fortunate enough to have to only work on the behavioral side. I was also blessed by the fact that you need a crisis to focus on the need for change. Basically what I said to people around here is: We just lost $17 billion and 150,000 people lost their jobs, and the media is throwing us on the junkyard pile. It appears that what we were doing wasn't working. Would you not agree? And, therefore, we ought to try something different. The ability to appeal to a bunch

of smart people, who obviously saw that the old system wasn't working, was very constructive.

What he tried—and this of course was very different—was to encourage IBM employees to adopt a new attitude toward the company, to be more serious about their work, and most of all, to be more willing to change their ways. He described the new IBM culture that he wanted to cultivate as one of "restless self-renewal." But could "restless self-renewal" be made a permanent part of the new IBM culture?

It has to be—if you want to lead during a period of great change. Remember, our market place is itself incredibly dynamic. It's protean; it constantly renews and reinvents itself . . . if you want to win this game, you have to wake up every day *expecting* change. In fact, you have to enjoy it.

It's the flip side of wanting to win them all, of never being satisfied with second, of wanting to score every point, of feeling every setback personally. It means embracing change. If there's something that's keeping us from growing and leading our business, change it—whether it's a process, or the way we work, or quite frankly, our own skills. IBM needs to be a high-performance culture characterized by restless self-renewal. And in some parts of the company, we're already there.

You have to expect change, and, Gerstner believed, you have to have a sense of urgency, being willing to change right away, where needed. Otherwise, it would be impossible to keep up with—and win—in the fast-changing computer industry of the 1990s.

Gerstner brought a sense of urgency back to a company that had come to equate aggressiveness with dishonor. The old IBM culture had bred a certain contempt for talking too much about competition; there was something wrong about seeming too pushy. Because of IBM's past confrontations with the Justice Department, which had sought to reduce its perceived monopoly over the computer industry, the company had discouraged its employees from thinking like monopolists, from behaving as if it were the proverbial six-hundred-pound gorilla pushing others around. Its sales force had been told not to belittle the competition, not to draw the government's attention. That could be counterproductive. The result was a company that felt it couldn't flex its muscles. But Gerstner wanted a different IBM. He wanted the competitive juices flowing again. He wanted employees to want to win. He took it personally when IBM lost a deal, and he expected others in the company to act the same way.

A Sense of Urgency

Urgency was a watchword for Gerstner. Not only did he want change, he wanted change quickly. He got it in part by forcing staff to think anew about performance, to think anew about how they got products to market; by letting employees know that their jobs were *not* 100 percent secure; by creating a more casual, less imperial environment, one where the conservative, cautious thinking of the past was out and risk taking and entrepreneurial efforts were applauded. To underscore how important he felt about all this, Gerstner tied executive pay and stock options to IBM's overall performance, forcing managers to focus on fixing their businesses. With regard to upper management, he required them to own stock according to a fixed formula: members of the Corporate Executive Committee had to own three times their annual base salary and bonus; the worldwide Management Committee, two times; and the Senior Management Group, equal to their annual base salary and bonus. Gerstner imposed a heavy ownership requirement on himself—he had to own four times his annual base salary and bonus. There was no parallel ownership requirement for nonexecutives; instead, Gerstner expanded IBM's stock option program to nonexecutives; in the past those options had been reserved only for senior management.

How did Gerstner change the old ways at IBM? What did he do to break the old culture? First and foremost, he abandoned the decades-old no-layoff policy, which, more than any other part of the corporate culture, bred lethargy and indifference. No longer would IBM employees enjoy the luxury of having a job for life; of coasting along in an environment that did not keep them on their toes; of being assured that no matter how lax they were, no matter how many hours they took off in a day, their jobs would be secure. By dropping the no-layoff policy, Gerstner stripped away the protective covering that cloaked many IBM employees who were not pulling their weight. Now he could identify them—and send them on their way. Only the truly talented remained behind. He moved aggressively in July 1993, announcing a one-time plan to dismiss 35,000 employees. This plan was different from those of the past because it did not simply use normal attrition and attractive early-retirement packages to reduce payrolls. This plan actually laid people off. Gerstner expressed regret, but offered no apologies.

In the fall he announced his eight guiding IBM principles. Significantly, number eight read: "We are sensitive to the needs of all employees and to the communities in which we operate." That was in stunning contrast to the values established by founder Thomas Watson Sr. who placed "respect for the individual" at the top of his own list of priorities. Gerstner would show respect for employees all right, but he expected them to work hard and demanded that they produce results. His no-nonsense approach contrasted sharply with the past. Gone were the days of "We appreciate what you did. We know you tried your best." No longer would arguments go on forever and decisions get put off and put off. He brought a new toughness, a brusque take-no-prisoners style that many found intimidating and downright unpleasant. But Gerstner did not care. In fact, he was pleased if others felt terror in their hearts upon meeting him. Under such pressure, they were bound to perform better.

Getting Things Moving

What mattered to Gerstner was performance, not offending employees. He was, for IBM, a breath of fresh air. For so long, IBM's executives had gone through the motions of restructuring, cutting costs, starting one program after another until the media and the financial analysts concluded that the company's problems were simply insurmountable. Lou Gerstner scoffed at such thinking. He understood from the start that the problems weren't insurmountable; the problems existed because no one had been willing to tackle them head on. He had figured out how to transform a big company when he was at RJR Nabisco, and he was confident that he could do the same thing at IBM.

Gerstner challenged the old IBM culture in a number of significant ways. He worked to destroy the turfs and fiefdoms that had grown up at the company. "You can't have politicians," he said. "You sack politicians." To get his point across, Gerstner employed another tactic: "We had a few public hangings of people who didn't want to get on the new programs. That told everybody we were serious." One of those public hangings involved someone very close to the new CEO: his own brother, Dick Gerstner.

Cain and Abel

Dick Gerstner was warm, gregarious, and popular—the epitome of the old IBM. At one point people thought Dick, not Lou, might be the Gerstner who would replace John Akers.

Dick began his career in 1960 as an industrial engineer, rose to become the head of IBM's Asia Pacific Group, and in 1988 was chosen to fix the troubled PC business. Even before taking that latter job, he had become sick with a mysterious illness that kept him from work for three years. It was diagnosed as Lyme disease, but not before he had undergone two spinal surgeries. Dick left IBM in November 1992, but came back the following spring for a 90-day consulting project which gave him a ringside seat to brother Lou's arrival.

Both brothers found the situation bizarre: with Lou running the company, Dick was in a position to let everyone else at IBM know what the new boss was really like. Lou wasn't happy to have his brother around—not that Dick was overly chatty about the new boss. Lou loved his brother, but he wanted to get off to a good, clean start, and Dick was in the way. Lou planned to use a new broom to sweep IBM into action. People like Dick had to go. But they were brothers. Dick and Lou. Cain and Abel.

Even though he decided to sack thousands of employees, Lou might have made an exception in Dick's case; he might have let him continue on in consulting jobs at IBM. But Lou felt he couldn't in good conscience preach to IBM's employees that big changes were in the offing and at the same time keep his brother around.

Dick remembered their first meeting at IBM. "It was a little spooky for both of us," he acknowledged. "Lou and I both felt it didn't make sense for me to stay. I was ill. I hadn't worked much in three years. I was part of the team that had messed it up. The last thing Lou wanted was somebody from the old guard who happened to be his brother." Beyond that, Dick says, he was ready to leave. "Everybody was asking me what Lou was like and how should they part their hair. It was madness. I was very happy to see my three months come to an end." Such talk was only to be expected in public. Even so, Lou Gerstner's behavior struck many IBM employees as, well, unbrotherly, to say the least.

If the decision to let his brother go was agonizing, Lou Gerstner showed no signs of it. What he *did* show was a determination to breathe new life into IBM. Others called him hard-hearted, a tough bastard who would sell out his own brother just to make a point. Well, they were right—but it was a point that Lou Gerstner was eager to make. He was on the warpath, and he expected to be taken seriously. Otherwise there would be more public hangings.

Gerstner's Guerrillas

Gerstner wanted change, and so did IBM's employees. That much was clear from the e-mails they sent to the new CEO. They just didn't know how to begin. Gerstner planned to give them some help. During his first few months on the job he called for 5,000 volunteers to help him bring about change in IBM. The "volunteers" would be expected to influence thousands more, recruit others, and so on. He did not intend to launch a formal program—it was more of a challenge, a call to arms, Gerstner's way of encouraging an ongoing grassroots campaign within IBM to change the company's culture. To effect real cultural change, Gerstner sensed that he would have to start small, and hope that his cadre of volunteers would create a movement that would grow over time.

Gerstner received letters from hundreds of employees who responded positively to the overture, asking to sign up. One writer dubbed them "Gerstner's Guerrillas." In response to the offers, Gerstner penned a letter of thanks to those who answered his call. He asked them to think twice before agreeing to join the effort because the membership requirements were tough. He wanted people who were...

Committed to the long-term success of all IBM in a fast-changing, intensely competitive global business environment. Commitment to your career and to your business unit are not enough.

Zealous in making things work for the customer, especially when the customer's needs require the involvement of several different parts of IBM. Turf barons and baronesses need not apply.

Undeterred by bureaucracy, obstacles and this-is-the-way-we've-always-done-things thinking. I can assure you, there are some in the company who will fight you at every turn. I'm looking for people with the guts to go above, below, around or through internal hurdles.

Willing to take risks in the face of conventional wisdom and practice.

Constantly looking at everything we do with a critical eye, finding new ways to do things better and more productively. I need people who spend company money and use IBM resources as prudently as they spend their own money and resources.

Aware that the race goes to the swift, and are willing to set the pace in an already breathless environment.

Looking to the future with confidence. (No handwringers!)

How can these volunteer change-makers take the first steps?

Basically, you need to change the way you think and act, every hour of every day for the rest of your IBM career. Make a constructive and critical evaluation of everything that happens in your unit, and make it better.

Toward the end of the letter, Gerstner issued an implicit warning that those who couldn't stand the heat of change, who were too comfortable with tradition and procedure, might find themselves in trouble at IBM. "If you are ready to set tough goals and reach for high standards of performance, I'd be proud to have you at my side as we move forward," he wrote, adding that he wanted only those people who were willing to follow his business approach.

To really be successful, people have to change. Our culture has to change. And you know what that's all about.

We can't share knowledge, we can't reach out to customers, if we continue to operate in silos inside of IBM. If we're going to share knowledge, if we're going to increase our speed, if we're going to have a complete connection between our customers and us, we have to integrate inside of IBM. We've got to work as a team. We can't be part of a division or a product; we've got to be part of IBM—coming together, delivering solutions.

The New Stealth IBM

To Lou Gerstner, it seemed as if everyone was showing up for work at IBM dressed as if they were going to a funeral. Indeed, IBM's conservative, stodgy, dress code had been one of the most ingrained and annoying of company habits. Changing that habit, Gerstner decided, would help break down other parts of the old corporate culture. So the word was passed down to employees on the back pages of IBM employee publication *THINK* magazine: The dress code was out. The starched white shirt had been replaced by the more casual striped shirt. Gerstner was walking through an open door. Even before he had arrived on the scene, many IBM divisions had already shifted to a more relaxed dress. In public, he rarely made any references to the way staff workers were supposed to dress. Dressing for work called for a certain common sense, he told colleagues in private, and he trusted employees enough to know how to dress without issuing specific instructions.

Still, it did not take long for everyone in the company to understand that Gerstner had quietly ended the crusty old dress code. The employees at IBM headquarters rejoiced that their unstarched wardrobe at home could now be put to good use. The men could wear slacks, sports shirts, and loafers and the women could wear blouses and pants without feeling that their jobs were threatened. Essentially, Gerstner was trying to tell his troops to lighten up. His theory was this: by rallying behind a change in the dress code, he would have an easier time convincing the staff to make other, more significant changes throughout the company.

The real message behind the style change was this: IBM's sales personnel should forget about their trappings of power, their suits, their slide presentations—and figure out what customers required. In short, stop acting as if you know it all. As one observer noted: "IBM has become a casual company. It's not a structured, button-downed company any more. That didn't just happen. Lou Gerstner mandated it. He wanted to break the mold. He said, 'There will be no more dress code. Do what you want.' The new dress code became his way of saying that from now on things are different. The code went from white shirts to blue shirts to plaid shirts. Part of what he was trying to do was to get IBM-ers to think more like the rest of industry because in California they were not dressing up."

A Building That Stresses Openness

Along with the more relaxed dress code was a new lack of pretentiousness around IBM, symbolized best in the new corporate headquarters, which were to be built not far from the old headquarters. Ground was broken in September 1994, and the new headquarters opened in the summer of 1997. The new building was smaller and more open than the previous headquarters—less stodgy, less formal, and more intimate. *The Economist* described the new headquarters, made of polished granite and burnished stainless steel, as "modest." "IBM's new headquarters at Armonk in New York state is so discreetly tucked into a valley that it cannot be seen until you are almost upon it. It politely curves in an S-shape around trees and rocks that could more easily have been blasted away. For a company that employs 270,000 people and brings in revenues of nearly $80 billion per year, it is implausibly tiny. Inside, it is light, open-plan, discreetly high-tech, and very, very calm. It is a stealth headquarters, the antithesis of the swaggering IBM buildings from before."

The old building had, in Gerstner's view, too many offices and too little space to accommodate meetings with customers. It was embarrassingly obsolete, with wiring that was too old for the fast modems needed to handle computer communications traffic. Nor was the building wired for cable, video conferencing, or satellite broadcasts, hardly the infrastructure required for the giant computer firm. (When Gerstner decided to broadcast a worldwide New Year's message to employees, he was forced to do it at IBM's Manhattan's offices.)

In the old 420,000-square-foot headquarters, where 900 IBM employees worked, Gerstner's office was in a cloistered space at the end of a lengthy corridor of offices. In the new 280,000-square-foot building, Gerstner and other senior executives occupy offices on the top floor in the central portion of the three-story Z-shaped building. Most of the other 600 employees work in cubicles. Gerstner's idea was to have as many employees as close to him as possible. One sees few walls and few doors. The theme is openness. If wiring was a problem in the old building, the new building has done away with the need for wiring altogether in some cases: now employees can take their laptops anywhere in the building and be connected wirelessly to the Internet. Here and there were remnants of the old IBM—a THINK sign on a glass table in a waiting room for customers—but for the most part, this was Lou Gerstner's monument to the new IBM: toned down, less formal, state-of-the-art, a more unassuming company. Visitors walking into the building encounter a wall of poster-size photographs of IBM CEOs, the monumental names from the past: Watson Sr., Watson Jr., Learson, Carey, Opel. But conspicuously missing is a photo of IBM's new CEO, Lou Gerstner. Why the omission? Has Gerstner decreed that he wants to be a stealth CEO to go along with the stealth IBM? Does he feel that he has not yet earned the right to join the pantheon of IBM superstars? Or has he made a calculated attempt at modesty to keep employees from making the same criticism they had made of Tom Watson Sr.: Why do we have to see his photo at every turn? No one at IBM has any quick answers, but whatever the reason, it certainly seems odd that someone who takes enormous pride and satisfaction in what he has accomplished for IBM would insist on this kind of anonymity.

The old corporate culture was crumbling. A new one was taking its place. The old culture had turned IBM into an empire around which barriers had been erected: barriers that had been designed to keep the outside environment from impacting on Big Blue, barriers that were meant to keep the old culture in place. As he set out to weaken the old culture, Lou Gerstner did not pretend to be a revolutionary. His thinking was short-term only. Many would have preferred that he spark a revolution to save IBM. But Gerstner was too conservative, too cautious, too careful, to make such leaps. For the time being, he was content to shelve many parts of the old culture. That was revolution enough for him.

Chapter 11

———◆———

Don't Worry about Grand Visions

"The last thing IBM needs right now is a vision. What IBM needs right now is a series of very tough-minded, market-driven, highly effective strategies in each of its businesses."

*I*BM WAS IN such desperate straits when Lou Gerstner became its chief executive that few believed the company could be saved. Still, the very fact that a new CEO had been named to replace John Akers produced a certain amount of hope. A conventional wisdom arose that just as Lou Gerstner had turned around other companies, he would do the same for IBM. Many were adamant that Gerstner should march into IBM with a blueprint for recovery in his hip pocket. A strategic vision, if you will. The trouble with such thinking was that Lou Gerstner wanted to take a go-slow approach with the computer giant. His modus operandi for turning companies around in the past had not been to overhaul them; was rather to take as much time as needed to learn what made the company tick, and then and only then, begin to attack problems. Strategic visions, as far as he was concerned, had their place. But CEOs should only articulate them after giving much thought and time to learning how a company functioned.

Gerstner had gone through a transformation in his thinking on the question of how quickly a CEO should articulate a strategic vision. In earlier days, when he was at American Express in 1985, he saw the virtues of setting out such a vision as quickly as possible.

You have first to decide what kind of a company you want to have. If you don't have a vision you believe, you can't achieve it. People just won't believe you and you won't communicate it effectively in everything you do.

And even when he took over as CEO at IBM in April 1993, he felt it was necessary right off the bat to know where he wanted to take the company.

We must have a clear sense of direction, a sense of priorities, a sense of mission—for IBM as a whole and for the individual parts of IBM. Without strategy you fail, and without strategy in a rapidly changing industry, you fail rapidly.

The media and the financial analysts agreed with him. Gerstner looked more and more like the proverbial knight on a white horse. It was unthinkable that he would not have a readymade long-range plan for IBM's recovery. They felt that Gerstner was required to set out such a strategic vision for IBM, and they seemed to be suggesting strongly that the new vision would have to differ radically from the failed strategies of the 1980s and early 1990s.

I've Got to Immerse Myself in the Company

On March 29, 1993, a day before the IBM board formally voted him the new IBM chairman and CEO, Gerstner sat in a fortieth-floor office at the company's midtown Manhattan skyscraper and in an interview with *Business Week* offered some early insights into how he would behave in the first days and weeks of his stewardship. From that interview it became clear that he would drop no bombshells in those first few weeks. He really wanted to take his time, to learn, to get a feel for the company. He would decide on what steps to take at IBM only after completing a major reconnaissance mission.

I've got to immerse myself in this company. I want to see as much,
hear as much, and feel as much as I can in the context of the
ongoing business of this company.

He found the media's zeal for news about plans for the company
frustrating. "I have no idea how best to organize IBM," he commented,
perplexed at what he termed the "frenetic, maniacal press announcing
everything weeks and weeks in advance." By the time he had joined
IBM, he joked to colleagues, "I was old news." Always, he was asked
about his goals. When a *Fortune* magazine reporter asked him if he
planned to stick to John Akers' goals for IBM, which included a return
on shareholders' equity of 18 percent; a return on assets of 8 percent;
cutting expenses by 23 percent, and leaving $4 billion in free cash flow,
he replied that this was the first time he had heard of such goals and he
certainly felt no obligation to stick to them.

I haven't spent any time setting goals. I'm spending my time trying to understand our competitive position and how we're serving customers. Out of our competitive strategy will come the
right set of financial objectives.

Did he have a timetable in mind? Did he have a deadline by which
time he would articulate his strategic vision?

Not really. He could not imagine that after only thirty days on the
job he would be expected to lay out a timetable for making changes in
a company so large and complex as IBM.

Besides, I really do want to disabuse your readers of the concept
that there's going to be this grand plan that's going to emerge
from the new management at some point. It isn't going to happen.
It's time for IBM to perform and then talk, instead of talk and then
perform. We are going to be very, very parsimonious about talking,
and we are going to be maniacal about doing what we want to do.

No Vision Required

The "perform first, talk later" approach may have sounded modest, but
it did not sit well in some quarters of Wall Street and certain segments

of the media. Why the go-slow approach, they wondered obstinately, when IBM was in such trouble? Even some customers weighed in with concern that Gerstner was being too vague: they wanted to know how IBM's technology and products would evolve. Potential customers wanted to know whether IBM was going to get out of the mainframe business. Gerstner owed them clear, quick answers, they felt, and none were forthcoming.

Here and there, Gerstner shed light on his overall plans for the company, but they were meager and mostly unenlightening. For example, on July 2, 1993, he wrote a memo to his top executives, declaring that IBM would keep doing what it had been doing under Akers, only more efficiently: "I do not want to undertake a major reorganization of IBM at this time." The company should focus on customers, markets, and competitors over the next twelve to eighteen months, he urged, and not on internal changes. He was not interested in spending a great deal of time on tinkering with IBM's organization, with what he called its "internal plumbing," adding: "I want to make sure the current system is implemented well before we try alternatives."

He saw no benefit to fomenting change all at once. Asked if he saw himself as a revolutionary, he replied:

Oh, no, no, no, no. I'm just somebody trying to help our customers. I didn't create those changes. Those changes are created by this very, very significant science known as information technology, and it is an extraordinary science. We're trying to take the science and really direct it to groundbreaking applications. And if you want to say that's revolutionary—the revolution from IBM is not that we're so enamored with the technology and that we're predicting that, again, everybody will be connected to everybody else and all these predictions of—I mean, that's not a great interest to us. What's of interest to us is: How do you really create breakthrough applications for our customers? How do you create revolutions for our customers?

Gerstner felt that he had to concentrate on measures that would stabilize the company. He was willing to think about what strategies might be best for IBM, but he was still not ready in late summer 1993 to divulge his long-term thinking. He was all too aware that the IBM of the 1980s had gone through one strategic vision after the other—always planning to redefine the company, always misjudging what the competitive environment was like. He had no interest in offering up yet one more "strategic vision" meant to overhaul the company. A strategic vision was no magic bullet, it would not solve the company's immediate problems overnight. In time, he would come up with his blueprint for long-range growth, but for the moment he had more immediate problems to tackle, a company with an out-of-control cost structure, a company that employed far too many people. For now he would be content to straighten out these short-term problems. Gerstner did not conceal his contempt for strategic visions. "There's been a lot of speculation on when I will deliver a vision," he said during one press conference in the summer of 1993. "The last thing IBM needs right now is a vision. What IBM needs right now is a series of very tough-minded, market-driven, highly effective strategies in each of its businesses."

"The last thing IBM needs right now is a vision"—financial analysts seized on that one sentence as proof positive that the IBM chief was a disappointment, at least during his early months in office. Believing that only a sweeping set of strategic visions could save IBM, the analysts could not understand why Gerstner was holding back. They did not buy his arguments that he needed to go slow. They wanted to know what his plans were, and when he let them down, they constantly pointed to that one sentence to illustrate the continuing sense of drift at IBM.

Strategic Imperatives

Gerstner did lay out a set of eight principles in the fall of 1993, though together they hardly constituted a strategic vision:

- The marketplace is the driving force behind everything we do.
- At our core, we are a technology company with an overriding commitment to quality.
- Our primary measure of success are customer satisfaction and shareholder value.
- We operate as an entrepreneurial organization with a minimum of bureaucracy and a never-ending focus on productivity.
- We never lose sight of our strategic vision.

- We think and act with a sense of urgency.
- Outstanding, dedicated people make it all happen, particularly when they work together as a team.
- We are sensitive to the needs of all employees and to the communities in which we operate.

None of these principles, however, provided a clue about the direction Gerstner wanted to take the company. Did he want to remain mainframe-oriented? Did he want to put all of IBM's resources in services and solutions? What about personal computers and software? The principles were designed more to encourage employees to work better and to keep in mind that IBM was making products for *customers*, not for itself. As for the direction of the company, Gerstner was playing his cards close to the vest. Such caution was characteristic of this contemplative, slow-to-act leader.

In the 1994 Annual Report, Gerstner was a bit more concrete, unveiling what he called six "strategic imperatives"—the road map for IBM's near-term future. But even these left much to the imagination.

- Exploiting IBM's technology
- Increasing IBM's share of the client/server computing market
- Establishing leadership in the emerging network-centric computing world
- Realigning the way IBM delivers value to customers
- Rapidly expanding its position in key emerging geographic markets
- Leveraging its size and scale to achieve cost and market advantages

Six months later, in March 1994, Gerstner addressed Wall Street analysts and again suggested that he had no intention of announcing broad-based strategic visions for the company this early in the game. "You must understand I am not trying to create a complete IBM makeover, a brand-new IBM. But rather, a sense of urgency, direction and engagement." He was focusing his energies on getting the various parts of IBM to work better. The job, he admitted, was like "draining a swamp." Grudgingly, perhaps in an attempt to calm the nerves of analysts who had such high hopes for Gerstner, the IBM chief declared what some might have called a vision statement: IBM would "be the world's most successful and important information technology company, would introduce technology to customers and continue to be a technological pioneer."

Thinking like a Businessman

After nearly one year in office, Gerstner still seemed unsure of what direction he wanted to take IBM. He had been credited with taking solid, if cautious steps. Yet, when *Gannett News Service* polled a dozen analysts, industry experts, and computer consultants, some said Gerstner had acted too slowly and ineffectively. Most, however, gave him the benefit of the doubt and said a year was too little time to right such a ghastly situation. His focus on stabilizing the company, they believed, was proper and, for the time being, sufficient. Wall Street seemed to approve of Gerstner's approach: IBM's stock had risen 40 percent in the year since Gerstner assumed office. Best of all, IBM had racked up a profit of $382 million in the fourth quarter of 1993 after it had lost money every quarter since the summer of 1992. In place of a strategic vision, Gerstner had worked hard to avoid making any big mistakes, and strived to give Wall Street and the rest of the world the feeling that he was tackling IBM's problems. Edwin Black, publisher of *OS/2 Professional*, a national computer magazine in Rockville, Maryland, praised Gerstner's overall performance, noting: "He's thinking like a businessman and IBM hasn't had someone at the top thinking like a businessman for many years. IBM's chairmen have for years treated the company like an institution that couldn't be changed. But Gerstner is going through a methodical, unsentimental resuscitation of IBM."

Eighteen months into the job—in the fall of 1994—Gerstner was still very much the nonrevolutionary. He liked to describe himself as a "general manager," implying that he was riding herd over a situation, not preparing for a revolution. And the results looked quite good. Profit margins were rising, and better yet, the stock was soaring. Some cynics argued that it was simply luck that had improved IBM's financial picture. For example, there had been an unexpected surge in demand for mainframe computers—something that Gerstner could not have influenced.

Gerstner knew that meaningful change took time, and though he preached a sense of urgency around IBM, he did not fault himself or the company for falling far short of its targeted $8 billion in cost reductions. He was quite pleased that IBM had cut $4.8 billion, or 20 percent, of its total expenses.

> Our results on expense reduction have been more than satisfactory. Transforming IBM is not something we can do in one or two years. The better we are at fixing some of the short-term things, the more time we have to deal with the long-term issues. You can't really start addressing the long-term issues unless you've got a stabilization.

Explain Yourself!

It was ironic. The financial analysts and the media wanted Lou Gerstner to explain himself, to draw a road map of where he planned to take IBM over the next decade or so. But he thought such road maps were foolish, and was not afraid to say so. When he balked at their demands to learn of his specific plans, many accused him of being just like the old IBM leaders; vague, unsure of themselves, complacent—yes, even paralyzed. Gerstner listened to all that criticism and shrugged his shoulders. He knew that he was different from Big Blue's previous leaders. And in time people would come to appreciate the difference.

Chapter 12

Nothing Is More Important Than Executing Business Plans

"The fundamental issue, in my view, is execution. Strategy is execution."

G RAND VISIONS WERE worthless to Lou Gerstner. They were just words on paper. Who had time for long-term plans and strategies when the patient was on the operating table? He had no choice but to focus on the here and now. Maybe if all went well, if IBM got its house in order, if the bottom line showed steady improvement over a prolonged period, then perhaps he could get around to the grand vision part of the job. Gerstner knew there were people out there—in the media, on Wall Street—who felt that he could not lead IBM successfully without a vision; but he couldn't have cared less. Right now, he believed he had no choice but to be pragmatic, to spur the company to action, to execute.

Despite its problems, the chief had a lot of faith in IBM, in its products and its people. No company could have amassed nearly $63 billion in annual revenues (as IBM had in 1993) without doing a great deal that was right. He believed there was nothing inherently wrong with IBM. In the past it had done the job of coming up with the right products, marketing them properly, bringing in the massive revenues and the healthy profits. So what *was* wrong?

In his view, IBM was simply not executing properly. It was as if a football coach had designed the greatest plays, put the best players on the field, but then neglected to give the team time to learn and practice the plays. When he made the rounds of IBM in the early weeks of his tenure, Lou Gerstner was dismayed at what he found: here were all sorts of solid product and marketing plans just lying around on people's desks. Time and time again, when he asked how had the product done once it got to market, he heard a recurring theme: The products had never been launched; they had never seen the light of day and had racked up zero sales. For God's sake, why? Gerstner kept asking. All he got in return were forlorn looks and shrugs of the shoulders. It didn't take long for IBM's new CEO to figure out what was wrong: lack of execution. People were asleep at the job. People were not carrying out their assignments. The plays were there. But the team wasn't learning them or running them properly.

Executing Is Working Hard on the Right Things

Gerstner knew that before he would be articulating any grand visions, he would have to get IBM functioning again. To do that, he would have to teach the company the true meaning of execution.

> **Execution is not going to meetings, convening task forces, debating issues, studying opportunities and escalating problems. Execution is closing deals, calling on customers, shipping products, meeting (and exceeding) targets. It is not working harder or longer hours. It is working on the right things, the ones with the highest marketplace impact.**

Anyone caught not focusing on "the right things" would be in serious trouble. Either the person learned to execute—or there would be an execution. That was Lou Gerstner's attitude.

Some had put forward the idea that IBM ought to become a services company, that although it had been the premium technology business in the world, it no longer was able to come up with the products. Gerstner rejected such thinking, insisting that IBM was the technology leader in the industry. The way to get IBM back on track was not to get rid of its manufacturing side but to improve the way products get to market.

Our customers know we are the technology leader. The problem is, we haven't brought the technology to market quickly enough, and quite frankly, when we have, we've often had some quality problems. So we must also reassert our commitment to maintaining consistently high standards of quality.

Again, the best way to fix things, Gerstner believed, was to execute properly.

In any transformation like the one IBM is making the hard part isn't getting started. It's seeing change through. We've got a lot of work behind us, and we've learned a lot—from cultural change to how to make better use of our own IT systems, to getting more involved in the higher-growth areas of the business.

As he learned more about the company, Gerstner began to understand why IBM was not executing properly. A set of roadblocks, some obvious, some more subtle, had constricted IBM, making it more and more difficult to implement business plans. One, of course, was the no-layoff policy. When the company faced good times, the policy was not that harmful; but in tough times when IBM's sales suffered, the company's costs were still immense while revenues dropped. When outright dismissals were required, all the Akers regime did was to implement a series of measures that allowed employees to take generous retirement packages, which served to eliminate jobs through normal attrition. Finally putting an end to IBM's long-standing no-layoff policy, Gerstner announced the actual firing of 35,000 employees during the summer of 1993.

To get IBM employees to execute properly, Gerstner felt he had to convey a sense of urgency. He felt he had his work cut out for him:

We still take too long to make decisions. We still talk too much in large committees. We still study things too much. And we don't have a uniform sense of urgency across the organization. More

than at any other time in history, victory today goes to the swift. Being fast can be better than being insightful. I don't mean ready-fire-aim recklessness. I mean moving projects and activities along with a passionate commitment to get it done today. We need a massive dose of constructive impatience at IBM!

To turn IBM around, Gerstner did not feel he needed any fancy strategies. All he had to do was to get IBM's employees to do their jobs better.

The fundamental issue, in my view, is execution. Strategy is execution.

Reshuffling the Deck

Eventually, IBM executives began to take Gerstner seriously. Sam Palmisano was put in charge of the personal computer division in April 1996 in the hope that he would find ways to spur growth. Recalling Gerstner's theme of urgency, Palmisano set an ambitious agenda for himself: in order to attract new customers with exciting new products, a minimum of half of the products his division produced that year would be new. He was in the job only three weeks when he realized that he had set an impossible task for himself. One visit to the personal computer manufacturing complex in Raleigh, North Carolina, conveyed to him the seriousness of the situation. Things were proceeding at a snail's pace and he was desperate to speed the process up. At 7 A.M. one day he gathered his manufacturing team together and delivered a short speech that echoed his desperation: "We've got to do this. If we don't, we're going to have to kill our kids." ("I didn't really mean kill the kids," he explained later, "but you get my point.")

He began reshuffling the deck, reassigning his senior executives to take different responsibilities. Employees were no longer expected to show up for useless meetings; instead, they had time to do more testing of the products, and to accelerate the pace of testing overall. He prodded the sales force to start pushing products seriously even before those products were ready for market. "Sam," said one sales rep, "if we do that and miss [the marketing deadline], we won't be considered a reliable supplier." Palmisano had an answer for that one: "If you guys don't push the product now, we'll lose sales." Six weeks later the PCs rolled out the door. For the first time this decade, IBM's PCs were first to market; as a result, the unit gained a full share point in each of the last three quarters of 1996. Palmisano hosted a large celebration and gave his employees bonuses—the first they'd seen in years. But he remained cautious: "Ten months is not a trend. We have to continue to execute. These aren't slouches in this business."

By the end of 1996, Gerstner was pleased to note that IBM was showing marked improvement in a vital area: speed. "I would argue that there's not a company that has come close to what we've done. The culture has become very focused on speed." Analysts began to notice a difference too. Frank Dzubeck, president of Communications Network Architects, commented: "I make calls there at 6 P.M. and people are working. You now have people giving home phone numbers out so you can talk to them at night and on weekends. You get responses to e-mail back from Europe and China."

Part of executing properly was not promising something you couldn't deliver. This was another important aspect of the Gerstner management philosophy and it was something he had learned during his pre-IBM years. Overpromising, he had learned, was counterproductive. It was a way of damaging one's reputation, and ultimately of losing customers. "I don't understand. At the other places I worked, my lawyers would tell me I would go to jail for things people say they're going to deliver in this industry and then don't."

For that reason, though he stressed the need for urgency and quick decision making in his early days at IBM, Gerstner was always careful not to overpromise. He made sure not to promise shareholders that he would turn IBM around immediately. He believed that turning the company around would take five, or possibly ten, years. In fact, he achieved remarkable results far more quickly than that. Not overpromising made him look that much better.

Gunning for Leadership

At the 1996 shareholders meeting in Atlanta, Gerstner noted that he had indeed tried to proceed slowly, not promising a revolution overnight:

Three years ago, when I joined this company and addressed shareholders for the first time in Tampa, IBM was on the endan-

gered species list. I talked about the hard actions necessary to save our company. Two years ago, we talked about stability. Last year, growth. Now, we are gunning for leadership.

In an interview he gave in the fall of 1998, Gerstner had not abandoned his theme. He still believed that if IBM employees did their jobs as well as possible, the company would flourish.

The single biggest challenge at IBM is making it all happen inside at IBM. It's making execution. We are arguably the most complex company in the world. Not just because of our size and breadth but because of this technology. . . . The real issue is how do we execute in a company of 300,000 people across the 170 countries. In an industry that changes as dramatically as ours does. When we can execute to do what we want to do in front of the customer, we're unique. We win almost every time. It's a huge managerial challenge.

If he could shorten the meetings, get his executives to make decisions faster, get products to market more rapidly, Lou Gerstner knew that he would be able to move IBM in the right direction. To get IBM moving, he had to instill a new brand of urgency in the new company. But urgency was not enough. Employees, top to bottom, had to focus much more sharply on what they were trying to do: keep expenses down and make the company grow. Gerstner was confident that if he could just get his employees to do their best, the rest would follow.

Part I

Overcoming Corporate Complacency

———◆———

"I asked a great deal from our people. I asked them to do more with less ... to change a culture that took success for granted ... one that had become easy pickings for the competition."

———◆———

Chapter 13

———◆———

Stop Wasting Time,
Get Right to the Point!

"We ... have too many sign-offs, too many reviews, too many task forces.... And we still value 'face time' over results."

*L*OU GERSTNER DOESN'T like to waste time, his or other people's. If there's a faster way of doing something, he's in favor of it. If others are obstructing him from getting a job done, he doesn't want them around. To him, people who spend time talking and talking are the kind who can kill a business.

When he was at American Express he made sure to invite only those he truly wanted at vital brainstorming meetings, even if it meant irritating those who weren't invited. At times, he would call a three-day retreat and invite a small, select group.

> I know the people I want at that meeting. There will be a dozen or more people who will be upset that they are left out of this meeting. The more vocal of them will come into my office and say, "My career is over. Why have you done this to me?" That is a problem. I will say to them, "Look, I wanted to have a small meeting. I think that you make contributions in other areas. I do not

think it is critical for you to be at this meeting. You are part of the senior management team, so as the results evolve from this process, you of course will participate in reviewing them to the extent that they impact on your area of business. You will have a say in them. But this is an important brain-storming session and these are the people I want to have at the meeting."

Gerstner knows that even such kind, soothing words will irk his listeners. But he doesn't really care.

I am trying to avoid the concept of reward being associated with these meetings. In the regular shirt-sleeve sessions that last three hours, I have consciously driven out the reward. They are tough, hard-nosed meetings. A lot of people come out of there wrung out; they do not see them as a reward.

Eyeball to Eyeball

As he assembled his management team at IBM, Gerstner told executives: "I don't care whether you're the next star or on your way out. You start clean with me." Senior executives who had been with the company for years did not like hearing such things. But they paid attention to him.

Remember the IBM meetings before Gerstner? They were congenial but produced no great results. Well, Gerstner-led meetings are anything but congenial. Almost always, before he meets with anyone, he requires something in writing that establishes the facts, defines the problems, and allows him to skip the small talk and get immediately to the matter at hand. To embattled IBM employees accustomed to skirting problems, meeting with Gerstner was a frightening prospect.

"Oh, my God, now I've got to look at this guy eyeball to eyeball" was how one former IBM employee put it.

He wanted decisions to come out of meetings. "In the past," noted Jim Cannavino, the former IBM senior vice president for strategy, "when you sat down at a meeting at IBM, you felt like the decision had already been made. Not so with Lou. If he had a meeting, he expected to make a decision. If he had enough facts, he'd make a decision. He did not come to the meeting with preconceived notions. Meetings were shorter and a lot smaller. In the old days, if a guy three levels down had information, the next two higher-level guys were expected to come to the meeting. Lou changed that, and it was hard for people in the beginning. Everyone was paranoid, but they got used to Lou's ways."

In keeping with Gerstner's desire to get to the business at hand, he abolished foils (overheads) and charts at meetings. "I don't want a feel-good presentation where you show me your best shot. I want to know where your business is going. Eyeball to eyeball." Once, a senior executive showed up with his overhead projector. As he approached the machine, he was startled to find Lou Gerstner approaching the projector as well. The IBM chief snapped the machine off, adding these no-nonsense words: "If you can't explain your business, of which you are the expert and manager, without all kinds of props, you don't understand your business."

Before he came on board, IBM executives gave lengthy oral reports at meetings, leaving little time for analysis. But the new boss liked compact reports—this was a holdover from his McKinsey days, when he demanded that no presentation to a client exceed fifteen pages. His favorite phrase is "Never confuse activity with results." Results always had to be real with him. "You don't get points for predicting rain," he liked to say. "You get points for building arks." As a result Gerstner greatly improved the quality of thought at IBM.

What the Hell Is This?

Phone calls from the IBM chief were no better. When the call came, he never offered a compliment. Instead, it was curt and to the point, and sometimes harsh: More than one Gerstner call began, "What the hell is this?" Walking the corridors when Gerstner was in the building was no picnic either. Former IBM managers recalled that he would catch them on the run and ask for an off-the-cuff evaluation of a colleague, even including one's boss. It was tremendously flattering but also tremendously frightening. Gerstner noted: "There's no question that, during the first year, there were some attempts to feed me intellectual arsenic— some bad ideas, some pet projects."

Gerstner admitted to all of this in a *Fortune* magazine interview:

I'm tough-minded. I'm tough in business situations. I'm really focused and have little time. I guess I'm also relatively blunt, so if

you want to know if I'm intense, competitive, focused, blunt, and tough, yes. That's fair. I'm guilty. Quite frankly, I am not very comfortable in chitchat. When I go to Board meetings, I arrive two minutes before, and I leave when it's over. I don't stay for lunch or go early and have coffee. But if arrogance means pride, wanting to take credit for everything, not seeking others' advice, I don't think those are fair characterizations.

IBM officials suggested that Gerstner was referring to nonprofit boards, not the IBM one.

No Putting on a Pretty Face

He hated to waste time. And he did not like it when someone wasted his time by skewing the truth. Gerstner seemed to know precisely when he was being told half-truths. "He's an exceedingly bright person," said one former IBM executive who had worked with Gerstner. "More than any other executive, you did not put bullshit past this guy. He instinctively knows when you didn't know the answer." Employees learned pretty fast that the way to survive at IBM was to tell the boss the truth. No spinning. No putting a pretty face on the business. If you were frank with Gerstner, you would be fine. Added the executive: "Lou is not a person who everybody feels is warm, friendly, fuzzy. He's not that kind of personality. But he is a person who you'll get along with great if you don't spin him, and if you're smart and you go to him, tell him what's going on and come up with solutions to fix a the problem. He is very results-oriented. He's a hands-on kind of guy. But IBM hadn't been that way. He's not a sweetheart of a guy. But the company didn't need a sweetheart of a guy. It needed a tough, bright, no-nonsense person who could motivate."

Gerstner made many people nervous because they could no longer get away with sub-par performance. He would separate out the spinners from the truth-tellers. His senior management team was an interesting mix of insiders and outsiders. For the supporting roles, Gerstner reached out to key people from his past to fill senior staff positions. David B. Kalis, his senior public relations man, and Lawrence R. Ricciardi, his general counsel, were both at American Express and RJR. Abby Kohnstamm, head of marketing, had been at American Express.

Richard Thoman, who replaced York as CFO and who is now the heir apparent at Xerox, had worked with Gerstner since their McKinsey days. He also held onto his executive assistant, Isabelle Cummins, who had worked alongside him since 1978. "Having done this three times, let me tell you, it's pretty lonely parachuting into a company all by yourself," Gerstner admitted. "It's extremely helpful having some people you can shorthand and rely on because you know them well."

When he wanted to distance himself from someone, he did not resort to outright firing at once. Often he assigned the person an inconsequential task that sent a clear message: You're not wanted around here.

Gerstner brings his no-nonsense discipline to his personal schedule as well. He doesn't seem to waste a minute. He reads huge amounts of material each day, visits IBM customers often, and rounds out his calendar with frequent visits to IBM sites. He is so busy that John M. Thompson, the executive responsible for software, once had to wait an entire month for a routine meeting with the boss.

Too Much "Face Time"

Spending five years trying to change things at IBM, Gerstner knew that he had a long way to go to make the company more efficient.

> **My surveys indicate that where IBM is worse than the industry in general has to do with our bureaucracy and culture. We still have too many meetings. We still have too many sign-offs, too many reviews, too many task forces, which add work but not much value. And we still value "face time" over results. We need to have more trust in one another—confidence that our colleagues can lead and do the right thing, so we don't have to attend every meeting and check every detail.**

He was being harsh on himself and harsh on IBM. No longer did IBM executives take joy in sitting around for hours at a meeting. No longer could those executives study a problem to death—not on Lou Gerstner's watch. He was determined to keep a tight rein on all that went on at IBM. He prided himself on that. "I don't view the role of the CEO

Chapter 14

Set High Expectations: Don't Settle for Mediocrity

"It comes back to win, execute and team....
You do not get up every morning and salute them.
You get up every morning and live them."

L OU GERSTNER'S take-no-prisoners management style was tailor-made for a company in trouble. He did not tolerate time-wasting activities. Just as important, he did not tolerate employees who did not pull their weight. He had always detested mediocrity. He had always believed in setting high expectations. These were the values that he had learned from his days in the consulting business at McKinsey. He believed firmly that businesses had to face reality, get rid of dead wood, and insist on running as productively and efficiently as possible. He made much the same point as chairman of American Express Travel-Related Services when he addressed a meeting of his division's star performing sales managers in Fort Lauderdale, Florida. His main theme that day in 1985 was "redefining excellence." He emphasized how important it was for every employee to rise to new challenges, both personal and professional. Likening American Express to Roger Bannister, who had succeeded in breaking the four-minute mile, he said:

> **We have no peers. We have done something unique. Now what? We must now set our own standards, explore new boundaries, develop new approaches, support the self-renewing persons who feel like they're always striving for the ultimate goal.**

Banning Boasting Terms

Patience was not Gerstner's strong suit. He was, to say the least, not easy to please. When he was running RJR Nabisco, he once told a cigarette salesman, "No one has ever met my expectations, with the exception of my wife." That may have been an exaggeration, but Gerstner's reputation as a no-nonsense type of guy was widely recognized. At RJR Nabisco, he and fellow executives banned certain "boasting terms," phrases that might convey the impression that expectations had been met. Among the forbidden phrases:

We had an excellent year.
I'm proud…
I promise…

When he took over at IBM, Gerstner quickly sensed that the leadership had become far too kind to its employees. In the past senior executives found it easy to say, "Thank you, we know you tried your best," but Gerstner would no longer tolerate such compassion. That was a sure-fire way to guarantee that workers *didn't* do their best. No longer would he tolerate sloth, or mistakes, or a lack of enthusiasm. And he would certainly not tolerate those who did not seem to be up on their jobs. On one occasion, attending a meeting of 400 IBM managers from various countries, he asked the managers to hold up flags with the names of their toughest competitors. Gerstner was aghast at the paucity of flags being held up. How could it be that IBM managers didn't know, or worse yet, didn't care, who their chief rivals were? From that gathering, he drew the conclusion that he would have to work hard to shake up the complacency at the company.

Dictatorial and Autocratic

Gerstner made it clear to everyone that he wouldn't settle for second best. "Each business has to be successful," recalled Jim Cannavino, the former senior vice president for strategy and development at IBM. "Each thing you do has to be world-class. The businesses that he got out of weren't mediocre; they were just not generating cash."

He passed the word that those who did not perform up to his standards would be fired. "He put an awful lot more power in the line guys," Cannavino noted. "The corporate staff had become very powerful and had a lot of power over the line guys. Lou made a big move to shrink the corporate staffs and get the line guys to run the businesses. He told them: 'Get the job done or you're out.' "

Performing up to Gerstner's standards meant many things, but one thing above all. It meant a willingness to adjust to change—change in the way IBM conducted business, change in the business environment, change in general. IBM had fought tooth and nail against change in the past, and Gerstner was determined to make sure that that didn't happen on his watch. At one stage early in his tenure at IBM, an internal survey was conducted showing that 40 percent of the managers doubted that radical change was needed. Fuming at the results, Gerstner passed word to the "40 percent" that they should think about leaving the company—or get with the program. Needless to say, a number of IBM executives found the Gerstner management style harsh, excessive, autocratic, and dictatorial. It was a style, they grudgingly acknowledged, for managing a crippled company that needed to be whipped into shape. But behind closed doors they were whispering far harsher words against the IBM CEO: He would only get so far with his tough-guy tactics; he might turn the company around, but he would not be able to return it to its preeminence in the industry.

For Gerstner, such questions seemed irrelevant. He knew what action had to be taken immediately, and that was all he was concerned about.

> **When I joined IBM in 1993, I asked a great deal from our people. I asked them to do more with less . . . to change a culture that took success for granted . . . one that had grown complacent and had become easy pickings for the competition.**

One of Gerstner's Big Tests

Gerstner's message of perform-or-you're-out filtered down to one of the company's most important business segments, the personal computer division. The PC effort was IBM's largest hardware unit and accounted for almost one-sixth of the company's revenues.

When Gerstner came on board, he found this division to be in sorry shape. At one stage IBM's personal computer division had been the dominant revenue leader in its market. But by the mid-1990s, it had dropped to number four in the United States and number two (Compaq was number one) in the world. Standards were indeed low. Forecasting left much to be desired: there were far too many computers in inventory that were not moving, and too few of the ones that were. Product development was also in terrible shape: personnel in this field moved far too slowly, missed critical deadlines, and cost the company a great deal of money. Designs that arrived at the manufacturing stage came only two-thirds complete, making engineering changes expensive and leaving insufficient time for product testing.

Gerstner knew that the PC division represented one of his greatest tests: if he could right the wrongs there, he would have a good chance of fixing the entire company. The IBM chief knew that all eyes were on the troubled PC division. Gerstner's strategy was simple: he would select someone with an excellent reputation to run the unit; he would then set very ambitious goals; and, most important, he would settle for nothing less than unmitigated success.

To deal with the PC mess, Gerstner put G. Richard Thoman in charge in January 1994 and gave him one sweeping mandate: Transform the business. Thoman had wanted to be a diplomat and had picked up a doctorate in economics, but he had joined McKinsey and there had crossed paths with Lou Gerstner. They stayed together at American Express and RJR Nabisco—and then at IBM. Thoman's task as head of the PC unit was a tough one, since Gerstner had set such lofty goals. Gerstner insisted that he get the products to market far more quickly, that he fix the inventory problems, and that he adopt a far more aggressive pricing strategy in order to make sure that the products moved.

The Saturday Morning Conference Call

Thoman engaged in the kind of micromanaging that he hoped would lead to better results. When he took over, he was astonished to find that the division gathered only monthly inventory figures, which led to two disastrous problems. Inventory stacked up, and IBM was simply unable to modify prices quickly enough to respond to changes in the market. So every Saturday at 8:30 in the morning, he held a weekly conference call to some dozen managers around the world, in Raleigh, North Carolina, in Paris, and in other cities. Together they pored over a forty-four-page document that detailed daily production and sales figures. Thoman quizzed each manager, one after the other:

How many computers had he built that week?
What kinds of computers?
Which factories were making them?
How many of the computers had been shipped?
Had deadlines been met?

The conference call lasted well into the late morning and by the time it was over Thoman had a clearer idea of how things had gone the week before. This was certainly a new development.

Thoman established a system in which IBM PC managers received a report of what had been manufactured the day before in each of their plants. A plant manager could expect an irate call from Thoman if production numbers were down from the day before. At first, IBM's reports were so sketchy that Thoman was unable to tell how many laptops and desktops were in inventory. By improving reporting procedures, he afforded plant managers a way of finding out which product lines were moving and which were not.

Thoman then set out to tackle other PC division problems. By tightening up internal operations, Thoman produced some wonderful results: finished-goods inventory plummeted 65 percent; procurement and distribution costs dropped 50 percent; and the division closed thirteen European warehouses. Gross margins, a profitless 13 percent in 1994, were up to 19 percent and were fast approaching Compaq Computer's 25 percent margins.

Just as important, the research and development teams at IBM were now creating new products for the personal computer division at a much faster rate. Gerstner and Thoman had taken the crucial step of bringing them all together in Raleigh rather than have them work, as in the past, at nine locations around the country. The Butterfly subnotebook was the best example of the new accent on speed pervading the PC unit. It had gone from a lab project to a finished viable commercial product in just a year and a half, setting an IBM record.

Thoman was determined to meet Gerstner's high expectations. For example, when visiting factories, he insisted that plant managers send their products to dealers and customers at the promised time. Accordingly, IBM personal computers arrived on time four out of five times by the summer of 1995; that was a great improvement over the year before, when slightly more than one out of two arrived late.

Thoman had one more huge challenge: fix the mess in the factories. The problem was that IBM produced a staggering number of different models of PCs: 3,400 to be exact. By the end of 1996, the IBM PC chief had reduced that to a far more manageable 125. That was no easy feat considering that IBM shipped 6 million PCs alone in 1996.

I Won't Tolerate Failure

Perhaps the most crucial step Thoman took in the resurrection of the PC business was to get across to everyone, senior executives included, that he would not tolerate failure. He seemed mild-mannered and some thought he looked more like an academic (he is the son of a college professor) than a high-level computer executive. But his looks were deceiving. He fired one product manager who did not measure up, and of the twenty-four senior managers who were working in the PC division when he came on board, only nine remained by the summer of 1995. "We have clear accountability to Lou Gerstner," he asserted. "If I can't turn this business around, then Lou should move me on, and I shouldn't be here." He did move on in 1997—to become president and heir apparent to the CEO of Xerox Corporation.

A Personal Commitment

In his pursuit of a new, vastly improved IBM, Gerstner did not plan to give employees a pep talk every day. He expected them to become self-motivated.

What's really important is the personal commitment that each of us makes about how we're going to behave, how much we care, how much we're willing to give, how much we're willing to learn and adapt, what we think about every day that drives what we do operationally.

It comes back to win, execute and team. Those are not slogans or even institutional values. They are personal commitments. They're not things of the head, they're things of the heart and the gut. They are behavioral, not intellectual. You do not get up every morning and salute them. You get up every morning and live them. We have completed, for the most part, the task of restructuring the institution. Our success now is going to be a function of personal behavior—the behavior of each and every one of us. We can't fix it with systems anymore.

Under Lou Gerstner the IBM employee was a far different breed from that of his predecessor. It was not only that the dark suits and white shirts were gone; or the fact that the ethereal presence of Thomas Watson Sr. was not monitoring his every sip of liquor or puff on a cigarette. The IBM employee was more motivated to work hard, to figure out what the job was, and to get it done as quickly and efficiently as possible. Gerstner had one huge advantage over former IBM leaders: he was free to fire people. With that kind of power, it became much easier for him to set higher expectations and make sure that each and every employee live up to those standards. After all, the competitive climate of the 1990s was a far different environment than that of the 1950s. Gerstner could ill afford a complacent workforce that took jobs for granted.

Chapter 15

———◆———

Communicate Self-Confidence, Demonstrate Leadership

"If we're going to lead, we must set a direction, and go there. Whether competitors follow isn't important. Winning in the marketplace, with our customers, is."

*L*OU GERSTNER UNDERSTOOD that implementing the right business strategies was important, but so was demonstrating leadership. And the way to demonstrate leadership was to radiate self-confidence and to communicate effectively—to his employees; to outsiders like the media and financial analysts; to everyone, in fact. Gerstner knew that the best business strategies in the world would not work without effective leadership and meaningful communication at every level. He understood very well that communicating was the essence of leadership. He liked to say that leadership was not a birthright. The only way to claim leadership was to demonstrate it.

He knew what leadership was *not*. It was not letting oneself be influenced by rivals..

Leadership isn't a popularity contest. Our competitors may not share our views. We can't be distracted by what they say or do (or

more often, what they say they will do). They may lurch off in directions that are right for them but wrong for us. If we're going to lead, we must set a direction, and go there. Whether competitors follow isn't important. Winning in the marketplace, with our customers, is.

The real test for Gerstner—and he knew it—would be not just in coming up with the right strategies but in gaining the loyalty of his workers. He could then leverage that loyalty to make sure that, among other things, products got to market on time. Missing deadlines had been a major IBM problem in the past. To gain their loyalty, Gerstner would have to communicate effectively and be respected for his leadership abilities.

Communicating effectively would also bolster IBM's image, and this was key to winning customers in the marketplace and securing the crucial support of Wall Street. Gerstner understood and was pleased that his image and IBM's went hand in hand, for unlike other more modest and humble CEOs he had no trouble with being identified as the sole cause of the company's success. Gerstner had lofty ambitions for himself. In fact, he often pondered how history would judge him. He wanted to go down in history not only as the man credited with one of the greatest business turnarounds ever but also as one of history's top business leaders. "Lou wants to be in the very top echelon of business leaders," according to James W. Johnston, his tobacco chief at RJR. Jerome B. York, IBM's CFO during the crucial initial phase of Gerstner's turnaround, told people that Gerstner could become the Jack Welch of the 1990s. To be favorably compared to the legendary GE chairman and CEO was music to Gerstner's ears.

Hungry for Some Candor

From the start, Gerstner proved that he was a good communicator. Even as he was learning the business, he was able to stand up in front of an IBM audience and talk forcefully and convincingly about his views of the company. He spoke *sans* notes and seemingly from the heart. He seldom asked his communications staff to prepare a draft of a speech. Nor were talking points offered to him. He had little trouble conveying his message, and was able to convince his audience of his sincerity. He knew that his audience was often packed with managers eager to protect their own turfs, but he sought to transcend turf issues by getting his colleagues to put the customer first. People who heard him speak recalled that the crowds seemed hungry for such candor. He instinctively cut through to the points that the audience wanted to hear. And what the audience wanted to hear was how he planned to turn IBM around. While he wasn't too specific, he was brimming with optimism and self-confidence, and that was enough to win most audiences over.

Gerstner was determined to get the media to treat IBM with more respect. The company's image, under Akers, could not have been worse. The death plunge of IBM in the early 1990s led the media to turn its spotlight on every flaw, every weakness, and every dismal financial downturn. If IBM was a runaway train heading for disaster, the media seemed eager to record the carnage in living color. The train wreck still seemed a likelihood even after Gerstner's arrival in 1993. The very fact that he was the new kid in town helped IBM's image somewhat; now the focus was less on the possible derailment, more on the effort to get the train functioning properly. Gerstner understood that his handling of the media would have a great deal to do with how IBM was perceived in public, so he went to great lengths to make sure that the media wrote only positive things about the ailing computer giant.

A Great Story Unfolds

Under John Akers, IBM had a simple media policy: When things go bad, head for the bunker. In other words, the best response to an embarrassing story was no response at all. Gerstner had no use for a "no comment" media strategy. He understood that an important part of selling IBM to Wall Street and the public at large was to toot the company's horn. He got off to a good start since his very appointment as chief executive sparked a flood of upbeat news stories. Journalists loved the IBM drama: Here was an American icon in free fall now in the hands of a new leader, an outsider, chosen not because of his expertise in technology, but with the hope that his brand of financial re-engineering would save the place. With journalists eager to cover the story, with Gerstner able to grab the media's attention, one question remained: Would he be able to exploit the media's newfound interest in IBM beyond the spate of stories surrounding his arrival at the company?

By taking media relations so seriously—a new departure for an IBM CEO—Gerstner signaled the beginning of a new era. Peter Thonis, who was on the IBM communications staff when Gerstner was appointed, sensed immediately that his new boss understood the role the media could play in building IBM up. "Before Lou came along, we [the communications staff] were considered the ugly stepchildren. We didn't feel like we were a central part of the organization." Most importantly, Gerstner brought in a professional communications person, David Kalis, as his vice president for communications. In the past, IBM had given the communications assignment to marketing and salespeople, failing to grasp the fact that it took a professional communications specialist to handle the media. Gerstner also made sure to involve himself personally in media issues. Thonis recalled that "When it came to the prior senior management, if you had a problem they wouldn't back you up. They would say, 'Well, that will work itself out.' But, Lou would stand up and kick butt if you needed him to. Lou would get involved. He would fire people. He would do whatever it took to turn the company around. We quickly realized that he would stand behind us. I could get things done that I couldn't get done for years because Lou stood behind us." Thonis cited one example. At the time of Gerstner's arrival, IBM had eight spokespeople talking to *The Wall Street Journal.* The communications staff knew that was absurd and asked Gerstner to arrange for only one spokesperson to deal with the paper. It was not easy to get the edict implemented. The staff asked Gerstner to make some phone calls to people who hadn't gotten the message the first time. "You only had to have him phone someone one time and the word got around," noted Thonis. "That could have taken five years to fix without a forceful CEO. It took us about five months. That was more than a little refreshing."

As it turned out, Gerstner's media strategy was short-lived and eventually he exhibited some of the same reticence toward the media as earlier IBM executives. It certainly seemed ironic for someone who appeared to understand the clout and significance of the media, for Gerstner to become so distant from journalists. Worse yet, he got into angry fights with them. His attitude toward the media fit his tough-guy image, but at times he shot himself in the foot by antagonizing the very people who could have boosted IBM.

At the outset, even though the media was hungry for details about how he planned to turn IBM around, he spoke cautiously and vaguely.

Journalists wanted to speak to him at every turn. But he insisted that he had a business to run, and he preferred to spend time behind his desk or traveling to various IBM sites. The media began to demonstrate some impatience with the new man at the helm.

I'd Rather Talk to Anyone but a Journalist

Gerstner seemed far more comfortable talking at industry events than one-on-one to journalists. When he delivered speeches, he did not have to answer questions. He did not have to be put on the spot. Moreover, he believed that the speeches afforded him the time and opportunity to talk broadly about the industry as a whole. He seemed happiest when sizing up the industry's past and future; it's no wonder, since he was often described as one of the industry's leading figures. Because of the battles he was winning at IBM, Gerstner frequently showed up high on magazine lists of the most powerful figures in the computer industry.

But when it came to the media, he seemed openly uncomfortable. He clearly preferred talking to customers and his own employees than to the media. One financial analyst believed Gerstner would help IBM's cause by being interviewed more in the media. One day the analyst cornered Gerstner and pressed him for an answer: Why don't you talk to the press more? Gerstner answered unflinchingly, "My time is best spent with customers." Still, he did hold a number of news conferences, and he opened up financial analysts meetings by inviting a select group of journalists. And at times he seemed to enjoy sparring with the media. "He liked the notion of getting in the media's face and saying something that was provocative and would draw attention," observed Peter Thonis. "He's not the least intimidated by the media. He tells the media what he thinks." The media dogged him. Reporters followed him to trade conventions, asking customers and others what the IBM boss was really like, where he planned to take IBM, if he had a vision. He was seldom a dull story.

Still, the IBM chief rarely gave interviews. He waited four and a half years before granting an interview to *The Wall Street Journal.* He simply did not like being in situations where he could not control the agenda. Granting an interview to a journalist created the possibility that Gerstner would be asked all sorts of questions that he had no desire to answer. The media felt it carried a mandate to keep score of

IBM's wins and losses, and Gerstner thought such scorekeeping was shortsighted. He knew he needed time to bandage IBM's wounds and get the patient on the road to full recovery, much more time than the media seemed willing to grant.

Controlling the Interview

On those rare occasions when he did grant an interview, he sought to control the entire process. Gerstner's aides demanded that journalists confine their interviews to one or two topics and let the aides know in advance what topics would be covered. Gerstner claimed that he wanted to bone up on those topics in advance of the interview. Some journalists balked at the constraints. But Gerstner had the ultimate advantage. He could always cancel the interview if the journalist did not submit to his demands. So the journalists got nowhere. "Lou doesn't work like that" was the only explanation his aides would give to journalists who sought free rein in their interviews. Every journalist was required to submit a list of questions in advance. Gerstner also limited the length of the interview—never more than 45 minutes. Journalists who asked questions that rubbed him the wrong way met with a frown and a dismissive wave of the hand for their troubles. He always gave terse answers. Journalists found his behavior toward them odd; they had heard that he could be funny and even warm when talking to customers. But to journalists he seemed distant and cold.

Gerstner seemed obsessed with IBM's image to the point that he would complain about the use of a single word in a news story that he believed to be anti-IBM. Once a reporter suggested that he had engaged in "financial maneuvering" when IBM repurchased its stock and shifted tax categories. He hated the word "maneuvering" because it seemed to diminish Gerstner's achievements. The word also seemed to imply that Gerstner had practiced some kind of gimmickry in his turn-around of IBM. But that was not all. Gerstner also assailed a reporter for his apparent sarcasm. The journalist had written that the IBM chief seemed to cheer when he learned that Bill Gates' computer had crashed at a public event. That sort of barb irked the IBM chief, and Gerstner was not afraid to vent his anger.

Fortune's Bad Fortune

However, his most bizarre reaction to the media came with the publication of a *Fortune* magazine cover story on Gerstner and IBM in April 1997. The tone of the story was generally upbeat and for the most part portrayed IBM in a favorable light. But the magazine had no intention of deifying Lou Gerstner, as the headline of the *Fortune* cover story made clear:

> **He's Smart. He's Not Nice. He's Saving Big Blue. Lou Gerstner Isn't Easy to Love, but You Have to Respect Him. He's Done the Job No One Wanted Better Than Anyone Expected. But Will He Finish It and Restore Growth and Glory at IBM?**

While the story documented in great detail the Gerstner turnaround, he was bitter at the way he was described personally. The first adjective used to describe him was "uptight." He was later described as the "ultimate free agent," implying that he did not like staying at one job for too long. The story also suggested that he was rude and boastful, and even criticized his golf etiquette. The magazine wrote that in one round of golf in Florida, a foursome playing ahead of Gerstner was a bit slow. According to golf etiquette, slow-playing golfers should really allow those playing directly behind to pass them. When they asked Gerstner if he would like to pass them, "he grumbled something about an open hole ahead, and proceeded on without so much as a thank you." According to Gerstner acquaintances, he went ballistic over the article. He banned IBM advertising from *Fortune,* forbade IBM personnel to speak to the magazine's writers, and even canceled a speaking appearance when he learned that *Fortune* was a sponsor of the event. IBM would not confirm any of this. As for *Fortune,* one of its senior editors enlisted the help of a financial analyst, asking him to smooth the path for a reconciliation between the magazine and Gerstner. When the analyst approached someone at IBM, he was told to "leave the whole thing alone." (A *Fortune* spokesperson noted that the magazine had made no comment on Gerstner's actions against *Fortune.*) The *Fortune* affair has proven to be Lou Gerstner's own March of

Folly for here is a major business figure who has chosen to declare war against one of the business community's most important journals, an act that hardly seems in Gerstner's best interest.

The IBM chief had some of the same difficulties in communicating with another major force in the business community: the financial analysts on Wall Street. These were the people whose views of IBM would play an important role, even a crucial one, in determining the overall perception of the company. Yet, no matter how hard the analysts tried to understand Gerstner and what he was all about, he gave them trouble, believing that it was better to avoid overpromising, convinced that he would bring himself and IBM harm by sounding too sure of himself. Even if he didn't feel compelled to tell the media what his grand vision for IBM was, the financial analysts felt they were entitled to know— indeed, he had an obligation to share with them—his views and plans. The analysts were accustomed to CEOs being more open. Gerstner had asked the analysts to be patient, but three months into the job, he still insisted that he had no grand vision for IBM.

The group with whom Gerstner communicated most effectively was IBM's customer base. He talked freely and openly with customers and made sure to listen to what they had to say to him. They told him time after time that IBM's salvation lay in providing customer-friendly services and solutions, not in simply selling more and more products. So Gerstner insisted that IBM would measure its success not by its revenues, but by how much more productive and efficient the customer became as a result of relying on IBM solutions to their business problems. Customers knew which way IBM was heading long before the media and the financial analysts did—and that suited Gerstner just fine.

Chapter 16

———

Get Combative— Develop an Aggressive Acquisition Strategy

"You're running the place. Do what you want."

ONE OF THE strongest features of the IBM culture had been the not-invented-here syndrome. For decades, IBM had manufactured products that had been the stars of the computer industry, from the earliest mainframes to some of the new personal computers and laptops. IBM had no need to look elsewhere to acquire companies because its senior executives genuinely believed that no other company could produce Big Blue's quality. Lou Gerstner had no qualms about destroying cultural icons, especially if those icons did not fit into his plan for the IBM turnaround. As far as he was concerned, if IBM were to stubbornly adhere to the not-invented-here syndrome, its chances of rising from the mire of mediocrity would be stymied.

He wanted IBM to get more competitive and combative. And one of the best ways to achieve that, he thought, was to acquire other companies and gain ownership over the products they produced.

An Early-Morning Phone Call

It was 8:25 A.M., Monday, June 5, 1995. Lou Gerstner was about to make one of the most important phone calls of his IBM career. He picked up the phone to Jim Manzi, the CEO of Lotus Development Corporation, the leading developer of applications for IBM's new OS/2 operating system for computers. This was a call that the unsuspecting Manzi would later look back on with horror. Gerstner was calling to inform Manzi that in just five minutes IBM planned to announce that it would launch a takeover of his company for $3.3 billion—and he hoped the Lotus CEO would cooperate. If not, IBM was prepared to carry out a hostile takeover. Manzi later complained to friends about the extremely short notice. What he failed to take into account was the new pugnaciousness at IBM.

IBM had decided to acquire Lotus after some internal task forces had portrayed their own software business in less than flattering terms. With thousands of programmers hard at work around the world, Gerstner felt it a crime that IBM still had no major presence in desktop software while one of its main rivals, Microsoft, was about to launch a software product called Exchange. The Microsoft product resembled Lotus Notes, which was Lotus's most important cash cow. If IBM could gain control over Lotus, Big Blue would obtain several popular software programs that would run on its operating systems, including Lotus Notes and the Lotus 1-2-3 spreadsheet program. In short, buying Lotus gave IBM a crucial opportunity to catch up to Microsoft.

Founded by a Disk Jockey

Lotus was a recognized and highly regarded name in the computer industry. Founded in 1982 by a former disk jockey and transcendental meditator, Mitch Kapor, the company gained fame not just for its hip, young corporate culture but also for its revolutionary "1-2-3" spreadsheet program. Although Lotus had lost some market share since then, it remained an important player in the world of spreadsheets and word processors. Recently, it had come up with Lotus Notes, a piece of software that many said was as innovative as its early spreadsheet, for it permitted geographically scattered people to work on the same documents and projects through networked computers. One wag called it "e-mail on steroids."

The mid-1990s seemed an ideal time for IBM to make the Lotus acquisition. While Lotus had posted $970 million in revenue in 1994, it had lost $17.5 million in the first quarter of 1995. IBM could offer the software maker the deep financial pockets it needed to stay in business. Gerstner had asked John M. Thompson, IBM's senior vice president and senior software official, to make improvements in IBM's software operations in January 1995, but the CEO realized that the fastest way to make those improvements was to purchase Lotus.

So for the next five months, IBM secretly conducted negotiations with Manzi and other senior Lotus officials to purchase Lotus. The talks got nowhere. Part of the problem may have been the clashing corporate cultures: the solid, venerable IBM versus the laid-back upstart, Lotus. Lotus possessed a culture that was considered hard-driving and irreverent. The firm's name was adopted from the lotus flower, an important symbol in transcendental meditation. When John Thompson first met with Lotus development officials early in 1995 he made sure to dress down in jeans and a T-shirt. Much to Thompson's surprise, the Lotus executives had donned the traditional IBM uniform: dark suits and ties. The attempt to please by dressing in the other's uniform did not augur well for the planned merger. It appeared that the two companies did not know what to make of each other.

After it became clear that a friendly deal could not be struck, Gerstner phoned Jim Manzi, and a few minutes later made the announcement: Big Blue was offering $3.3 billion (all cash) to purchase the software maker. This was IBM's very first hostile takeover bid, and the largest in the software industry. It took Gerstner only a week of fairly easy negotiations to win Lotus for IBM. By June 18 it was all over. To make the deal more attractive to Lotus, Gerstner promised that Manzi would be retained and that Lotus would continue to function for the most part as a separate entity. In short, it would not be swallowed up by the IBM bureaucracy, as Lotus officials feared.

Notes to You!

Wall Street wondered why IBM had paid such a high price for Lotus. After all, IBM was paying $64 a share for a company with shares wallowing in the low 30s, a price that was three times Lotus's 1994 revenues. Yet, for IBM there was a good reason to buy Lotus. Although it was selling $11 billion worth of software each year, it was having a hard time developing new products for the PC and client-server markets. At one point it thought of trying to develop its own products to compete with Lotus Notes groupware, but rejected such a project as far too expensive, lengthy, and risky. But by grabbing Lotus, IBM jumped to the forefront in the increasingly important groupware segment of the industry. It also gained the highly successful Lotus development team. IBM overlooked the fact that it had paid more than ten times Lotus Notes revenues. It seemed likely that IBM could sell more of Notes than Lotus would have on its own—and the hope was that the surge in sales would spill over into sales of all kinds of software, services, and even computers.

At a news conference that day, Gerstner explained why it was important for IBM to acquire Lotus. He began by noting that the computer industry had passed through two revolutions: first mainframes, then personal computers. And, he noted, the information technology industry was now entering a new phase, in which all of the computing power of an enterprise is linked together so that the mainframes or servers and the PCs become linked in a network.

> **Not just a hierarchical network, so that the PCs can talk to the mainframes or servers—but very importantly, a world in which all of the users can talk horizontally to each other, and to work together in what is known as "collaborative" or "team" computing. That is a very, very powerful need of our customers around the world.**
>
> **Now, what does it take to be successful in that third phase? Well, it takes the industry delivering some very important products. First of all, the products must operate across a very heterogeneous set of hardware and software platforms that today don't work together.**

For such fully collaborative computing, there must exist software that can operate on multiple platforms. It must be open, fully compliant with broad industry standards, and supportive of the full industry range of products. Moreover, said Gerstner, it must possess the strengths of the desktop—phase two: ease of use and ease of application—along with the strengths of large-scale systems—phase one: reliability, security, and robustness. Finally, these products must work across very small local networks all the way up to cross-border, multinational global networks, including publicly switched networks like telephone company networks.

Gerstner thought such a transaction was unique, because both Lotus and IBM had been investing significantly in this new model of computing. Lotus brought a very strong position on the desktop—strong products, and experience, and a solid reputation—while IBM had been delivering and continues to invest the critical industrial-strength resources to make this model work: network management skills, data management skills, systems management skills, etc. All this meant that it would operate both on the smallest computer and the largest computers.

Soon after the June 5 announcement, IBM posted a message on its Web site meant to reassure Lotus workers of their autonomy. The site received thousands of visits. Within twenty-four hours Gerstner and Thompson flew to Cambridge, Massachusetts, to Lotus headquarters, to soothe employees who now feared for their jobs. The Lotus staff appreciated Gerstner's willingness to pay them a visit.

Most important for IBM, the Lotus deal would provide both IBM and Lotus with one last chance to prevent Microsoft from dominating networked computing the way it had dominated the field of desktop PCs. Lotus had been hoping for some time to gain a foothold in the new world of networked computing, but it lacked the organization and resources to promote Notes into that environment. Gerstner offered Lotus the organization and resources to push Notes sales way beyond its present level.

The acquisition of Lotus—at a price that was three times its 1994 revenues and twice its stock price—sent a strong message to Microsoft. IBM would go to great lengths to become the leader in efforts to link PCs, workstations, servers, and mainframes into a network that could share information and tasks.

IBM had counted on Lotus getting off to a smooth start after the merger, but things came undone that fall. Lotus employees became frightened by the takeover, viewing IBM with suspicion. IBM sought to reassure Lotus workers but to little avail, and many Lotus employees left. While all this was happening, Jim Manzi was trying to gain more influence within the new alliance. He tried to convince Gerstner to unite the software businesses of IBM and Lotus and to put him in charge of the overall unit, a surprise reversal of what Lotus had asked for at the time of the merger, namely, keeping IBM at arm's distance. Manzi now realized that his firm desperately needed IBM's deep pockets, and uniting their software businesses would, Manzi believed, make IBM more generous.

You're Running the Place

For three days in late September Gerstner and his colleagues met with Lotus executives to figure out how to mesh the two businesses. At a certain point, frustrated by his inability to get his way, Manzi resigned. Rather than bring in its own people, IBM indicated that Lotus could choose an insider to replace Manzi. Lotus executives were grateful and replaced Manzi with one of their own.

Soon thereafter, Lotus was again challenging IBM. This time, the software maker sought to slash Lotus Notes' price in half, hoping to take advantage of Microsoft's delay in delivering a competitive product. By making Notes cheaper, Lotus hoped to gain market share. What would IBM think of the idea? Gerstner and Thompson told the Lotus leadership, in effect, "You're running the place. Do what you want." The price took effect that December and the results topped even Gerstner's usual lofty expectations: Lotus sales doubled in 1996 to 9 million units.

Some cynics were convinced that IBM, seemingly unable to turn large profits from an $11.3 billion software business, was unlikely to succeed at running Lotus. Gerstner, aware of that perception, sent a memo over the Internet to Lotus employees pledging that Lotus would not be changed and indeed would become the focus of a new IBM PC software operation. Notes developer Raymond E. Ozzie was optimistic: "I've spent ten years of my life nurturing this product. We have a Goliath coming into the market with Microsoft. I want to do everything I can to make sure that Notes is a rip-roaring success."

Gerstner had more at stake in the Lotus deal than the $3.3 billion that he eventually paid for Lotus. Once he began telling analysts and customers that the future of the company depended in large measure on its ability to lead in network computing, he became even more reliant on Notes' success, since Notes was vital to network computing.

How much of a help was Lotus to IBM's overall financial picture? It was hard to say, but clearly Lotus's impact was growing. In 1995, IBM was headed for a record profit year until the third quarter when it took a charge for the Lotus acquisition. IBM watchers felt that Big Blue was still too dependent on mainframe software, that it still had not made a recovery in the personal computer field, and that its presence in the PC software industry was way too small.

Early in 1996, IBM began marketing a new version of Lotus Notes that permitted Notes to both read and create information for the World Wide Web, making it much more useful for electronic commerce. The new version also facilitated electronic data interchange between companies or individuals using the Internet in two ways. Web pages could be created using Notes, and individuals could click onto the Web while reading e-mail from a colleague. To head off competition from Netscape and Microsoft, Gerstner negotiated agreements with eleven communication companies to carry Lotus Notes on their networks. He wanted to make Notes the envy of the industry, a product that every company wanted for its laptops, workstations, network servers, PCs, and mainframes.

As 1996 wound down, Gerstner won praise for the Lotus deal. Although the acquisition had shocked the whole high-tech industry (since Lotus had been losing market share and money), the new IBM-Lotus enterprise now ranked as one of the three biggest players in the Internet technology market (along with Microsoft and Netscape). Encouraged by the Lotus merger, Gerstner set his sites on other companies as well. In 1997, IBM acquired a majority stake in Web developer NetObjects, which made Web development tools. IBM was also investing a good deal of time and money in trying to develop state-of-the-art Internet software, including security and encryption programs and online retailing applications. It also had obtained full ownership of Advantis, the network services unit it once jointly owned with Sears, Roebuck. By now, IBM, with $13 billion in sales, had become the largest software company in the industry. Unfortunately, that figure was somewhat misleading, for IBM's aging software for mainframes, a lucrative, but slow-growth market, represented three-quarters of the total amount. The figure that troubled Gerstner most was his software business's rate of growth: while the software industry was climbing at

12 percent, IBM was growing at an anemic 4 percent. Meanwhile, the database software maker Oracle and Microsoft were both growing many times faster than IBM: in 1996 at 38 percent and 25 percent, respectively.

Gerstner had by now spent $5 billion to acquire companies in the fast-growing software markets. In early 1996 he also bought Tivoli Systems, a maker of software that managed client-server computer networks. In client-server technology, individual users, called clients, are "served" over a network by a central computer that acts as the common repository of programs and information. Gaining an important stake in network computing made sense for IBM, as client-server networks were quietly replacing the mainframe computers that had been the traditional bastion of IBM sales.

Gerstner never let up in his effort to boost software sales. On April 15, 1997, IBM announced a whole new game plan, centering on software, to turn all of its hardware—from PCs to parallel computers—into sophisticated Web servers ready for Internet commerce and other uses. It was introducing a new line of powerful Web-server programs, called "Go" after the Japanese strategy game, which would become the high end of IBM and Lotus's Domino Web-server software. While IBM rivals were purchasing browsers and Web TV, IBM was focusing on the less glamorous aspect of the Internet known as middleware, the software "plumbing" that linked business programs and processed thousands of transactions a second—for banks, airlines, and other big customers—to the Web. By 1998 it was clear that Lou Gerstner had been correct in destroying the "not-invented-here" icon at IBM. Lotus was fast becoming a huge success for IBM, thanks in no small measure to his decision to refrain from imposing IBM's culture and will on the Massachusetts software enterprise. As a result, Lotus still maintained the identity of a medium-sized software house. Gaining IBM's cash and distribution clout, Lotus watched happily as its 2 million user base in 1995 grew to an astounding 22 million by 1998.

In addition to all of the Gerstner plans and strategies, his nononsense, tough-as-nails exterior sent a clarion call at IBM. He would no longer tolerate lackluster performance. Period. He conveyed this message every day, not only by what he said, but by how he acted. Because his very demeanor contrasted so vividly with the gentlemanly Akers 9 to 5 regime, his personality played a leading role in helping

IBM to overcome its complacency. His staff simply had no choice: Either wake up and get with the program, or they might find themselves searching for new jobs. This was not a man to be trifled with. Because his personality is so central to the IBM turnaround, we will now take an up-close look at the personal side of this enigmatic leader.

———•———

Chapter 17

What's Lou Gerstner Like: You're Not Getting Inside My Head!

"A desk is a dangerous place from which to view the world."

*L*OU GERSTNER HAS what every great commu-
nicator needs and wants, a powerful presence. When he walks into a
room, everyone knows he is in their midst. When he talks, people listen.
As a public speaker, he is able to distill large amounts of information
easily and pass on that information to an audience in simple phrases
and ideas. He has been called "a tightly coiled package of high-voltage
brainpower." His face is boyish, giving him the appearance of a younger
man. One writer described him as "a fleshy, impeccably groomed man
with thick, black hair, hazel eyes, and smooth, round cheeks." Another
said he had the body of a mainframe.

Lou Gerstner's tough, suffer-no-fools personality keeps everyone
alert. A surprising number of his acquaintances admit that he is brusque,
sometimes to the point of rudeness. For evidence, they point to the
fifteen-minute meetings and the one-minute phone calls—and his insistence that subordinates come to meetings prepared to give solutions to

problems, not simply to go over old material again and again. Undeniably, such attitudes breed a certain amount of discomfort. William J. Milton Jr., an analyst at Brown Brothers Harriman, notes that Gerstner is always accompanied by a small entourage of senior executives at meetings, and just by looking at their body language, Milton can tell they're afraid of him. No one had ever shown signs of being afraid of John Akers.

People who have gotten to know Lou Gerstner say he is uptight, intense, abrupt, impatient, ambitious, and driven. A demanding boss, he expects results yesterday. He is above all orderly and a stickler for detail. He plans his highly regimented schedule down to the minute.

Unlike some other business leaders, Gerstner can live without being in the company of celebrities—movie stars, heads of state, and the like—yet some colleagues at RJR Nabisco accused him of having an imperial air. He was selective not only about who got to ride in the corporate jet with him but also about the seating arrangements. No wonder those executives dubbed the desk where he worked at the back of the plane "the throne."

You're Not Getting Inside My Head

For all of his desire to be publicly recognized as a great business leader, Gerstner is intensely private. He almost never talks about himself in public. When a reporter introduced himself to Gerstner, the IBM head snarled back at him, "You're not getting inside my head." A few months later, the same reporter, hoping that Gerstner had softened by now, asked, "Where does your ambition come from?" Gerstner shot back: "I have no idea. I'm left-handed. Where did my left-handedness come from?" Most other CEOs are more sensitive to the media and would never dream of talking in this gruff manner to journalists; instead, they would go out of their way to put them at ease. But Gerstner has a strong aversion to anyone writing about him, an odd reaction if only because most of what has been written about him down through the years has been largely favorable.

He is especially annoyed (to say the least) when anyone in the media tries to describe him personally. *Fortune* magazine sought to do just that when it wrote in its April 1997 cover story: "Talk about contrasts. He is drawn to the limelight like a moth to flame, yet he is belligerently private. He has lived a great Horatio Alger story, but doesn't want to tell it. He is a devout Catholic who attends Mass every week but often flouts the golden rule.... He intimidates many who work for him, yet a cadre of loyal executives has followed him from company to company. He hates for anyone or anything to waste his time, yet he's a gardener who enjoys the painstaking process of growing asparagus." As noted earlier, he was so appalled at the way *Fortune* described him that he exacted his own kind of punishment on the magazine.

The consensus among his business colleagues is that Gerstner is an excellent CEO, but difficult to be around. A number of people interviewed for the *Fortune* magazine cover story suggested that while he had performed a miracle at Big Blue, he was not an easy boss. "He's done a hell of a job," one said anonymously. "He took a place that was totally into itself and got it to see reality." Unquestionably smart and a great listener, Gerstner was still frightening as hell. "Everyone's terrified of him," said a journalist who covers IBM. "He's more of a fear leader, he's not a warm and fuzzy manager," observed a financial analyst who watches IBM. "I hear from people who are close to him that he's a good guy. But if you don't know him, he seems standoffish."

Comfortable with his peers, especially other CEOs, Gerstner is less at ease with people further down the corporate ladder. Priding himself on being a businessman, he likes being among decision makers. He does not identify with nonmanagerial types. That's why he wants to meet with the CEOs, not their underlings, when he seeks out customers.

Tom Neff, who has done headhunting for IBM, admits that the man at the top can be exasperating. Neff finds it only natural that people are intimidated by Lou Gerstner because he exhibits such forcefulness and self-confidence.

The word "restraint" does not come to mind in describing the head of IBM. Even in his golf game, Gerstner exhibits a competitiveness that others find perplexing. Here Gerstner recalls one incident on the golf course that certainly must have perturbed his opponent, Vernon Jordan, the powerful Washington attorney and friend of Bill Clinton.

I had won almost 17 straight holes and I was beating him like a drum, and I hit the ball on the green, and he proceeds to hit the ball in the woods. At which point I hear this noise and clatter, and out comes a ball that miraculously goes into the hole. He beat me on that hole. And of course, he doesn't remember anything but

that hole. I can't believe he talked to you about that. I took it very gentlemanly until he started to crow about it, and he's still crowing about it years later. So he's leaning on a very thin reed.

Gerstner always wants to be the man in charge. This is as true now as it was when he was at American Express, in 1985, when he said:

On the discipline side, there is no question that I am a reasonably autocratic driver of the organization when it comes to strategy. I set the strategic agenda here. I am not going to let this ship get off its course. Sure, I will let some people play round with it, and I will, I hope, even be prepared to be convinced that I am going off in a wrong direction. But we have a handful of priorities here, and tough discipline toward our goals is very important to me.

He alone will determine IBM's direction, and he will also make sure that the people working for him don't gain too much individual power. No fiefdoms for Lou Gerstner.

Another aspect of project management is that I strictly avoid creating tsars. Let's say there is a strategic problem. The easy thing would be to take somebody, hired either from outside or internally, and say that he or she is going to be a staff person at headquarters. All of a sudden they will have five assistants and three vice presidents, and they want to be a senior vice president. They are going to be the "head" of this process. I don't want that. One of the things I learned at McKinsey is that the busiest people are those who can get the most work done. They are busy because they are good. I keep loading onto people who have full-time jobs.

Disdaining fiefdoms, Gerstner still wants managers with assertive personalities.

We have other kinds of change agents. We have people who are what I would call "china-breakers." They are bulls in the china shop . . . they are brilliant. They have strong convictions that we ought to do something in a certain way, but they are very tough on people. They tend to be tough on their peers. So you work at

supporting those kinds of people, not getting rid of them. You say, "You turkey, why do you treat people that way?" But you don't fire them. You don't let the organization kill them.

I'm No Workaholic

He prides himself on not being a workaholic: "A workaholic is someone who wants to be at work all the time and has no outside interests. I find time to do other things that I love to do." When his two children were in grade school, he left work early on the days that their reports cards were issued. His hobbies include gardening, golfing, and skiing. Yet when he worked at RJR Nabisco, he put in six-and-a-half-day weeks—and loved it. "I'm having a terrific time," he said then. He recalled being home one Sunday afternoon and saying to his wife, Robin: "I really can't wait to get to the office tomorrow." So eager was he, in fact, that on one occasion, when he was still at McKinsey, he cut off the tips of two fingers on his right hand with a lawn mower but was back at work the very next day. On another occasion, in April 1996, he had had surgery for a detached retina. Although he still could not see very well, he spent hours working on the phone from his home in Greenwich, Connecticut; soon after he showed up at work wearing dark glasses and plunged into a series of lengthy meetings.

At work, he is no nine-to-fiver, unlike John Akers, who prided himself on knocking off promptly at quitting time. "Lou is a voracious reader," says Jim Cannavino, the former IBM senior vice president for strategy. "He takes suitcases of stuff home with him. On Monday it's all underlined in red. It's amazing. Nothing is off his radar screen."

Gerstner expects everyone at IBM to work as hard as he does, if not harder. In December 1996, feeling very good about IBM's potential for the future, he noted:

I don't want to get too exuberant. I want to have a fairly strong dose of. . . . Well, what's the right word? Well, I don't want to use Andy's [Intel CEO Andy Grove] word [paranoia]. I want us to keep running, to keep moving ahead. Some may feel that because the wind is now at our back, it's time to coast. They are allowed a five-minute celebration, then it's time to get back to work for the other 55 minutes of the hour.

A Dangerous Place

When he's on the job, he seems to be in perpetual motion. He travels roughly half the time, visiting IBM sites. He is a firm believer in the words on a sign on his desk: "A desk is a dangerous place from which to view the world." In November 1996, for example, he raced around Europe, hitting four countries in seven days. He had already logged 542 flights in the corporate jet and over 400,000 air miles. But it's not only the hard work that appeals to him. He loves the thrill of the game.

> **Once I have a feeling for the choices, then I have no problems with the decisions. I love to make strategic decisions.**

When he made the move to RJR Nabisco, he explained why he was so thrilled to be going to a place where he might make some difference:

> **The idea of going into an already well-run company and taking the helm and steering it a few degrees to the right or the left— that doesn't have the challenge of [working at RJR].**

Lou Gerstner doesn't let people get into his head. He remains private, enigmatic. He can be short-tempered and overbearing. But whether people like him or not seems unimportant to him. He understands the need to set goals and never to waver in pursuing them. This often means speeding up the decision-making process, taking risky decisions, and making sure that people don't waste his time. He doesn't mind being described as tough. He knows he's tough, and he doesn't care if everyone else knows it too.

V

It's the Customer, Stupid!

"The first thing we had to do was reorient ourselves from a highly introspective view of the world to an obsession with the marketplace. . . . I want IBM to be obsessed with the customer."

Chapter 18

————•————

No More Arrogance, No More Distance

"We are going to approach the market from the customer's perspective, which is: 'Give me a solution, not raw technology.' "

IT WAS FAR easier in the old days to spend time holding customers' hands. When IBM rented mainframes to a few hundred select businesses, it was possible to get to know each and every client personally. Customers changed mainframes often enough that it made sense for IBM's sales force to keep in close touch with them. Thomas Watson Sr. always contended that he was far more interested in customers than in machines; he wanted to make IBM a customer-friendly company. Watson encouraged his sales force to practically move in with a customer.

Because Watson believed so strongly in the importance of customer relations, IBM had always boasted a massive sales force. And because Watson sought to avoid the usual pejorative image of the American salesperson—lethargic and slightly shady—he insisted that his salespeople dress in the IBM "uniform" and follow strict rules of conduct regarding drinking, smoking, and marriage. Watson was striving to create a new breed of salespeople who would set new professional standards in their dealings with customers.

More Than Just Salespeople

Watson trained his people to be much more than just salesmen. He wanted them to be friendly guides through the arcane world of computers, always making sure that the customer understood just how the new technology could help his business. It was not unusual to find IBM employees showing great dedication to a customer, even taking up residence in the customer's business. Many sales reps developed strong ties to the senior management of those companies. "I had access to all executives of all the companies that I dealt with," said John D. Loewenberg, a sales rep for IBM in the 1970s and now a senior vice president for information technology services at Aetna Life Insurance & Casualty. "Part of my relationship with my customers was understanding their business problems and working with them to solve them. IBM represented integrity and quality—things that became part of the IBM culture, that the whole world saw IBM as."

Yet, with IBM's incredible success, in the 1980s the company began to make the near-fatal mistake of disregarding the customer. Indeed, all the sales force seemed to want to do was to sell as many computers as possible, and the customer be damned. Though IBM's prices were high, so was the quality of its products, and customers had little choice but to go with Big Blue. IBM kept a vice-like grip on customers, cleverly insisting that anyone who purchased a mainframe had to purchase IBM software as well. Why bother with hand-holding? It wasn't going to increase sales. Sales—repeat sales—were already guaranteed. The customer *had* to buy IBM products, so why bother keeping close tabs on customers? There was certainly little incentive.

Sales reps developed the attitude that "If I'm not selling products to you, it's because I am not doing a good job of *persuading* you that these are the best products for you; it has nothing to do with how many customer calls I make." According to this logic, it was easy to stay away from customers. Furthermore, customers made few demands on the sales force in the early days of computers. They knew very little about the workings of the complicated mainframes, making it easy for sales reps to tell them what to buy.

But once IBM stopped renting computers and began to *sell* them, customers had more reason to get to know the equipment. And with the advent of the personal computer, customers became more conversant with the technology. To be fair to the IBM sales force, when the number of computer buyers had swollen to the thousands, staying in touch with customers became an impossible task. When a sales rep would ask an executive to join in a customer call, the superior often found an excuse to skip the meeting. The message was beamed loud and clear to IBM staff: customer calls just weren't that important. Accordingly, the vaunted relationship between the IBM sales force and the senior figures of American corporate life began to come unhinged. IBM was shifting away from "solutions" and focusing instead on a high-growth strategy of selling hardware; unfortunately for IBM, its hardware was often not the best or the best-priced. IBM would have been much better off trying to help clients with their business problems instead of pushing undesirable merchandise on them. But arrogance prevailed.

IBM had always prized itself on having a deep understanding of its clients' business needs; but with the advent of the PC and the cheaper, more flexible Unix servers, IBM lost this edge. And rather than face the new market, IBM tried to buck it, sinking its resources into hardware, which was what had always driven the business and produced those fat margins and bonus checks.

Pushing "Big Iron"

With IBM software largely designed to run only on its own computers, it had strong incentive for the company to push "big iron." Although they seemed arrogant, in truth IBM salespeople didn't know any other way to behave when they sold products. The system had worked in the past, so why change it? Unfortunately, what customers wanted increasingly were inexpensive PCs that could put word-processing and spreadsheet functions on every office desktop. Some senior executives eventually resigned in the mid-1980s, fretting that they were being asked to insist on solutions that they knew were not in their customers' best interests.

When salespeople did go to a company, they visited top management less and less and dropped in on the people who ran the computer operations more and more. In general, though, the sales force was spending significantly less time with customers. Indeed, one IBM-sponsored survey in the 1980s showed that sales reps had been spending less than a third of their time with customers. As a result, IBM's strong ties to corporate America weakened; it lost sales and market share and its reputation suffered significant damage.

Long before he arrived at IBM, Lou Gerstner had been a customer of Big Blue, and he knew that the company was in trouble. He had watched as the company turned its back on customers. When Gerstner became CEO in 1993, no one had to tell him that one of IBM's most pressing problems was winning back once-loyal customers.

> I was basically the first customer that had ever run an information technology company. And I said: We're going to change the way the industry has been approaching the customer. The way the industry has been approaching the customer for the last 15 years is [with] a bunch of piece parts that were sold to customers, and the customers had to do the integration inside their own organization. There are, I don't know, 60,000 competitors in this industry today, and most of them make individual little boxes with little pieces of software, much of which doesn't fit together.
>
> So we said we were going to approach the market from the customer's perspective, which is: Give me a solution, not raw technology; give me something that adds value to my business as I see my business; and I don't see my business from a pure technical point of view. If I'm a pharmaceutical company, I want to increase the speed of my molecular research. I want to be able to model molecules faster. If I'm an oil company, I want to get value out of my seismic research faster. If I'm a bank, I want to reach out to new customers in new ways, less expensive distribution systems. That's what customers worry about.

He was convinced that IBM's products were sound, and that its employees had great potential, but he also knew that they had fallen on bad habits. They had become so arrogant and distant that they had frightened off customers. "I want to take IBM back to its roots," he said often. To Gerstner, IBM had been focusing far too much on its internal workings and not enough on the outside.

My view is that the company had been so successful for so long it stopped comparing itself with competitors and started gauging itself by internal measures. That's a recipe for trouble. So the first thing we had to do was reorient ourselves from a highly intro-spective view of the world to an obsession with the marketplace, both customers and competitors. . . . I want IBM to be obsessed with the customer.

From the start, Gerstner sensed that IBM had to repair its damaged relationships with customers. "The marketplace is the driving force behind everything we do," was the first of the eight new IBM principles Gerstner articulated.

If there is one thing that best summarizes what happened to IBM, it's that we missed changes in the marketplace. It wasn't that our technology wasn't good. It wasn't that our people were somehow deficient. It was that we failed to adapt quickly to fundamental change in the marketplace. . . . We must let nothing stand in the way of driving IBM against a set of actions defined by what's going on outside our doors. We should be prepared to change every organization—every process, every IBM myth—as part of a con-tinuing path of evolution.

Gerstner wanted his sales force to pay much more personal atten-tion to customers.

We need to spend a whole lot more time with customers. Every one of the senior managers has a little assignment from me regarding customers. We're going to try to squeeze out whatever arrogance remains in the selling approach of IBM. And we're also going to start talking to our customers about what we think we can do to define for them the computing model of the Nineties, which right now nobody is providing. IBM used to be the company that did that. IBM could be the company to do it again.

IBM had to focus on the outside and that meant focusing on cus-tomers. Focusing everyone on what was outside the company was nothing new to Lou Gerstner. He had faced a similar problem when he was at American Express, where he saw...

> ...an enormous amount of mythology in the management structure. "Why do we do this? We do it because we always did it that way." Or "We do it because the consumer wants it." Or "We just do it." But when you started to think, "Well, what do you mean, the consumer wants this? Which consumer? How often? Where?" the analysis just fell apart. It was clear to me that we needed to get more external focus on what we were all about.

IBM needed to look outside the company for measures of success.

> We don't rely on our own internal sense of satisfaction nor on internal measurement systems. Our success is driven by customers who, by doing business with us, tell us that we are the best at giving them what they want and need.

He strongly believed that change was healthy, and that by its very nature, it tended to shake people out of their slumber, forcing them to look at the world differently. And it would force them to give more thought to the outside world.

> I believe in organizational change. I don't do it just for the sake of doing it, but if you consistently and regularly change the home base and the way people view the world, they tend to think more externally than they do internally.

Gerstner, no technology visionary, liked to say that he "came with the mindset of a customer." Soon after he became the head of IBM, Gerstner changed the direction the company was heading, calling off the plan to split it into thirteen autonomous units, and keeping it whole. Keeping IBM united, Gerstner would say later, was the best thing he could have done to attract customers. Indeed, John Akers' plan to break up IBM overlooked a central reality about the company: It had been a united, whole IBM that had attracted such a steady, loyal, and large customer base.

Just five years ago, IBM was on the verge of scattering its businesses to the four corners of the information technology world, to
live—or die—within their own industry sectors. We know now
what a mistake that would have been.

Our unique value proposition to customers has been—and
will continue to be—precisely our ability to offer integrated solutions that draw on sources and strengths across IBM. Today, with
the shift to a networked world, our customers again need inte-
grators. They need secure, reliable, scalable technology—in other
words, IBM-style enterprise computing. And they need partners
who understand how to apply technology to address basic business issues—our heritage. I believe IBM's comeback is a direct
result of our decision to swim against the tide, to stay together.

As Gerstner set about rebuilding ties to IBM's biggest customers, he
was also laying the foundation for what would become an enormously
successful service strategy. IBM had certainly demonstrated a keen
ability to supply computer services; indeed, in 1992 it had made money
selling $5 billion worth of services. But for service to become the focus
of IBM's business the company would have to undergo a major attitude
adjustment regarding what Gerstner deemed one of its most vital
assets: its customers.

The Personal Touch

It was not simply that Lou Gerstner placed a new emphasis on the customer. It was something far more important—and more personal—
than that with him. He decided from the start that he would get
involved himself in massaging the old customers and winning new customers for IBM. That marked a major departure from the past, when
John Akers left customer relations to underlings.

Lou Gerstner vowed to spend as much time with customers as he
could. And he does just that. And like IBM's best salespeople, he often
comes back with billions of dollars in orders for hardware and services.
By his own estimate he spends 40 percent of his time talking to customers and hosts several CEO conferences every year to discuss the
information technology issues facing senior executives.

Gerstner talks to CEOs on a regular basis. If some of those CEOs were uncomfortable talking to customers, Gerstner was not. To him, there was simply no substitute. As he told George F. Colony, the president of Forrester Research, a consulting firm in Cambridge, Massachusetts, "I won't listen to executives tell me about customers. I will listen to customers."

I Don't Want to Be in Armonk

He made sure to use an office in Manhattan because, as he told Colony, "that's where my customers are. I don't want to be in Somers or Armonk. I want to be in New York, close to the customers."

He told his senior executives that he considered meeting customers his most important task. When one manager invited him to come to part of a two-day meeting with American-based IBM customers in May 1993, Gerstner replied that he would be there for the entire session. He knew he would never be able to observe customers casually, as he had at RJR by visiting supermarkets. But he would do his best to figure out what IBM customers really wanted. His workweek often included several phone conversations with key customers, and senior executives were obligated to get out of their offices to meet with clients—executives who delegated that task to subordinates did so at their own peril. Gerstner commented: "When I arrived here, I said, 'Who is talking to customers?' "

Among the steps Gerstner took in the early days to ease the confusion of customers was renaming some of IBM's organization units whose names were either vague or misleading. He banned the term "line of business," routinely abbreviated as "LOB" and replaced it with "division." He changed unit names too. For instance, the Rochester, Minnesota, Application Business Systems group that made the AS 400 was renamed, more precisely, the AS 400 division.

In the fall of 1998, Lou Gerstner made a rare television appearance on CNBC, the business cable network. When asked how he had turned IBM around, he focused on the company's renewed focus on customers.

We have focused this company maniacally on the customer. Everything we've done in this company has been driven by an

identification of who our customers are and what they want. And that's what got us in front of this whole network computing–E-biz world. That's why we're leading that. Because that's what our customers said. As we began to build the company from the customer back, we eliminated a lot of the internal focus that was in the company.

It's as if Lou Gerstner put a sign on the main bulletin board at IBM with just four words: "It's the customer, stupid!" That's all that he was saying. Don't assume you know what's best for customers. Don't tell customers what they should be buying. Today's customers are far more sophisticated and knowledgeable, but they still require assistance in resolving business problems, big and small. As Lou Gerstner preached, helping customers solve their problems just happened to be IBM's number one strength—and he was determined that the message would stick.

Chapter 19

———

Listen to Customers—
They Know Best
What They Need

"The information revolution will happen, but only when the industry stops worshipping technology for its own sake and starts focusing on *real value* for its customers."

TODAY, PEOPLE INSIDE and outside IBM speak in awe about a watershed event that took place in May 1993. "You know about Chantilly," one person after the other says in hushed, conspiratorial tones, as if talking about some secret conclave where the president of the United States had gathered with his most senior aides to plot a nuclear attack against China. "That's where it all started. Everything began at Chantilly." Everything dealing with IBM's customers, that is.

A Meeting in Chantilly

A few weeks after he assumed office at IBM, Lou Gerstner arranged an unusual meeting at a retreat in Chantilly, Virginia. The chief information officers of IBM's top 200 customers were invited. Even if the attendees were not planning nuclear warfare, few people that attended the meeting have forgotten it. It was at that meeting that Gerstner shattered certain IBM cultural icons, and forever altered the course of the computer giant. It was the first time that the company had dared to admit that it didn't know everything about everything, the first time that IBM executives stood in front of a group of customers and asked two simple questions:

1. What have we done right?
2. What have we done wrong?

Lou Gerstner didn't care what others thought. He was not impressed that people couldn't remember an IBM chairman ever meeting with customers en masse like this. He viewed the encounter as essential. He wanted the facts, and he wanted to hear them unfiltered, directly from the people who mattered most—IBM customers.

At the session, customers pulled no punches. They told Gerstner and the rest of the IBM employees that it had not been much fun dealing with IBM in the past few years. It was too difficult to work with the hordes of salespeople who kept calling on them. Worse yet, none of those salespeople were very responsive to their needs. Take the mainframes. Rather than explain why their companies needed mainframes, the sales reps had been known to badmouth their own products and suggest that IBM might get out of the business altogether very soon. Gerstner could not believe his ears: Who badmouths his own products?

The guests at Chantilly also told Lou Gerstner that they would prefer dealing with a single IBM salesperson, as they had in the past, instead of dozens of reps. They wanted one person who was able to talk knowledgeably about the entire scope of IBM products and services, everything from mainframes to notebooks.

When Gerstner finally spoke, he made it clear that IBM was in mainframes to stay, that he planned to aggressively cut prices and focus on helping customers set up, manage, and link systems together.

Learning What the Customers Wanted

Gerstner had been building up to the Chantilly meeting ever since he took over IBM the previous April. A few days after he joined IBM, he asked his twelve product managers to write a one-page summary of their businesses. At a meeting held the following day, he asked for details on how they hoped to sell their products. Most of all, he wanted to know what their customers wanted. Too many of them didn't seem to know. Gerstner was seething. Some of the more ill-prepared managers received the brunt of his anger. Several of their names were on the list of the 35,000 employees fired the following July.

The ill-fated meeting with the product managers led Gerstner to make a major decision: IBM would spend far less time on internal debates about what kind of technology to develop, and instead focus on finding out what customers really wanted. He was adamant that IBM put customers first.

Soon after Chantilly, when he was visiting an IBM plant, an employee approached him with a question: "One of your key things, Lou, seems to be getting closer to the customer. Frequently we find that we need to trade off customer requirements in favor of strategic decisions—platform support. Can you make specific recommendations for how we can achieve a successful balance?"

Gerstner stared at the man, as if he only half understood what he said—and what he understood he didn't like:

I don't know what "platform support" is, but let me answer your question very simply. If there's a key customer requirement, do it. Whatever this thing is—"platform whatever"—get it out of the way.

Gerstner knew that it would not be enough to hold Chantilly-like retreats, and that he could not be the only one at IBM to meet with customers; it would be important for many others besides himself to reach out to customers, as IBM had done in the old days. He began to think about how to improve IBM's huge 70,000-strong sales force, almost half of which was based overseas. Once able to explain IBM's complex machinery to customers, salespeople had become increasingly frustrated by their inability to impart good advice to customers in the post-mainframe computer world. Gerstner urged them to get closer to customers, to spend more time and effort getting out into the field and away from their desks.

The Vertical Marketing Approach

It took Lou Gerstner a solid year to resolve the marketing problems at IBM. By the spring of 1994, however, once he had decided what was wrong with the way IBM was marketing its computers, he moved to revamp its worldwide sales activities with incredible speed. It was in May of that year that he announced what was perhaps the most sweeping reorganization of IBM's mammoth sales force in decades. He reassigned them to "vertical marketing" groups that would cater to the specific industry of their clients. Over the next eighteen months, IBM planned to have 80 percent of its customers reached by the direct sales force covered by one of fourteen sales teams dedicated to such segments as financial services, travel, health care, utilities, and insurance. The new industry teams would cover the 5,000 largest IBM customers and account for 75 percent of the company's worldwide revenue. Besides the sales force, each industrywide unit included researchers from IBM labs, software engineers, and industry consultants hired from outside firms such as McKinsey. The man who headed up the new industry units, William A. Etherington, suggested that Gerstner had solved one key problem IBM had faced in the 1980s. Now, thanks to the infusion of the extra personnel, the newly organized teams could talk to customers, not just as commodity salespeople but as professional consultants.

In the past, IBM sales reps were organized along geographical lines: for instance, an IBM sales rep in Spain sold mainframes only in that country. Under the new scheme, sales reps were assigned to one of the fourteen global teams—perhaps the one for banking clients, or for the travel industry, or for multinational oil companies—and each team provided customers with information-processing systems tailored to their industry. The arguments for this "matrix management" were strong. Multinational clients disliked the geographic approach, because they found that too often an IBM subsidiary in some country would establish its own prices and write its own contracts. To make matters worse, salespeople for different IBM products and services did not offer coherent systems solutions. Customers were getting little benefit from IBM's worldwide reach. "The kind of clients we have don't necessarily care about your geography," says Robert Timpson, head of the marketing and product development team devoted to banking and securities firms. "They want to talk to somebody who had lunch with Sumitomo Bank in Tokyo the day before." The new industry teams, among them thousands of newly recruited business consultants, were better able to influence the design of new systems.

Gerstner found that it was not enough to restructure the sales force. He had to deal energetically with recalcitrant personnel as well. One such person was Hans Olaf Henkel, the 54-year-old Paris-based chairman and president of IBM-Europe. Henkel had resisted a panEuropean sales structure, let alone a worldwide one, so in September 1994 Gerstner removed him and replaced him with Lucio Stanca, who was committed to Gerstner's new industry marketing approach. The effect of the change was to weaken the authority of Europe's country managers, who had previously reported via Henkel to headquarters in Armonk, New York.

Having shifted to the industry approach to selling, Gerstner found it easier to woo back some of IBM's old customers. One example was Prudential Insurance of America, one of the nation's ten largest buyers of computer equipment. For years, Prudential had bought IBM computers, but by the late 1980s, the insurance giant was purchasing two-thirds of its mainframes from rival companies at lower prices. Under Lou Gerstner, IBM had a powerful new weapon in its arsenal to lure Prudential back as a customer—its problem-solving ability. IBM hoped to use that ability to solve industrywide problems which would then trickle down to help companies like Prudential. In one case, researchers at an IBM lab in Belgium began working with several insurance companies to develop a new way to manage data and improve industry efficiency. Prudential responded favorably and decided to buy IBM mainframes exclusively. Then in September 1996, it decided to award IBM a five-year contract and $340 million to run its computer systems.

In the 1994 Annual Report, Gerstner announced that he was embarking on a companywide crusade to win customers over to IBM's new technologies. There was no question that information technology would revolutionize every institution in American society.

But it will not happen the way, or as fast as, predicted by the pied pipers of this industry, who are obsessed with and endlessly pro-

mote electronic utopias and who are covered breathlessly by some in the media. What is possible is not always desirable—particularly if it costs too much money. . . .

The information revolution will happen, but only when the industry stops worshipping technology for its own sake and starts focusing on *real value* for its customers. We must provide products and services that improve customers' competitive position; that enhance their own customer service; that increase their productivity; that enrich their personal lives. These benefits are what will drive the revolution, not faster and faster silicon or millions of miles of fiber optics.

There was no reason, he said, why IBM's products couldn't be as simple to use as household appliances. It was his goal to make technology easier to use, easier to manage, in order to help customers embrace advanced technology and put it to work in the real world. It was crucial to think more about factors outside the company, and that often meant the customer.

Gerstner prided himself on listening to customers. When he heard customers complain about the high prices of mainframe software, he immediately ordered cuts up to 30 percent. He listened also as customers balked at investing so much in proprietary hardware and software, and pushed for more industry standards, such as Sun's Java programming language. He listened as potential customers complained that they were having trouble running complex computer networks. Once again, Gerstner moved quickly. He bought Tivoli Systems for $743 million to improve IBM's systems management skills. He listened as clients assailed IBM for forcing them to spend so much on technology, which brought little in the way of results.

Prestige for the Boss

Huddling with customers boosted Gerstner's prestige within the company. "It gives him tremendous power over the culture, knowing what customers want," noted George F. Colony, the president of Forrester Research. "No one could suggest to him that he had no idea what was going on in the business environment." No one dared. "His thoughts revolved around customers," recalled Jim Cannavino. "I thought I was one of the more customer-oriented guys in the company, but he was a welcome addition. He knew that if you can't describe something in the customer's values, you can't do it."

Above all, Gerstner practiced a "go to the customer" approach. He wanted to meet the customer personally, talk honestly about the company's needs, suggest ways in which IBM could help.

I came here with a view that you start the day with customers, that you start thinking about a company around its customers, and you organize around customers.

Circling the Globe

Three weeks after he took over IBM, he met with a group of chief information officers and talked to them about IBM. He still did not know enough to speak in detail about IBM, so he talked about a CEO's view of the technology and a customer's view of the technology. After the meeting, a number of the CIOs told him enthusiastically, "You need to get your message to our bosses. Our CEOs have got to hear your view of information technology—information technology as a strategic investment."

He heard the same comment three months later in Phoenix when he addressed another CIO conference. He was still lukewarm about the idea of inviting CEOs to hear him speak. "Well, I don't know. I'll be happy to do it, but I don't think if I call a meeting anyone will come."

"Try it," said the chief information officers. And he did. The first CEO conference was held early in 1994, with ten CEOs in attendance. The conferences eventually grew to be one of the most successful forums for Gerstner to meet with customers. At least 180 CEOs have now attended similar Gerstner conferences around the world.

In pursuit of customers, the IBM chief often set out on whirlwind journeys. On one such trip Gerstner set off from his Greenwich, Connecticut, home just after dawn and arrived at the Westchester County Airport. The morning was cold and rainy. Gerstner boarded IBM's Gulfstream IV, which took off a few moments later at 7 A.M. He had advanced the time of departure three times to make sure he would not be late. Shortly thereafter the plane landed in Toronto, where he was to meet with twenty senior executives from such organizations as Rubbermaid and the University of North Carolina.

Arriving by car at Toronto's King George Hotel, Gerstner raced to the conference room upstairs, where the CEOs were seated around a horseshoe-shaped table. Over the next ninety minutes, Gerstner talked enthusiastically about the Internet and the technology issues that these people faced. His jacket was off. He seemed relaxed. He had brought no slides, no presentation, and he gave no long discourse on technology. Instead, his topics included the quality of public schools and the changes technology was bringing to financial services companies. He wanted to convey to his listeners that he and IBM knew how the twenty-first-century high-tech society and economy would develop. He was there as an educator, but as a salesperson as well. As far as he was concerned, everyone in the room was a potential IBM customer.

Ironically, despite his original concerns about whether CEOs would come to his meetings, Gerstner was forced to *limit* attendance. At each meeting, Gerstner begins by telling the CEOs that he came to IBM as a customer; that he believes that the newly emerging electronic world will transform every institution in the world; that it is one of those technologies that come along every century that truly revolutionizes society and every part of society. He then tells the CEOs that the electronic world will create winners and losers in every industry. He talks of the implications for change this technology will bring, the enormous pressure on middlemen—insurance agents, travel agents, and so forth. He asks how they will all fit into an electronic world.

He tells the CEOs that the new electronic world brings competition to institutions from places they never expected. The new technology will effectively require every institution to become an information company as well as a product company, so whatever product these CEOs make and sell, they also have to use information technology.

What should a CEO do? What should the CEO's agenda be in dealing with the information revolution? In a talk he gave in 1996, he summarized the answer he routinely gives to these questions:

We focus on what I believe every CEO needs to worry about, the first of which is: Is information technology—its power and threat—an integral part of your strategic thinking? Is it there at

the table when you make strategic decisions? Do your senior managers understand it? Not bits and bytes; but its power to change? Is your CIO [chief information officer] at the table when you're doing strategic planning? Are you on the leading edge? Are you going to be a follower? What are you going to do with your old distribution system versus new distribution systems? That's number one. Then we get into another discussion which I tell all these CEOs I was unaware of when I was a CEO of a non-technology company: the battle of organization within large institutions, the battle of control of decentralization and central-ization. Where should decisions be made? Where should resources be purchased? Where should data be? Where are secu-rity standards set?

Gerstner tells them that this is a tough issue, but it's no different from any other organizational issues CEOs face. They have to decide what is centralized and decentralized in manufacturing and in market-ing, what standards are set by the central finance group and how much local discretion to allow.

The third thing he says is that CEOs should be aware of the issue of standards in the information technology industry. The CEOs get very upset, surprisingly, when he tells them that he discovered upon arriving in the industry that it is the only industry that doesn't live by and pro-duce common standards for the customer's benefit—and the customer ends up paying because of fights over competitive standards.

Now, they get very upset about this. And then I tell them to for-get it. Don't get into this stuff. Just recognize your CIO is wrestling with it.

Finally we move on and spend the bulk of our conversation, at least in the last year and a half, on networks. And they want to know: What is this Internet thing? And what should I be doing about it? What does it mean to me? And what we talk about ini-tially is fairly simple. . . .

What all the excitement is about is that standards issue I talked to you about: with almost all of the world seeing that maybe for once we will create what the industry, including IBM, should have done years ago. And that is the ability to have platform-

independent applications and true connectivity: any computer to
any other computer.

Apart from the forums, Gerstner spoke in person with CEOs on an individual basis, sometimes as often as three or four times a week. Sometimes he struck up a conversation with a CEO at some business function. The conversations sometimes paid off handsomely. In one such instance, in December 1995, Gerstner and his management team visited Procter & Gamble in Cincinnati, Ohio, where they were greeted warmly. It marked the first time an IBM CEO had taken the trouble to visit the company in decades—even though P&G ranked as one of IBM's best customers. Gerstner had bumped into P&G chairman and CEO John E. Pepper at a business function where Pepper mentioned that he and his senior managers were wrestling with a thorny challenge: how *could* they exploit new technology such as the Internet to streamline operations, speed innovation, and reach customers through new channels. A few days later, the IBM chairman called Pepper and proposed that he bring his management team out to P&G for a full day of briefings on how IBM views the burgeoning era of electronic commerce. Pepper was impressed at Gerstner's willingness to deal with all of them personally. Thanks to the visit, IBM had cemented relations with the consumer giant and improved its chances of winning new business with the company.

Gerstner worked his charms on other firms as well. When Ameritech was looking to farm out its data processing operations, Gerstner made a sales call at the Chicago-based Baby Bell. He also phoned Ameritech chairman and CEO Richard C. Notebaert several times before closing the deal. Of all the companies bidding on the $2.6 billion, ten-year contract, Gerstner came across as the only CEO who was deeply involved. His hands-on approach paid off in new IBM business: he quickly put together a $400 million joint venture between Ameritech and IBM that offered help-desk services to other corporations.

Gerstner knew that companies like Procter & Gamble and Ameritech and a host of others were under steady pressure to become more productive. But they couldn't achieve that goal if they had to spend huge amounts of time worrying about installing and then monitoring computer systems throughout their companies. That was where IBM came in. As he explained to an interviewer in *U.S. News & World Report:*

[There are] tens of thousands of competitors, some of which only make a little card that slips in the back of a PC. Some of them make just a single application software. Some people just make databases. Some people just make communications software. Yet the task inside the customer hasn't fragmented. The task is still the same. They need to get their business moving. It's just moved the integration from the industry to inside the customer.

And because of a couple of things, the customers are saying: We don't want that anymore. They are under pressure in their own companies to increase productivity. And, secondly, the proliferation of this technology and the pace of change of this technology has gotten to the point where the risks of kind of putting it together yourself are far more significant than the customers want to take on, which of course is one of the reasons that outsourcing has grown so enormously in the business, and it's also the reason our services business has grown so rapidly. . . .

Lou Gerstner was indeed listening to customers. Mostly what he heard from them was the complaint that while computers were essential to their businesses, they were getting way too complex. If IBM really wanted to help out its customers—and win back those who had jumped ship in the 1980s—it would strive to make life easier for them. It could work on solving some of the many problems these customers faced, not just throw a lot of hardware and software their way. Lou Gerstner heard that message loud and clear, and he responded aggressively. A thousand times a day, the IBM chief seemed to be saying: It's the customer, stupid.

Chapter 20

———•———

Choose Products That Customers Want to Buy

**"You take my mainframe away,
and my business is dead."**

ONE OF THE key ways of making IBM more customer-oriented was to make certain that the company made products that customers wanted to buy. But Lou Gerstner faced a critical decision at the outset of his tenure: What to do about mainframes?

No product was of more importance and more sensitive for IBM than the mainframe. IBM's profit margins on mainframes were as high as 70 to 80 percent; they were indeed the engine of the company's growth over the years. IBM and mainframes were almost synonymous. But by the 1980s, the mainframe business seemed to be disappearing. By the latter part of that decade the boom in personal computers appeared to spell an end to the product that made IBM the most successful company in America. Year after year new PCs hit the markets, more powerful than the year before, and government institutions and increasingly businesses were scrapping their "big iron" for PC networks. By 1992, IBM was taking in only $10 billion in revenue from mainframes.

Upon taking over at IBM, Gerstner faced two options regarding mainframes. At the time IBM mainframes were based on bipolar technology. One option was to sell off the remaining bipolar mainframes and then reduce the mainframe business to a lesser priority. The second option was to switch over to CMOS (complementary metal oxide semiconductor) technology and press ahead with the mainframe business.

"It was not an easy decision," an IBM official recalled. "We could let the mainframe die and invest in other server platforms or we could save the mainframe by investing in CMOS." CMOS technology was cheaper than its bipolar counterpart by a factor of ten. It was also the same technology that IBM used in all of its midrange and UNIX-based servers, so there would be economies of scale. But opting for CMOS technology meant taking a short-term hit because it would take five years for the technology levels of CMOS to reach the performance level of bipolar technology.

Gerstner was told by a number of people that mainframes were not dead, that they were not the dinosaurs that others thought they were. Gerstner had been a mainframe customer for years and had an appreciation of what the big machines could do. He decided to keep IBM in the mainframe business, betting that the enormous interest in the Internet and internal networks (intranets) would translate into a demand for the kind of "big iron" only IBM could make and service. By replacing bipolar technology with CMOS, IBM would be able to get a significant increase in the 70 to 80 percent gross profit margins it already gained from its traditional mainframes. The choice seemed clear. In July 1993, Gerstner cut loose the bipolar technology, writing off the investment in that technology.

In April 1994—right around the thirtieth anniversary of the System 360 mainframe that assured IBM's dominance of the computer market—IBM rolled out its first two CMOS-based mainframes. Built around a new microchip that used the same low-cost technology as the mass production PowerPC chips but capable of running the software of existing IBM mainframes, the new computers cost 25 percent less than conventional IBM mainframes.

Mainframe Rex

Addressing a thousand customers at the New York Hilton one morning early in July 1994, Gerstner declared reports of the mainframe's demise premature. "IBM and you all deserve a shot in the head for allowing this mythology that mainframes are dead," he said with a note of humor in his voice and continuing more seriously, "You take my mainframe away and my business is dead." Veteran mainframe customers loved the speech. Later, Gerstner was given a T-shirt emblazoned with a Tyrannosaurus rex and the words "Mainframe Rex." He beamed, raised the shirt, and shouted: "Dinosaurs are back."

But Gerstner knew that he had a long way to go. Mainframe revenues had been on the decline since 1991. In order to keep total mainframe revenues up, IBM raised its prices for related software. As it turned out, this was a shortsighted decision that angered IBM customers. Chief information officers retaliated by deciding to work less with mainframes and more with personal computers, so demand fell and sales of mainframes dropped—from a $12.6 billion industry in 1990 to a $10.9 billion one in 1991. It rose to $12.3 billion in 1992, but then dropped precipitously to $9.5 billion in 1993. Revenues for the entire mainframe industry would continue to drop: down to $7.7 billion in 1994, $7.2 billion in 1995, $7.4 billion in 1996, $6.6 billion in 1997, and $7.3 billion for 1998. For IBM, the two-year period from 1992 to 1994 were the killer years. That's when the industry experienced its worst downturn ever, dropping a whopping 50 percent from $12.3 billion to $7.7 billion.

The cost of the machines relative to their power dropped precipitously: from $109,000 per MIPS (millions of instructions per second) in 1990 to $5,900 per MIPS in 1998. Such a cost reduction would have been impossible with bipolar technology.

IBM continued to manufacture and sell bipolar technology during Gerstner's first few years, but by 1996 sales of CMOS-based mainframes topped sales of bipolar machines for the first time.

I Won't Give Up on Mainframes

At the end of 1996, most growth in computers was coming from small firms using networks with inexpensive computers selling for thousands of dollars, not millions. Dell led in market share, not IBM. Nevertheless, Gerstner refused to give in to the pundits or give up on mainframes. He recalled how hard it had been to come to the support of mainframes when he joined IBM.

> When I arrived at IBM, it was politically incorrect in this industry
> to say anything nice about mainframes. But customers never said
> mainframes were dead. They said they had to be changed. And
> we've done that in three very fundamental dimensions. First, by
> successfully migrating to the parallel CMOS microprocessors, our
> large systems now have the same price performance curve as
> UNIX or Intel-based servers. Secondly we've opened up the archi-
> tecture at the high end to support UNIX application development
> and the Internet protocols. And thirdly, we've taken aggressive
> pricing actions on [System] 390 hardware and software.

In June 1994 IBM brought a new generation of mainframes to market, and Gerstner registered fresh optimism about mainframes. Known
internally as G4—for fourth generation—the machine cost less
because it used the kind of chip and disk-drive technology found in
personal computers. IBM was trying to learn other lessons from the PC
industry—accelerating product cycles and using industry-standard
software. The introduction of the G4 helped the company remove
some of the psychological baggage it had been carrying for the past four
years around mainframes. Suddenly, mainframes were in again. It was
even OK to use the word "mainframe," as Linda Sanford, general manager of the System 390 division, noted: "People are talking about mainframes again, and everyone kind of wants to be like mainframes,"
Sanford said. "It's a good word again, a good term again, even though we
call ourselves enterprise servers." The new G4 could perform about 20
to 33 percent more work than the previous generation.

For IBM, mainframes were still its top profit center. Analysts
guessed that IBM's share of the $7 billion mainframe business came to
70 to 86 percent of the total, which meant that IBM sold $5 billion in
mainframes in 1997. It was estimated that IBM would sell another
$5 billion in mainframes in 1998.

We're Kicking Ass

Not only was IBM tackling the mainframe business head-on; it also set
its sights on capturing a greater share of the personal computer market.
As recently as 1994, it had lost $1 billion in that business. Even after
Gerstner took over, the personal computer business was an embarrass-

ment. Bob Stephenson, senior vice president in charge of PCs, acknowledged those early failures: "We had a reputation of being a laggard with products and a wholly unreliable supplier to both dealers and end customers."

But after Sam Palmisano took over as general manager of the PC division in April 1996, there was fresh optimism. Seven months later Palmisano boasted: "We have a reliable supply of hot products, excellent relationships with retailers and corporate resellers, and competitive prices. We're kicking ass." The reason was simple. Lou Gerstner had convinced senior executives that IBM had to produce products that customers wanted to buy, and that's exactly what was happening. The new 4-pound ThinkPad 560 was considered the best combination of light weight and functionality yet produced; they sold so well that IBM couldn't keep them in stock. The latest IBM consumer PC, the Aptiva-S, was perhaps the most innovative yet; it separated the floppy and CD-ROM drives from the box that held the computer's brain, enabling the customer to store the bulky box away from the desk. In addition, IBM was getting the products to market fast by simplifying the machines, making them easier and faster to produce.

The customers had spoken—and Gerstner made sure IBM was listening.

Our traditional businesses represent multibillion dollars of revenue and maintain healthy margins. They're good generators of cash, but growth is a challenge. These include the System 390 line of large servers and the software, storage, and network subsystems that are attached to these large computers. When I arrived at IBM, a lot of people were saying these businesses were liabilities, dead wood. I got a lot of advice that basically went: "Get rid of 'em, Lou, or at a minimum, milk 'em."

IBM, he explained, had a very different view, based on what its customers said. Customers said, quite loudly, that there were problems with this set of offerings. Large problems, starting with price and lack of interoperability with other companies' products. They also said they needed these systems; they counted on them and needed them to run their businesses. And they needed IBM to fix the problems, not to abandon the field.

> So we went to work. Today, Systems 390 and the products asso-
> ciated with it is a very strong business. . . . Customers remain
> committed to the 390, and they are migrating to newer genera-
> tions at a steady pace.
>
> A few years ago our storage business was on the rocks. We'd
> done everything but formally spin it off. What a tragedy that
> would have been. IBM created the storage business. We've
> invented every significant piece of storage technology in use
> today and continue to lead in new patents. Today, the turnaround
> in that business is truly startling. We are making significant
> billion-dollar investments in storage because our storage team
> has proven they can win—they can generate leadership, revenue
> growth and good returns.

Yet, there were dissenting voices within the industry who simply
believed that Gerstner was putting too much effort into rebuilding
the mainframe business. One such voice was that of Jon Oltsik, an
analyst at Forrester Research. "The problem is, Gerstner is not a tech-
nologist, so he depends on people to give him advice who don't operate with the same set of rules that he does. He's taking technical
advice from career IBM-ers who are notoriously bigoted about what's
going on in the market. But they are operating with a mindset of 1980,
not 2000. For instance, it's a mistake for IBM to try to reinvigorate the
mainframe and the AS 400 market by claiming that they are Internet
servers. They will play a role in the Internet, but it will be the same
role they always played as the back-end system of recordkeeping, etc.
So there's not much growth potential there. IBM has really cemented
the mainframe as a legacy system in the minds of large companies,
but that's not where the new activity is going. Every time IBM says
the Internet is reinventing the mainframe, customers say they don't
get it."

Banking on E-Commerce

In trying to stay ahead of the competition, in the mid-1990s IBM bet
that E-commerce would become a major factor in the near future.
There certainly seemed to be heavy demand for computer networking

and the Internet. Hence, managing and integrating complex systems—something IBM excelled in—had fresh appeal.

Toward the end of 1997, Gerstner took his dream of E-commerce to the marketplace. In a $200 million-plus marketing and ad campaign, he debuted his new products in an eight-page advertising insert that appeared in twelve large newspapers nationwide. In the past, Gerstner had promoted E-commerce to CEOs and in speeches to industry meetings. Now, he was taking his campaign to the rest of the world. The ads envisioned a world in which a company was wired to customers, employees, vendors, and suppliers—whether by intranets, extranets, or over the Web. The ads suggested that IBM was best equipped to deliver those companies into this wired E-commerce world, using IBM's hardware, software, and expertise.

It should be noted that the fully wired world Gerstner envisioned remained a far-off dream, although electronic business was growing exponentially in the United States. Internet trade was expected to skyrocket to an estimated $105 billion by the year 2000. IBM hoped to be the company that would dominate E-commerce, but for that to happen Gerstner felt that customers would have to change their buying behavior. To help customers through this transition, Gerstner has tried to bring vendors into the decision-making processes—a major cultural change.

> **It requires a whole change in the way people think. I've talked to a number of large manufacturers who have . . . brought their vendors right into the basic engineering, production, and inventory data of their company. The vendors have access now just like insiders. It's a huge cultural issue. Are you willing to open the boundaries of your enterprise and bring in your extended team in a truly collaborative way?**

IBM, Gerstner promised, would help businesses adapt to the changes required by the advent of E-business.

> **E-business moves the agenda of the IT industry back into the CEO's office. The new mantra is growth—globalization, cycle times, and competitiveness. What we keep saying to our customers is that E-business is not a technological change. It's a fun-**

**damental change in the way business will be done in their indus-
tries, aided, abetted, supported and enabled by technology. It's
an end-to-end reshaping of their companies to take advantage of
an electronic marketplace.**

IBM's goal was to get as many people as possible to buy and sell on
the Internet. Fundamental to IBM's strategy was delivering three cross-
industry solutions: electronic commerce payment systems; supply-
chain services and software; and customer-relationship solutions,
which included data mining and speech recognition and call-center
technologies.

**When the time comes where the E-business industry moves from
a browser opportunity to a commerce opportunity, it's coming
our way.**

Choosing products that customers want to buy—it would seem, on
the surface, to be such a fundamental business precept that one need
not spend much time on the subject. Yet, for IBM, the precept was crucial. Lou Gerstner had sensed when he joined IBM in 1993 that the
company was not tuned enough to the wishes and demands of the marketplace. He had vowed to change that. But which products should IBM
emphasize, and which should it not? Gerstner made one of his most
important decisions early on, arguing that IBM should keep mainframes as a core business. Keeping IBM intact and retaining the emphasis on mainframes set the tone for the Gerstner turnaround of the
mid-1990s.

Anchoring a Company's Future in Growth

———◆———

"We act in a way that is consistent with the marketplace: fast, entrepreneurial, with a sense of urgency and minimal bureaucracy."

———◆———

Chapter 21

We Need Teamwork, But It Must Allow for Entrepreneurial Spirit

"Entrepreneurial companies ... innovate and take prudent risks. They encourage and protect their risk-takers, mavericks and china breakers."

*L*OU GERSTNER WAS on the prowl for growth. The turnaround was over, though no one quite knew when it had ended. What everyone inside and outside the company did know was that the second and final test for Gerstner was approaching: making IBM grow. Many doubted that this was possible.

One way to spur growth in an organization of IBM's girth was, in Lou Gerstner's view, to reduce bureaucracy and maximize entrepreneurial spirit. He pinned his hopes for growth on creating an entrepreneurial organization that would emphasize productivity. Long before he took over at IBM, he commented on how wedded he was to the concept of entrepreneurship.

Entrepreneurship is not something I set out to do at American Express. I don't think I ever said, "Well, I am going to become a

corporate entrepreneur." But it may be that I started out with a management style and philosophy that one could subsequently look at and call entrepreneurial. Some of it goes back to my first 12 years of full-time work at McKinsey. It was a small company with almost no hierarchy, which placed an overriding premium on problem-solving and on people—whatever their level—with good ideas.

Less Red Tape

After arriving at IBM, Gerstner stressed the same theme.

We must move with less bureaucracy. We must be entrepreneurial. We must have a constant preoccupation with productivity. . . . We can't have [the] sort of red tape at IBM as we do now in abundance. We need to drive decision making in the company as close to the customer as we can get it without all sorts of second-guessing and checking and obstacle building from the sidelines.

He knew that it was easier to talk about the need for entrepreneurship than to put the idea into action, because it required completely overhauling the way IBM staff thought and behaved. To help in the effort, however, he defined an entrepreneurial company:

Entrepreneurial companies are oriented toward growth—on all fronts. They exploit their growth businesses; they find new growth opportunities; and they find new ways to grow their older or stagnant businesses. They innovate and take prudent risks. They encourage and protect their risk-takers, mavericks and china breakers. Finally, they have motivation and compensation systems build around pay for performance.

Gerstner believed that to be truly entrepreneurial one had to believe that a company could grow.

The perception of capacity for growth in the marketplace has a profound effect on your ability to operate entrepreneurially . . . being an entrepreneur is a skill; you don't just say I want to be an entrepreneur. It is like saying I would like to shoot golf in the low 70s. That is a nice objective, but you have to have some natural and some acquired capabilities . . . the conditions we need to permit the real entrepreneurs to perform are: 1) a growth mentality; 2) rewarding performance right down through the organization; and 3) not "shooting" people who come up with ideas that are unusual and have some risks associated with them.

Make Entrepreneurship Happen Every Day

Gerstner understood that entrepreneurs did not just happen—they needed to be nurtured. And so he noted in 1985 . . .

If I left American Express tomorrow, the kind of discipline that we have built into the organization would definitely carry forward for a number of years. But the entrepreneurial side of it could falter because of its inevitable dependence on relationships. The entrepreneur constantly needs to be regenerated, nurtured. By definition, entrepreneurship does not come out of structure; it is not systematic. It is heuristic, it happens. You have to make it happen every day. It could die, because the relationships and messages stop with me. Now the next person coming in might be similarly inclined, so they would start it up again, but they would have to reaffirm relationships or create new ones. And the organization would clearly test for some time whether that person really meant it.

I am the locus of a lot, if not most, of it in supporting or nurturing entrepreneurial behavior and seeing that it happens. I am not the entrepreneur in the classic and creative. . . . I do not want to take credit for our entrepreneurial ideas, only for the entrepreneurial environment which helps produce and develop them.

He believed that Newton's First Law of Motion applied to everything people do. Things have momentum. You have to exert force against momentum or you can't change direction.

I think that the basic force within any organization of our size is toward the bureaucratic, safe approach. In large organizations, whether they are the government or the military, nonprofit organizations or profit-making companies, there is an inevitable process that leads toward rigidity, safe bets, non-risk-taking. Therefore the process of being a corporate entrepreneur is a constant task of changing the direction of something moving in a different direction from yours. It is important to have a sense of drive, zeal, and mission.

You've got to be out there creating an atmosphere of "can do." A great deal of my time is spent communicating this value—communicating it all the time, to all levels of management.

Entrepreneurs Don't Come in Packages

Gerstner wanted to be sure that IBM continued to foster entrepreneurial spirit, regardless of how large the company grew. In his opinion, corporate entrepreneurship required the presence and support of unconventional people. It was not easy to figure out where to find such people systematically.

I think it is important to recognize that entrepreneurs or entrepreneurial behavior don't always come in packages of creative brilliance. I am really talking about forms of nonstandard, creative behavior. I think you have to tolerate a lot of that in an organization. I have worked for some big companies where I was amazed at their lack of tolerance for aberrant behavior. You have to build a system that sends the message to the members of the organization that if you perform in an extraordinary fashion, you are allowed to be different. You don't have to abide by all the rules. There are certain rules that everybody has to abide by, but there are others that you don't have to abide by if you are an extraordinary performer in one dimension.

Why Are You Questioning My Subordinates?

He is perfectly prepared to shatter some of the traditional rules himself—such as scuttling the chain of command—as he makes clear in this story:

I remember going to early meetings at American Express where there were three or four levels of management present. Perhaps foolishly, I started behaving as I had at McKinsey. Somebody would ask a question or say something, and I would start probing around the table. Sometimes I would go to the third-level person and talk with him or her. Naively, I showed a disregard for the structural, inherent rigidity of the system. It seems that I shocked people some, and I had to back off a little bit. People would come to me and say, "Why did you do that? Why are you questioning my subordinates?" I started out with a distrust of formal bureaucracy and a positive attitude of "Let's have relatively informal problem-solving." But I wasn't sitting around consciously thinking about a management style. That was just the way I developed, so I was practicing the only behavior I knew.

He was the enemy of bureaucracy, for bureaucracy stymied entrepreneurship.

Even as he was deciding not to split IBM up, Gerstner knew how troublesome large organizations could be. He had noted this as early as 1985.

The biggest threat to entrepreneurship comes as the company grows to a size where my ability to intercede personally, both longitudinally and latitudinally, is limited. Four years ago I could reach down pretty close to the new recruits coming in. My message would be getting to their boss's boss if not their boss. Today, the levels between me and that first level are more numerous and more difficult to pass through. The new issue that I am now struggling with is: How do I create a team of corporate entrepreneurs? I do not want a team of individuals. How do I do that? Team work is one solution. My other concern is: How do I rethink the way I use my time? But the fundamental problem I face all the time is our size. Our growth and complexity are making it increasingly difficult for me to do something highly personalized. Some forces have been built into our system and structure which promote entrepreneurial behavior, but for the most part this was done by me personally.

Act As If You're Spending Your Own Money

To build teamwork and an entrepreneurial spirit, he presented his set of eight principles soon after taking office. His hope was to lessen the bureaucratic burden by giving IBM employees a set of guiding principles, rather than some unwieldy rule book to follow. With fewer rules, the layers of bureaucracy would be lifted and employees would be free to embark on entrepreneurial pursuits. That was Lou Gerstner's theory.

But did Gerstner expect his staff to tackle all eight principles at once? He appeared to say yes, suggesting that all eight were important for building a new IBM. The principles began, he noted, with the element that would most determine IBM's success: the marketplace—serving customers' needs. The principles also indicated that customer needs would be served best through technological leadership, through quality, and through a preoccupation with the measurement of customer satisfaction and a scoreboard of shareholder values. What precisely were IBM employees expected to do to live up to these principles?

> **We act in a way that is consistent with the marketplace orientation: fast, entrepreneurial, with a sense of urgency and minimal bureaucracy. To do that, we've got to have a strategic vision that aims us in the right direction. And we've got to have outstanding people working together, sensitive not only to our customers and our marketplace, but to each other and to our communities.**

Gerstner said it was not necessary to have rule books to tell people what to do.

> **We only have to tell them: "Manage whatever you do against this set of principles, and we will trust your judgment."**

Gerstner did his bit to cut bureaucracy when he combined all server activities under a single executive and formed two units that were developing common operating system technology and hardware components for IBM computers. He also consolidated most of IBM's software divisions into a single group. That left the company with three main product groups responsible for servers, desktop systems, and software. And he eliminated the separate American and overseas sales operations, hoping to reorient the computer giant toward a more global business approach.

Reducing bureaucracy was a prelude to getting the company moving again, getting it more productive.

Productivity simply means returning greater value to the business and to the bottom line for each dollar spent. It means every single employee doing everything he or she can to control costs and to find better and smarter ways to do things. It means treating every expenditure you authorize in this company as if you were spending your own money—because in a sense, you are!

Quality and productivity were not mutually exclusive, he insisted; they were complementary values.

We want—and we will demand—unmatched quality and unmatched productivity. Those who talk about business in terms of trade-offs between productivity and quality either don't know the right way to run a business or don't have the energy or ability to conceptualize a business in a more sophisticated manner. Our best IBM managers will understand and manage productivity without becoming bogged down in meat-ax expense reduction, or mindless ratio management.

A company that fought bureaucracy, that became productive, would benefit from teamwork—and out of that teamwork would come an entrepreneurial spirit.

Back in 1985, Gerstner talked about the concept of teamwork:

We all succeed together. If we do something right, there is plenty of credit to go around for everybody. A team of people working together to me is so powerful that it will always beat hands-down a group of uncoordinated individuals any day, even if the individuals are a bunch of all-stars.

Gerstner made clear that while he admired IBM employees for their sense of commitment, priorities, and urgency, "too often our personal instincts and commitments are stymied by bureaucracy and turf-ism." What was needed, he said, was to "rip down the barriers." Only then could IBM personnel pull together as a team. He said he was not interested in teamwork for its own sake.

> **This is not a soft objective for me. It's a very real, cutting-edge opportunity for IBM to overwhelm our competitors. We need to aggregate our collective strength through teamwork.**

He did not want the kind of teamwork that produced many meetings and that fed the bureaucracy and slowed everything down.

> **I want teamwork that is focused on performance, not activity, and that allows plenty of room for individual initiative and recognition.**

Lou Gerstner talked about teamwork at length because he felt it was crucial to overcome IBM's past—a past of turfs and fiefdoms, a past when IBM staff would simply ignore a request from the boss if they didn't like it, a past when there was little incentive to work as a team. Getting employees to work together, Gerstner believed, was the first step to reorienting the company toward growth. One former IBM manager had a more cynical take on Gerstner's version of teamwork, however: "Teamwork? Sure, but it was teamwork with intimidation. Let's not forget that."

———

Chapter 22

Shift Turnaround Tactics: End the Cost-Cutting, Search for Revenue

"The wind will turn. The wind that has been in your face will be at your back."

AT THE START of his tenure as IBM chairman and CEO Lou Gerstner came under a barrage of fire for not having a sound growth plan. By telling everyone that IBM didn't require grand visions, he seemed to be confirming their worst fears. Even as he turned IBM's losses into profits, many worried that he could do no more.

Yet growth was considered a vital ingredient in IBM's long-range success. For IBM simply to plod along with flat sales after so many decades of incredible growth would not do. Wall Street made this point time and time again. So the pressure on Lou Gerstner to foster meaningful growth at IBM was enormous.

He knew that before he could even think of making IBM grow, he would need time, perhaps as much as five years, to get the company back on its feet. Expectations, however, were very high. It was as if IBM were a boat battered by a storm at sea, on the verge of tipping over. The obvious strategy was not to turn the motor on, or even to get back to shore, and certainly not to build a bigger, better boat. The first priority was to figure out how to get the boat tipped back over onto its right side. Similarly, the first thing a turnaround artist had to worry about was the financial health of the company; he needed to be sure that there was enough cash to run the company comfortably. When Gerstner arrived, IBM's balance sheet was certainly in danger of "tipping over." The company had lost $16 billion from 1991 to 1993, with precious few signs of improvement. For his first two years at IBM, Gerstner was desperately trying to keep the "boat" from capsizing. Not until he had expenses in line and did some restructuring of the company could he even think of turning on IBM's growth engines.

Proving That You Are Creative

Gerstner understood that IBM's best hope for meaningful growth lay in its nonmainframe businesses. Though he had supported a major investment in the mainframe business, he believed that it would take fully five years before the investment would begin to pay off. He also believed that revenues for the total mainframe industry, which had been slipping sharply since 1992, would continue to plummet for the next few years. Wall Street, however, was in no mood to grant him a five-year honeymoon. Analysts demanded action and wasted no time communicating that to Gerstner and the rest of the world. Reflecting the same impatience, the media also harped on the need for IBM to grow. As *Time* magazine noted, "Gerstner has shown that he can be destructive; now he has to prove that he can also be creative."

One of the first signs that Gerstner had begun his growth quest in earnest came in January 1995 when he dropped a timebomb onto the senior levels of IBM management, essentially letting everyone know that the team he had chosen so far to run the company was simply not good enough. Their main failing: they had not developed the company enough. One big surprise: longtime IBM executive Robert M. Stephenson was given the high-profile task of running the software business. In all, nearly a dozen other executives switched jobs. Gerstner took other steps to promote growth, including unifying the company's worldwide sales and distribution network. Another key turning point in signaling the commencement of the growth phase was the departure on September 1, 1995, of IBM chief financial officer Jerry York. While Gerstner offered no overt signs that he wanted York to leave IBM, the CFO certainly felt that he had accomplished what he had set out to do in the cost-cutting department and he would be better off in other pastures. Meanwhile, Gerstner made clear he wanted to shift to a strategy that searched for revenue. "Lou's charter is, at this point in time, certainly the opposite [of mine]," York said.

Replacing York with Richard Thoman, who had run the personal computer business, seemed a good move if only because Thoman would be the first IBM CFO with solid international experience. This was a key segment of IBM's business, since 62 percent of its revenues came from overseas. Gerstner knew that the international arena could play a leading role in his growth strategy.

Gerstner had hoped IBM would be less dependent on the profits linked to "big iron" and would make up the earnings by increasing sales in potentially high-growth areas such as personal computers and software. But the prospects for software remained problematic. With $11 billion in revenues, IBM ranked as the world's largest software maker, but most of that revenue was linked to mainframes. While that business carried hefty profit margins in the 60 to 70 percent range, growth prospects were bleak. Unfortunately, the future for personal computers looked no better. The year 1994 had not been a particularly good one for IBM PCs. It had begun with a bloated $700 million inventory of obsolete models, which took six months to unload. When time came to launch the new Aptiva home PCs that fall, the company erred by not producing enough to meet the demand. Aptivas sold out before the fourth-quarter home PC boom started. Analysts estimated that IBM's PC hardware and software operations would lose as much as $2 billion in 1994.

But Gerstner wanted to shift IBM's emphasis away from mainframes and minicomputers to such potentially high-growth businesses as networking, software, and services. Much needed to be done. He was especially eager to turn the software business around; it contributed $11 billion a year in revenue and an estimated $2.5 billion in IBM profits, but those figures were declining in 1995. The IBM chief certainly had his work cut out for him.

Although it had invested billions of dollars in development over the past few years, IBM still lagged behind Microsoft in the high-growth markets for PC software. Critics suggested that IBM did not know how to market software and didn't understand the mass market nature of PC software.

IBM was still trying to score big on OS/2, its PC operating system. It had invested an estimated several billion dollars in its OS/2 operating program and in Warp, a new version for Power PC systems. Although IBM shipped 800,000 copies of Warp, analysts estimated that the heavily discounted program had generated a paltry $25 million in revenues.

If IBM had a window of opportunity in the software business, it was between 1992 and 1995, the three-year period prior to Microsoft's launching of the Windows 95 operating program. Sales in the software business rose a healthy 12 percent in 1995 after four years of stagnation, but that growth rate was not expected to last.

The Wind Will Turn

One of IBM's most promising businesses was its hard-disk unit. In 1995 and 1996, Jim Vanderslice sent the hard-disk business into orbit, proving that IBM, despite its size and complexity, could compete against smaller companies in a fast-paced business.

In late 1995, as IBM appeared to have turned a corner in its growth campaign, Gerstner delivered a pep talk to employees:

> **I told them that soon, something very important will happen: The wind will turn. The wind that has been in your face will be at your back. I said it will be a feeling of exhilaration that you won't understand unless you work through it. I said I didn't know when the change is coming, but when it does, you will feel it. You can feel it now.**

By early 1996 IBM appeared to have answered every naysayer, pundit, and critic. It had topped $70 billion in revenue for the first time the year before, achieving double-digit growth—its best in a decade. Earnings had doubled. The workforce had grown for the first time in years, and its stock price had soared 24 percent. In January, IBM reported fourth-quarter earnings in 1995 up 39 percent, to $1.7 billion, on a revenue increase of 10 percent, to $21.9 billion. From mid-January to March, its stock rose 42 percent to $119 a share. *Business Week* gave its stamp of approval to IBM's turnaround, leading off its late 1996 cover story on IBM by noting: "It's getting hard to remember the days when IBM was regarded as a national disaster." For all of 1995, earnings jumped 38 percent, to $4.2 billion, while revenues zipped up 12 percent, to $71.9 billion. It was undeniably IBM's best showing in a decade.

Investors seemed increasingly confident that Gerstner had weaned IBM away from a reliance on slow-growth products. IBM said that 57 percent of its revenue in 1995 came from such high-growth segments as personal computers, software, and services and that those businesses expanded at a 19 percent rate. Meanwhile, revenues for the more traditional slow-growth technology products were dropping by 3 percentage points a year. By far, its best performer was its $12.7 billion services business, which was expanding at a 30 percent clip annually.

As 1996 unfolded, IBM looked better and better. For that year, IBM reported record revenues of $75.9 billion, an increase of 9 percent after adjusting for currency effects—the company's highest rate of growth since 1985. The adjustment, known at IBM as "constant currency," is IBM's calculation of the various currency values weighed against the dollar in the 160 countries in which the company does business. With IBM doing 55 percent of its business abroad, Gerstner feels that the only accurate way to judge how Big Blue is doing is to take into account these currency fluctuations. While the adjustment for currency effects unquestionably makes IBM's revenue increases appear larger, IBM's growth still hasn't compared favorably with that of its adversaries. Some analysts believe that it is not helpful to use constant currency when examining a company's growth. In short, Gerstner has won few friends on Wall Street by insisting on a measurement that gives the impression that IBM is growing in greater percentage terms than it really is.

In April 1996, Gerstner reiterated that he was staking IBM's growth on network computers. IBM was the first major company to introduce a network computer—the IBM Network Station, a new kind of desktop device that provided access to networked applications and processing power while dramatically reducing the cost of desktop computing. Determined to keep IBM whole, Gerstner was confident that the network strategy, with its renewed emphasis on large computers, represented IBM's best bet for growth. After all, System 390 mainframe hardware and software accounted for 15 percent of IBM's sales and an even bigger share of profits.

Of equal importance, these large-systems sales drove a good deal of IBM's systems integration and consulting business—one of its faster growing segments. Gerstner hoped that a modest increase in mainframe revenue would lead to greater growth in other parts of the company.

By staking so much on his network strategy, Gerstner was taking a sizable gamble on big iron.

The PC Age Is Over

While IBM's $10-billion-a-year PC business brought in almost twice as much revenue as mainframes, Gerstner believed desktop machines were no longer the industry's driving force:

> **The predominant focus of applications for the last 20 years has been the individual desktop computer. That age is over. Corporate customers have discovered that [PCs] have produced very little productivity from the point of view of the enterprise. Now, I would suspect that all of us who use these devices feel like we've benefited a lot from them. But the data is overwhelming that the standalone PC is an enormously expensive proposition for an enterprise.**

IBM breezed through the summer of 1996 as profits reached unexpected highs; new IBM computers such as the ThinkPad 560 were moving off the shelves for the first time in decades; and the company's services business had booked an impressive $11 billion in business in the first nine months of the year. Even though Wall Street seemed uncertain whether Gerstner had really turned the growth corner, they grudgingly admitted that what he had done was remarkable. Since taking over in 1993, Gerstner's strategies had paid off handsomely. IBM stock had tripled, soaring nearly 84 percent in 1996 alone versus 22 percent for the Standard & Poor's 500 (Gerstner wasn't doing badly either: his stock options were now worth $90 million).

By the end of 1996, it was clear that IBM's hardware and software units were doing better than they had in years. Hardware had grown 2 percent. Software revenue grew 3.4 percent, driven largely by strong sales of Lotus and Tivoli products. The installed base of Lotus Notes doubled for the second year to 9 million. The company's income statement looked strong. Its greatest growth engine turned out to be the service division (24.5 percent growth). Most important, it no longer was burdened with the image of being the heavy-footed giant forced by its misjudgments to give way to smaller companies like Microsoft and Intel. Even these high-flyers had new respect for Big Blue.

IBM Is Back

The media picked up on the theme that "IBM is back." The signs were much in evidence. Its new line of smaller and cheaper mainframes was sold out by the middle of 1997; its services division, continuing to assemble and operate large computer systems, was expected to grow at a spectacular 20 percent in 1997 and in 1998.

IBM appeared to hold the lead in selling network computers, and it was beginning to exploit its acquisition of Lotus Development by enlarging the distribution of the Lotus Notes software program significantly. It was ahead in the competition to develop electronic commerce, having organized several key industry alliances that would facilitate business on the Internet. It was even making money in its PC division, which posted a 25 percent revenue increase during the second and third quarters of 1996. The company wasn't able to keep up with demand for its new home PC. The biggest growth segment continued to be services, which had gone from $12.7 billion in 1995 to nearly $16 billion in 1996, surpassing its main rival Electronic Data Systems. The stock was up to nearly $153 a share, with analysts predicting that it could rise much higher. Perhaps the most significant figure was market capitalization: In 1996, IBM's market cap grew $27 billion—to $77 billion—more than $50 billion since the July 1993 restructuring. Lou Gerstner was elated about the company's overall picture:

If you go back and read what people were saying when I took over in April of 1993 . . . some of them were predicting the demise of the company probably before the end of the decade. It certainly wasn't my expectation that we would have come this far, but I'm very pleased.

And the once skeptical media was becoming effusive. Here is *Business Week* in its December 9, 1996, story on IBM: "Why, it's as if Wall Street has found a new growth stock to love. And in a way, it has. The 7%-to-10% revenue increase that analysts expect from IBM this year may not be much by the standards of, say, Microsoft Corp. or Intel Corp. But the increase of $5 billion is huge—equivalent to adding another Dell Computer in revenues." Gerstner did not breathe a sigh of relief. He knew that he had won some important battles on the growth front, but pressure was on him from a host of quarters to rev up IBM's engines even more. Gerstner would have to show that 1996 was not merely a fluke.

Chapter 23

———

If You Don't Lead, You're Not There

"The most important development in the global economy at the dawn of the 21st century is going on right now, and IBM is at the epicenter."

GERSTNER KNEW THAT his performance would be scrutinized in 1997. IBM had grown the year before. That was not bad. But could Lou Gerstner keep up the pace? Could he really bring in revenue increases in the high single-digits on a continuing basis? That was his goal and the goal that would earn high marks on Wall Street. In an annual worldwide speech to employees in January, he said rather dramatically:

> There is no place to hide in 1997. This is the year of reckoning for all of us—1994 was the year we proved we could survive; 1995 was the year we stabilized; 1996 was the year we showed we could grow; 1997 is going to be the year we have to show we can lead. We have no more excuses. We can't say we're still getting our act together.

On April 14, 1997, Gerstner gave an interview to *Fortune* magazine in which he argued that IBM could grow in 1997, and indeed *was* growing. When asked, "What about top-line growth?" he replied:

> When I got here, one of the hypotheses on Wall Street was that our new businesses would not grow rapidly; our slow-growing businesses, like mainframes and midrange systems and the software that rides on them, would fall off too quickly; and our high-growing businesses, like services, PCs, distributed software, original equipment manufacturing, and licensing, wouldn't grow fast enough. We have shown that's not going to happen. We showed that the mainframe is not dead, and now we've got all kinds of people admitting that.

Challenging the Low-Growth Businesses

Did Gerstner have a target for his growth plans? Indeed, he did. He planned to challenge the low-growth businesses to re-create themselves as high-growth businesses and not permit the high-growth crowd in the company to look down on them. A company with $76 billion in sales, he suggested, is never going to increase its revenue at the rate of the comets in this industry. At the same time, IBM is not going to run into product obsolescence and competitive threats as suddenly as they do.

> Every single unit has a clear set of goals. It has to grow as fast as its relevant competition. We're not going to be a leader in every segment, and when we're not a leader, we're withdrawing from those markets or not funding them the way we used to. This is an industry where, if you don't lead, you're not there. People at IBM need to feel like they're leading again. [In 1996] we had to produce the kinds of results that people would say, "IBM really is back." And IBM really is producing the results [so] that we now kind of believe it.
>
> I've also been driving this network-computing strategy. The leaders of the networked-computing world are going to emerge over the next 24 months, and I want to see us step up and do that.

Holding his fourth annual meeting with Wall Street analysts that May in New York, Gerstner suggested that IBM's goal was to increase revenues in the high single digits. But he cautioned that it was not possible for the computer giant to grow as fast as smaller tech firms:

We have enormous opportunities within IBM. Our model is to procure high single-digit revenue growth. We are not going to be like most information technology companies. We are not going to grow 40 to 50 percent a year. That's hard to do. . . .

We are focused on growing shareholder value. We have a model that is not the model of the meteors.

Some of these fast-growing tech firms could be described as "meteors," he suggested, because they eventually burn up.

The analysts were especially eager to hear whether Gerstner thought that IBM's System 390 mainframes, once the company's biggest revenue and profit generator, would show growth again. In reply, he noted that over the last three years IBM had cut prices of mainframes by 80 percent, and this had helped spark stronger demand. As more and more computers were connected to corporate networks, demand would increase. He stopped short of predicting outright growth for the mainframes.

Software and Services Are Our Growth Engines

Software and services were the company's real growth engines. Software, he indicated, had not yet performed as well as IBM's services business because the company retained IBM software that ran on its mainframe systems and hadn't developed software distributed over computer networks. Referring to the sad-sack comedian who always claimed he never got any respect, Gerstner said:

We are the Rodney Dangerfields of the software industry. And to a certain extent, we deserve it. We gave software away on our hardware, we watched software go distributed and we hung onto our host stuff.

He felt confident that a new growth area for IBM would come in distributed and so-called middleware software, which linked its host mainframe software to other diverse computers. In pursuit of this goal, IBM had purchased Tivoli Systems and Lotus Development.

IBM's growth was not spectacular in 1997. It came in at only 3.4 percent. However, it did fare better on the revenue front. For the third straight year IBM reported record revenues—$78.5 billion, an 8 percent increase after adjusting for the effects of currency shifts. Earnings rose to $6.1 billion, up 12.2 percent from $5.4 billion in 1996, excluding a charge related to acquisitions in the first quarter of 1996.

In 1997 IBM's revenues ranked sixth on the *Fortune* 500 list of American corporations (it was sixth in 1996 as well) and seventh in profits. Its market value, which was ranked fourteenth, was over $98 billion. When he appeared before IBM shareholders on April 28, 1998, Gerstner called 1997 "a solid, a very solid year" for IBM. "In terms of technology performance, I think we can call it a great year."

What changed in 1997 for IBM was people's perception of the company. This was not because of huge increases in revenues or profits: the 1997 revenues and profits were both up only 3 percent over 1996, and the 1997 earnings were actually down 4 percent if adjusted for the lower tax rate. Still, the company appeared to be on the move: some product lines showed improvements, and the company seemed more innovative, more efficient. It was establishing a strong presence in the E-commerce businesses. It had just introduced copper as a better conductor that might ultimately replace aluminum in semiconductor design. It had doubled storage capacity to 11 gigabytes per square inch of disk space; only a year before it was 5 gigabytes. And it had created an illusion of prosperity with its stock buyback program. In 1997 alone, IBM spent $7.1 billion on its own stock; this was more than any other investment IBM made in 1997 and more than IBM *earned* that year. Since the start of the buyback program in 1995, the company had spent some $18 billion toward this effort.

The Real Star Is Services

Some divisions, however, were still struggling. Hardware grew only 0.2 percent; software, 1.6 percent. Once again, the real star was services, which grew 21.6 percent. Maintenance was down 8.3 percent, while rentals and financing grew only 0.2 percent. Services revenue increased to $19.3 billion, up 28 percent in constant currency. Gerstner noted that

Seven years ago, with revenues of about $4 billion, we were barely visible in the marketplace. Today, we are the market leader, and IBM Global Services has the highest customer satisfaction rating in the industry.

The outlook for services was indeed a bright one: As it was adding 15,000 people to its payroll in services during 1997, the company was also booking $43 billion in new services business for 1998.

The company's immense software business, $12.8 billion in 1997, was roughly the size of Microsoft's, but revenue had come mostly from areas of little or flat growth. More than $8.5 billion of 1997 software sales came from the 390 and AS 400 no-growth markets (in fact, those markets were shrinking). There *was* growth in IBM's $4 billion non-mainframe software business (showing a 30 percent growth rate). Some $2.5 billion of the other $4.5 billion in software sales came from Tivoli and Lotus. Analysts predicted that unless IBM came up with exciting, innovative products, software sales would continue to be flat.

Global Service revenue continued to be the fastest-growing segment and represented more than 28 percent of total revenue. IBM benefited from the trend of increasingly complex and geographically diverse computing solutions. With more than $5 billion in sales in the first quarter of 1997 and a backlog of more than $44 billion at quarter's end, this division was likely to see sales growth in the mid- to high teens for the next few years.

It seemed unfortunate that IBM couldn't exclude the PC division from its income statement. It faced continuing competitive pricing pressure and low margins. Sales were flat in 1997, with $13.91 billion in sales (compared with $13.92 billion in sales in 1996).

IBM's market valuation—to Gerstner, the ultimate measure of the company's performance—grew by $23 billion in 1997. IBM's stock price surpassed its all-time high and continued to climb, rising 38 percent over the year. Since IBM's major restructuring in 1993, its marketplace worth had increased by more than $73 billion.

The figures for 1997, while not as impressive as 1996, belied some of the major accomplishments of Gerstner's four years. Through April 1997, he had managed to buy back $10.7 billion in stock, helping to push the stock price to $168, close to its all-time high. When Gerstner arrived in 1993, the company's major businesses were losing $2 billion

a year. Those business—including the PC business—were all profitable by the spring of 1997. The microelectronics and OEM businesses had completely turned around and were growing, from $1
billion in revenues in 1993 to $5 billion in 1996. Disk drive sales were
exploding; PC sales were doing well. The network business was still
only mediocre.

Here's how a pair of Lehman Brothers analysts described the Gerstner turnaround of problem businesses:

> In 1993 many of IBM's main business areas were either unprof-
> itable or not competitive. IBM took bold action. Mainframes, which
> were based on expensive to design, build, and maintain processors,
> were replaced with a new line of much more inexpensive CMOS
> chips. Also, cost reductions over the last few years brought the
> price of mainframe computing down 80 percent for hardware and
> maintenance, and 30 percent for software, making this platform
> much more competitive with open server computing.
>
> Focus in the PC area was increased in order to compete with
> the best PC companies in the industry. In 1996 PC operations
> began to improve considerably and this has continued into 1997.
> International Data Corp. estimates that IBM's PC market share
> increased to 8.5 percent in the first quarter of 1997, based on
> worldwide unit sales, from 7.2 percent in the first quarter of 1996
> and unit growth year-over-year was over 37 percent.

Echoing their upbeat view was Laura Conigliaro, managing director
of the Investment Research Department at Goldman, Sachs:

> Gerstner is succeeding in his mission to refocus and leverage
> IBM's many strengths throughout the organization in order to
> once again be perceived as the most trusted, full-line vendor
> delivering a clear strategy around which its customers can build
> long-range IT plans—a title it seems to have ceded to Hewlett-
> Packard in the early 1990s.
>
> After years of suffering through badly declining margins and
> eroding influence, accompanied by massive restructuring
> charges, IBM has bottomed and has emerged as a strengthening

force within the industry and among its customers. An extremely strong services capability, favorable product cycles, a renewed respect for mainframes in the industry, improving margins, a no-nonsense management approach, and solid cash flow are the marks of today's IBM. . . .

Unlike a few years back when it seemed to be merely scratching its head and trying to determine what was wrong with itself, IBM now seems to have a much clearer view of what its goals and functions are.

Some concern was voiced that most of IBM's sales were coming from newer, lower-margin businesses such as PCs and that its revenues were growing slower than other big technology firms. *Vanity Fair* magazine, in ranking Gerstner seventh among its third annual top fifty leaders of the information age, noted: "Even IBM's once stuffy, white-shirt public image is improving: The company may have had trouble tracking the statistics for the Atlanta Olympics [massive computer glitches delayed IBM's vaunted "instant" on-line data] but it redeemed itself with Deep Blue, the computer that stunned the world by defeating chess champion Gary Kasparov last May."

And, despite the trouble Gerstner had given the magazine in the wake of its cover story the previous April, *Fortune* magazine sang Gerstner's praises in December 1997. "Big Lou Saves Big Blue" was the headline. Its first few lines read "When Gerstner took over IBM years ago, there were many who doubted that the brusque ex-McKinsey executive could turn this giant around. But Gerstner has succeeded beyond almost anyone's imagination (except his, probably)." The magazine paid tribute to two major milestones in Gerstner's turnaround which had occurred in 1997: The company's stock price had gone beyond its previous all-time high in the summer of 1987, $175 a share. And Gerstner had signed on as CEO for another five years.

How Much Longer?

Until November 1997, it had not been at all clear that Gerstner would stay at IBM for very long. He certainly didn't sound sure about what he would do, at least for a while. In April 1997 he said . . .

I've been here four years working seven days a week, 24 hours a day. I spent the prior four years working almost the same in the world's largest LBO. There are days when I ask, How much longer do I want to do this?

I've basically completed what I was asked to do when I came—maybe even exceeded some people's expectations. I have no plans to leave. But I go through the same emotions as everyone else. Now and then I think maybe I ought to take a little time off. Maybe spend a little time with my family. Maybe go work on my love of public education in this country. Then there are days when I think this is the best job in the world and there's nowhere else I'd ever want to be. Having completed an assignment, I need to sort out what I'm going to do next. The board has the same freedom. There are no commitments either way.

Five More Years

But on November 21, 1997, IBM announced Gerstner would stay for five more years—until he was 60 years old. In return for staying on longer, he was given a compensation package that included 2 million stock options. In the 1997 Annual Report, he noted that he had two reasons for staying:

First, the job I came here to do isn't complete. We've proved we could survive, when many had written us off for dead. We've proved we could grow, when most believed growth would come only to the small and fleet. And I believe we're proving IBM is relevant to the world of the future, when many saw us as an artifact of the past. Now, our task is to lead.

Second, I could not, frankly, think of anything else that would be nearly as much fun. If you love business—and I do—you want to be where the action is, where the marketplace is most dynamic, where the issues are the most urgent, where team creativity is at its most intense. The most important development in the global economy at the dawn of the 21st century is going on right now, and IBM is at its epicenter. This large, resourceful and vitally important company is coming into its own. Where else would anyone want to be?

As 1997 came to a close, Gerstner could well be pleased that IBM had reached a new plateau. He now had the confidence that came with achieving many of his goals. The company which so many had written off on the eve of his arrival, commanded increasing respect. It was moving toward leadership of the industry, making Gerstner look better and better.

VII

Searching for New Markets, New Opportunities

———◆———

"The opportunity is vast. We are number one in the industry, and we have 9 percent share."

———◆———

Chapter 24

There's Money to Be Made in Charging for Service

"There are a lot of people in IBM who tell me we can't sustain this 20 percent plus growth [in services]. I am not ready to accept that."

FOR DECADES, IBM was known as the premium manufacturer of computers. It was a *manufacturer,* not a provider of services. To be sure, it provided services, but they were an afterthought, something that the company felt it had to offer. But the services IBM offered were considered part of the overall product, and customers were only charged for the product. Few had ever imagined that IBM's service component might become a profit center on its own; no one thought that services in the 1990s would become *the* major profit center of the company. But that is exactly what happened.

It was only in 1990 that the service business got under way and IBM began charging customers for something that it had given away for free for years. Now, those same systems engineers who had set up new mainframes and didn't charge to keep them going were sending out bills for customer services.

At the start, the service business was never consolidated into one cohesive unit. While it grew, it lacked financial controls, and because of some bad contracts, it hardly made a profit. As a result, IBM remained a distant second to EDS, the number one computer service company.

Gaining Momentum

The service business gained real momentum in 1995 when IBM posted $12.7 billion in services revenues. Gerstner deserves credit for nurturing IBM's services business, but he did not start it. The service unit was already in place by the time he arrived as CEO. And after he took over, it was Dennie M. Welsh, the Tennessee-born engineer who ran IBM's contracts for NASA during the Apollo and space shuttle programs, who pushed Gerstner to make the service business a key IBM focus.

Welsh suggested that IBM offer the same kind of management services to firms that it had offered to NASA and other government agencies. He contended that IBM's expertise in running large computer systems for NASA and the government could be used in the corporate sector where EDS was faring very well. McDonnell Douglas, an aerospace firm and IBM's first services customer, liked the idea that it could draw on so many technological resources from IBM. Some worried, though, whether IBM could resolve the potential conflict between supplying the service that was appropriate for the customer and promoting its own products. Others also wondered whether the service division would be able to coordinate the various parts of IBM and offer the kind of integrated solution customers wanted. Accordingly, when Welsh and a few others cobbled the IBM services unit together in 1990, few paid much attention to it.

As the price of computers dropped, IBM's service unit took on even greater importance. The lower prices meant that there were far more computers purchased—and, accordingly, far more for service personnel to do. They needed to program the computers, maintain them, update them, and train employees to use them. Someone called the computers the razors, while the services were the blades that users needed to purchase on a continuing basis.

When Gerstner took over in 1993, listening to Dennie Welsh's arguments, the new IBM CEO agreed to give maximum attention to services in the belief that it would become a key growth engine—although its revenues that year came to only $7.64 billion. The services unit was in perfect synch with Gerstner's belief that IBM's revival depended upon capitalizing on its huge size. He chose not to break up IBM. A whole IBM was able to offer its large customers one-stop shopping for computer products—whether it was mainframes or microchips. And all of those products needed servicing.

Gerstner did not boost the services arm during his first two years at the helm, but eventually the service sector became IBM's main revenue driver, helping IBM to buy time while it decided what to do with the hardware and software segments of the business.

We're Not Monopolists!

Realizing that it had a good thing going for it, in June 1994 IBM asked a federal judge to lift a set of legal constraints that had been imposed on the company in 1956 to limit its monopoly power. The constraints were part of the settlement of a lawsuit that alleged that it was monopolizing the emerging business for data processing services. IBM agreed at that time that its service business would function separately from other segments of IBM and that it would pay the full price for equipment and software it purchased from other segments of IBM. By eliminating the constraints, IBM and its data processing unit could engage in the joint marketing of equipment and services; it could also pass on special equipment discounts to service customers.

The judge ruled in IBM's favor. On July 2, 1996, IBM announced that it had reached an agreement with the Department of Justice that would phase out all remaining restrictions placed on IBM from the 1956 consent decree within five years. Most of the provisions were terminated on that day, including computer services. (A few provisions from the original consent decree, like those that apply to the leasing of mainframe and midrange computers, will expire in 2001 when the decree ends.)

In 1995, Gerstner crowed about IBM's growth in services:

Services grew to become our second largest source of revenue, up 31 percent over 1994 [$9.71 billion]. Today IBM is the world's largest information technology services company, with more than

80,000 people providing consulting, systems integration and solution development services worldwide.

In 1995, the service business grew again—this time to $12.71 billion.

The service business exploited one of IBM's great strengths—its knowledge of product across all elements of modern computing, from the Internet to personal computers. Customers needed IBM to keep all these elements functioning together. By building up the services business, Gerstner reduced IBM's dependence on a single mainframe business. That had always been a daunting problem at IBM. He could have chosen other parts of the business to emphasize—building products for the Internet, for instance, or becoming a minicomputer company—but he chose services. Gerstner's overall success owes a great deal to that decision.

In 1996, Gerstner noted that IBM had become the world's largest computer service company:

Services now are our second largest source of revenue. And yet the opportunity is vast. We are the number one in the industry, and we only have 9 percent share. . . . We have more than 80,000 people in 159 countries providing systems integration, consulting, and solutions development. Last year IBM hired nearly 15,000 people, the majority in our sales and service business. . . . [I want to emphasize] why services are growing so quickly. It's because customers are fed up with piece-parts and raw technology, and they want solutions to their business problems.

Services, with revenues amounting to $15.87 billion as of the end of 1996, were just under 21 percent of IBM's total revenues of $75.94 billion. In the final quarter of 1996, IBM acquired a remarkable $11 billion in computer services business, winning four of the five deals it pursued.

By 1997, when service revenues reached $19.3 billion, the service business was growing at an annualized rate of 33 percent. The reason? IBM was equipped, as few other firms were, to handle all of its customers' computing needs—including their network needs. More and more companies wanted to "outsource" that responsibility—turn their computer operations over to IBM, EDS, or other companies that, for a fee, would run those operations.

In April 1997, Gerstner noted that the services division was . . .

. . . the fastest-growing part of the information technology industry. We are growing faster than the industry. Our challenge here is managing growth while generating good returns. Our services business grew 25 percent last year [1996], the fourth consecutive year it has grown 20 percent or more. Last year we signed long-term contracts with customers worth $27 billion. And another $3 billion signed in the first quarter of this year.

If the client prefers, IBM will buy and operate computers and use software made by other companies. It should come as no surprise that IBM personnel advise people to buy their own products, not their rivals'. IBM Services has become one of IBM's largest customers for hardware. A Goldman, Sachs analyst noted in 1997 that the Global Services Division, of which the Global Network was a part, embodied all that was working right in the new IBM, including Lou Gerstner's focus on customers:

If previously, IBM had been mostly a collection of loosely coupled segments principally aligned around mainframes, it now seems more of a tightly coupled confederation with services and solutions as its hub. . . . In the past, its services business was much less profitable—a misstep that IBM is still paying for as these unprofitable contracts are still winding their way through the income statement. . . . IBM's service business is quickly moving into a leadership position, threatening the long-term dominance of Electronic Data Systems. More so than at any other point in its recent history, IBM's strengths in large corporate computing and relationship building are being worked to the hilt.

As a separate company, IBM Services would have been the largest services company in the world.

In 1997, the company reorganized and streamlined the division from six service areas and 3,700 offerings to three business segments with 100 offerings: Professional Services (72,000 employees), Product Support (40,000 employees), and Network Services (8,000 employees). Services accounted for half of IBM's 240,000 employees. Though it had eliminated 200,000 jobs in the early 1990s, IBM hired 18,000 new employees for its services division in 1998.

A Shrewd Move

The service business has been IBM's only consistent growth engine. It reached $23.4 billion in revenues in 1998, a 21.4 percent growth rate over the previous year. IBM would not like to think of where its growth rate would be without services. As of the end of 1998, IBM had not shown meaningful growth in any of its hardware sectors; and it was only beginning to make some progress in some aspects of its software business.

Financial analysts thought Gerstner was shrewd in playing up the services business. Merrill Lynch's Steve Milunovich noted:

> **The main driver of solutions is services. IBM has tried to change the focus of the company away from hardware. They've moved it to a services company. IBM doesn't stack up well product to product in hardware. So they needed something else. They weren't going to win on product. So they turned to services. They needed to incorporate hardware, software, and services. They've differentiated themselves from EDS—and they've done it globally—not like EDS, which is less global. Today, 55 percent of the operating profit of IBM comes from services and software combined. Software is 35 percent, services 20 percent; the other 45 percent is primarily hardware, with some maintenance.**

Here's an example of how the IBM services division operates: In September 1996, Gerstner invites a number of CEOs to a day-long strategy seminar. The CEOs begin talking with Gerstner about research collaboration among companies in various fields. Robert B. Shapiro, the chairman of Monsanto, asks if his pharmaceutical and agricultural-products firm could benefit from IBM technology in its genetics research.

A few weeks later, IBM people travel to Monsanto's St. Louis headquarters and cite research projects undertaken in IBM's laboratories that could be used to help map the gene structure of seeds and human cells. One year later, IBM's executives, now with a foot in the door, are able to sign a decade-long service deal valued in the hundreds of millions of dollars with Monsanto. That contract was for the purchase of neither computers nor software, and gene research was the smallest part. IBM and Monsanto agreed that IBM would run Monsanto's mainframe computer system, install and maintain its 20,000 personal computers, operate the network that connected Monsanto's facilities, and write new application programs for Monsanto.

At the analysts meeting on May 13, 1998, Gerstner spent a good deal of time discussing his hopes for IBM's service business. At the time it accounted for 25 percent of the company's $78.5 billion in annual revenue. Gerstner knew that there were cynics out there who doubted that IBM could keep up such a pace in the services division:

> **There are a lot of people in IBM who tell me we can't sustain this 20 percent plus growth [in services]. I am not ready to accept that. Over the past 30 years as a consultant, as a manager, as a board member, I have been in and out of every industry in the world. I have never seen a better growth business than the information-technology-services business.**

Gerstner predicted that the sheer growth in services demand would lead IBM to double-digit revenue growth overall. One reason: a backlog in services contracts that stood at an impressive $44 billion. Estimates are that by 1999, services will represent almost one-third of IBM's revenues. (In January 1998, Dennie Welsh, the IBM executive who built computer services into the company's fastest-growing business line and its second largest, took a leave of absence for medical reasons. He was replaced by Sam Palmisano, who had been running the personal computer division. David Thomas was named to take over the PC unit.)

When Gerstner started out at IBM, he had no idea which parts of the company would prove to be the great growth engines, if any would at all. In time, he discovered one of the great growth engines right in his midst: the services business. Now that services has become IBM's most important revenue producer, most of the credit naturally goes to Lou Gerstner. What is forgotten is that he did not start the business, nor was he even certain at first that services were the key to IBM's future. In time, he came around to that belief, and he can be thankful that he did.

Chapter 25

———◆———

Don't Sell Products—
Sell Solutions

"Solutions require more than raw technology. They are combinations of hardware, software and services that we integrate to attack a customer's needs. . . ."

*L*OU GERSTNER DECIDED to keep IBM whole in order to exploit the company's size and diversity. Presiding over a unitary IBM, not a fragmented one, he would be able to provide customers not just with products but with the expert knowledge that IBM employees possessed to integrate those products (and at times the products of other firms) into computer technology solutions. In opting to make IBM a company that didn't just sell products, but helped customers with their business issues, Gerstner was reviving a strategy that had once been popular at IBM. Perhaps most important, committing IBM to a solutions approach meant that IBM was also committing itself to the services business.

While IBM was primarily a manufacturing company in its early decades, one of Thomas Watson Sr.'s favorite dictums was, "Don't talk machines, talk the prospect's business." He understood even back then that his customers didn't care half as much about machines or technology as what the machines could do to help their businesses.

Back on April 7, 1964, when the first real general-purpose computer appeared, the System 360, customers could hardly be expected to be knowledgeable about the new technology. The industry was far too new. So, IBM understood that delivering a product meant delivering not just the hardware. One had to deliver the operating system, the application software, and the services that taught customers how to run it.

Not a New Concept

So providing solutions was not a new concept. At the height of midrange and mainframe computing, from the 1960s to the early 1980s, teams of IBM systems engineers helped customers with many computing projects without charging in order to solve their technical and business problems. Many of these systems engineers worked full-time at the customer's site. But with the client-server revolution of the mid- to late 1980s, systems engineers turned into sales reps or consultants, as companies needed less and less help with the heavy iron.

By the late 1990s, however, many IT departments found that it was getting more and more difficult to deal with computer problems on their own, so the computer sales reps returned to their old role of business consultants and often proposed solutions that integrated hardware, software, and services. Vendors were often not even asked to bid on a project unless they could offer a complete solution. So although service was not a new concept in the computer industry, Gerstner pushed IBM to employ this approach far more energetically than it had ever done before.

It was IBM's depth and technological genius that provided the backbone for the solutions approach. Gerstner explained that what IBM brings in its services strategy is its laboratories, working with customers, thinking through how technology will evolve. When the cycle of technological evolution gets more rapid, the more IBM will be able to give clients a solution that achieves competitive advantage. After customers have gone through re-engineering, they say that the value is in fact in the system configuration.

The issue of whose workstation or PC it is becomes less and less of an issue, in Gerstner's view. What is important is to know how to bring about the change. The last thing customers need is one more piece-parts maker coming in to IBM flogging clock speeds on boxes. If that's what IBM's going to become, then potential customers will lose interest. What IBM had to do was convert its technology into products faster, and they had to be higher-quality products. That strategy, and that strategy alone, would lure in customers.

In Gerstner's first year running IBM, when the company suffered an $8.9 billion loss and had to borrow money to pay its dividend, it would have been easy to eliminate IBM's $6 billion-a-year research and development budget. That's what John Akers planned to do. Akers was sick and tired of spending all that money on R&D, with its esoteric projects, few of which ever reached the market. Gerstner kept an open mind about R&D when he took over. He visited its sites before deciding on its future. What he saw when he made his initial visit to the Watson Research Center at Yorktown Heights, New York, impressed him enormously. He saw research projects that, if tweaked in the right way, *could* be put to greater practical use. While he did cut IBM's R&D investment, Gerstner chose to keep the unit intact, admonishing the researchers to spend more time on figuring out solutions for customers.

Reducing Dependence on Hardware

When he took over in April 1993 Gerstner concluded that it was vital to make IBM the premier solutions company. He wanted IBM to address the specific needs of a bank or hospital, with special hardware, software, and services—even if the products were not all made by IBM. This was not a new solution. Most computer companies, including IBM, had been trying it out but with only mixed results. It was Gerstner's insight to use IBM's size and extensive technological resources to strengthen the company as a solutions provider.

Gerstner understood that IBM had to diversify, had to reduce its dependence on hardware. He has done that, and it remains one of the most significant things he's achieved at IBM. As of the spring of 1998, IBM was less than 45 percent hardware and less than 10 percent mainframe. Its primary emphasis is on solutions and software.

His goal was to create a workable organizational structure for IBM. That structure would focus around the idea that IBM could and would provide one-stop shopping to customers who sought solutions to their technology problems. By now, large companies had moved beyond the concept of office automation. In the past, these firms bought a lot of PCs, someone came and hooked them up, and someone else came in to consult. Gerstner realized that companies now wanted a unified strategy because access to information and the control of information were critical competitive issues.

The solutions strategy meant that IBM no longer simply sold hardware; it sold ways to get things done. As *Fortune* magazine observed in its November 4, 1996, edition, "If the old IBM was father Thomas Watson in his white shirt next to a multimillion-dollar mainframe, the new IBM is Uncle Lou, sleeves rolled up, getting the darn thing to work."

IBM's new rallying cry—offering customers solutions—was echoed in other quarters of the computer industry. Compaq had purchased IBM's old rival, Digital Equipment Corporation, primarily to obtain its 50,000 people in direct sales and service. The database firm Oracle had launched a services and consultancy division, and Cisco Systems, a networking company, now described itself as a "solutions provider." All of these firms agreed with IBM that, as products became more difficult to distinguish, service was a critical factor in increasing revenues and building stronger customer loyalty to products.

In the 1994 Annual Report, Lou Gerstner announced one of IBM's new strategic imperatives as "Expand market share in client/server computing." Then he explained that IBM had forty-two open systems centers in thirty-four countries, where it helped customers design and implement client-server applications. Its work with customers in these centers grew more than 50 percent in 1994, to about $1 billion revenue. It was focusing on ease of use, systems management, and software tools that improved the way products from IBM and other vendors worked together.

Two years later, in the 1996 Annual Report, Gerstner observed:

Solutions require more than raw technology. They are combinations of hardware, software and services that we integrate to attack a customer's business issues. . . . The networked world is also creating huge demand for services, our fastest-growing business. Customers want help in everything from consulting and systems integration to network services and education.

Gerstner kept pushing solutions as IBM's main approach to sales:

> The No. I thing that will drive IBM's growth in the future is a total commitment to solutions, not piece parts. We're not selling a browser. We're not selling a 3-D engine for your PC. We're selling ways for companies to make more money.

Pushing Solutions

Other companies were different. Other companies depended on one single core technology for their earnings and for their product lines:

- Microsoft pushed Windows.
- Intel pushed microprocessors.
- Netscape pushed Internet browsers.
- Oracle pushed databases.

IBM was different: It pushed solutions. It was counting on taking parts—IBM or otherwise—and creating networks to handle the critical sales or financial transactions that firms required. IBM called that solutions approach "E-business."

One interesting example focused on retail stock brokerage Charles Schwab. In December 1995, Schwab decided it required a World Wide Web site to allow customers to buy and sell securities and analyze their finances. Schwab executives talked to many people who thought they could help but finally chose IBM because it promised to get the site up within a reasonable time (it took four months). What ultimately sold Schwab was not that IBM would provide hardware or software, but that it offered the kind of consulting services that enabled Schwab to launch its Web site quickly.

With the advent of the Internet, IBM appeared to have a golden opportunity. Toward the end of 1996, it was estimated that companies would throw $250 billion at network-computing projects between 1996 and 2000. Of that, IBM said 65 percent would be spent for basic services and building solutions.

While mainframe computers are often written off as dinosaurs, IBM estimated that over 50 percent of all corporate data was stored on

IBM mainframes. Many companies need to find out how to take that data and make it accessible over networks. IBM was figuring out how to help those companies use the Internet effectively in a myriad of ways. For example, travelers are now able to use American Airlines' Web site to buy tickets. To set up the site initially, it was crucial to be able to feed data from American's Sabre system, which runs on a bank of ten IBM mainframes in an underground bunker in Tulsa. IBM was in an ideal position to help, allowing American to take the service quickly from its Sabre system and extend it to the Web.

When Lou Gerstner became chairman of IBM, skeptics in the industry wondered how this babe-in-the woods in technology would fare as head of the world's largest technology company. Not bad, as it turns out. In fact, his unfamiliarity with PC software actually helped him in one important case:

Back in late 1994, Gerstner visited the CEOs of two of the largest banks in the United States. As he sometimes did, he asked the executives who they thought their biggest future rival would be. Gerstner figured the answer would be Merrill Lynch or Fidelity or American Express. It wasn't any of them. Both CEOs mentioned Intuit, a maker of home finance software that had just been bought by Microsoft Corp. The answer surprised Gerstner. "I had never heard of Intuit. I mean, I had to fake it with the first guy," he said, smiling.

Gerstner quickly obtained a copy of Intuit's Quicken program and began playing around with it. He realized that companies such as Intuit would soon be able to do what banks should have been doing: offering home banking and other financial services to PC users. Unless the banks caught on, Gerstner believed, Microsoft and others could easily wedge their way between the banks and their customers.

Gerstner called Robert M. Howe, who headed IBM's $9 billion financial services organization, and told Howe that the company had to start thinking about what the banks needed to do to win in this new competitive environment.

For the next eighteen months Howe worked on the problem: helping banks provide online services. He envisioned a national network that all the banks could share. The banks would own the system jointly with IBM, split the costs, and avoid the hassle of inventing their own system. IBM would also be paid a fee for each transaction. Howe traveled around the country to drum up support among bankers. So did

Lou Gerstner, reeling in John B. McCoy, chairman of Banc One Corp. during a golf tournament in the winter of 1995. The two were part of a foursome, and through three holes Gerstner kept talking about this great electronic banking consortium. McCoy became so exasperated that he asked Gerstner if they could just play some golf—but eventually Banc One relented and joined the consortium.

On September 9, 1996, Gerstner and the CEOs of fifteen banks with 60 million depositors—including Banc One, NationsBank, and Bank of America—announced Integrion Financial Network, the electronic banking consortium. In addition to its Integrion network, IBM has created Insure-Commerce, which allows insurance agents, brokers, and buyers to shop for insurance. IBM's PetroConnect permits oil companies to buy geologic, weather, and other critical data.

In July 1997 Gerstner explained why customers need solutions:

Our customers are not in the technology business, and they don't have time to go door-to-door around IBM's product group to build their own solutions. They want someone to do that for them. This is what we mean when we talk about solutions. Now "solution" is a term that gets thrown around a lot in the business—even firms with a single-product line bill are offering a "solution" . . . but it all begins with an intimate understanding of what the customer is trying to accomplish—not in terms of IT strategy, but business strategy. That means we have to have in-depth knowledge of that customer's business and industry.

Lou's Greatest Legacy

Financial analysts were excited about Gerstner's solutions approach. "Perhaps," wrote Goldman, Sachs analyst Laura Conigliaro, "one of Lou Gerstner's greatest legacies will be his recognition of the importance of IBM's years of experience in delivering solutions."

Analysts understood that when the computer industry was less complex, as in the early 1980s when PCs were first hitting the market, customers were willing to learn how to use that product. But as products became more complex, with the growth of the Internet, users tended to prefer solutions. Gerstner had understood that point very well, so he was both lucky and smart. "One of the key things," said financial analyst Andrew Neff, senior managing director at Bear Stearns, "was Lou Gerstner's understanding of what IBM did well and why people did business with IBM. It wasn't because of its hardware. That's what IBM thought in the past. It was because it had armies of people that IBM would send out into the field; that was its strength: IBM would just swarm all over. But as the world moved to PCs, you couldn't send armies of people out into the field. But IBM still had this tremendous intellectual property and capital, whether it was technology or solutions or brains. IBM has always had very smart people; it simply lost focus on what the customer wanted from them. The people at IBM weren't idiots. They were just moving in the wrong direction."

Chapter 26

Exploit Cyberspace: It's the Next Big Business Challenge

"It will reshape the world as fundamentally as the invention of the printing press, the light bulb or manned flight. It will reshape every business and institution in the world."

*L*OU GERSTNER HAD constantly stated that he didn't like visions. He never said quite why. Perhaps he thought that the word "vision" was too vague or that it conjured up wild ideas. At any rate, he preferred to come up with what he called strategies. After leading IBM for several years, however, he was finally prepared to assert a vision. It had to do with network computing.

To explain himself, he delved back into his early days at IBM:

Almost immediately, there was a lot of whooping and hollering in the media about IBM wandering, visionless, through the wilderness. So it's with an enormous sense of irony now, almost three years later, I say this: What IBM needs most right *now* is a vision. I don't mean a slogan. I don't mean promises and vapor-

ware (announced products that don't exist now and never will). I don't mean here's-what's-good-for-IBM-and-therefore-it's-good-for you-too. Here's what I do mean:

We've seen great changes in computing before—from centralized mainframes to decentralized PCs to distributed client/server computing.

We now realize that client/server is not a full-blown phase of computing. It's the leading edge of what will be the next phase—what we call network-centric computing. I'll admit it's a cumbersome name, if not out-and-out dull. (I'd like to come up with something snappier, but I think it's too late.) But what we call it is less important than what it describes: a powerful change that has sweeping implications for individuals and institutions of all kinds. . . .

So this convergence of two powerful forces—customer need and advanced network technology—leads IBM to a strategy, or vision, that is simple and clear, and consistent with our company mission. IBM will lead the transition to network-centric computing by: continuing to create the advanced products and technologies needed to make powerful networks real; and working with our customers to help them fully exploit these networks.

Finally, the Boss Has a Vision

Gerstner was confident that he had found the right strategy and he was not going to veer from it. As he told *Business Week* in October 1995:

There is no question that the PC-based model is now not the future. The future is a network-centric model. The focus moves to a network that draws out the best of both worlds. The model drives the strategy of this company. When people talk about IBM, it's interesting to hear them say: "Well, I wonder if they'll get their new businesses to grow fast enough while their old businesses die." What they don't understand is, we are reconceptualizing our old businesses. We're bringing them into this new model.

Lou Gerstner did not just become a fan of networked computing overnight. He had spent eleven years running one of the world's most electronically based businesses. The American Express Card—one of his pet projects—was a great example of an E-business, a great example of a network business. It had tens of millions of people doing business in hundreds of countries with tens of millions of restaurants and hotels and airlines, all via electronic transactions. And it was done over a private network. Gerstner thought the idea highly transferable to the Internet:

> **The idea of a business that can run in—I hate the term—cyberspace, a business that can run in a digital world, not a physical world, was something that was very common to me. So I was thinking about this from a business point of view. Along comes this technology called the Internet, and it fit exactly into what we were planning to do. There are a lot of companies in this industry who sort of woke up one day and saw something called the Internet [and] said, "Gee, this is hot; we better go do something with the Internet." But we didn't come at it that way. We came at it from the point of view of the customer, and the Internet is just one of the tools and one of the assets we use to create these integrated solutions. It's a very powerful new tool, and quite frankly we were very fortunate that it has burst on the scene along with Java as tools we can use to expand and exploit this strategy we've got.**

The Central Organizing Principle

Lou Gerstner decided as early as 1994 that network computing would be the central organizing principle of IBM, its central integrating strategy.

In his 1994 Annual Report, Gerstner announced that one of his six new "strategic imperatives" was "Establish leadership in network-centric computing." To that end, he noted that IBM was moving on many fronts to define this new market and this new model of computing. It had created the IBM Global Network, the world's largest data network, with a presence in 700 cities in over 100 countries (in late 1998 it was sold to AT&T). It had begun working with telephone and cable television firms, field-testing IBM technologies that delivered interactive services to consumers and businesses. IBM was embracing the Internet and helping customers to do the same, by providing encryption technology, antivirus software, and "firewall" security products that would support heavy-duty commercial transactions and at the same time protect vital data from intruders.

Gerstner's big strategic bet, helping businesses create advanced computer networks, played to the company's strengths. Not only did IBM make some of the most important parts for these networks; it also had large numbers of salespeople and technicians to sell, install, and maintain the complex setups.

IBM realized the importance of the Internet about a year earlier than Microsoft. Irving Wladawsky-Berger, a veteran IBM guru who advised Gerstner on technology issues and was managing the Internet division, remembered that in 1995 his team felt "a sense of elation" at the arrival of the Internet. He sensed that the new phenomenon would mean a good deal more business for IBM.

To Gerstner, the virtue of the Internet was that it was open all the time. It was new and exciting, and easily accessible. But most important, what the Internet provided for IBM was a dramatic vision of networked computing. The Internet played to IBM's strengths, as it possessed huge storage capability and secure databases, had massive processing power, expert systems integration, and strategic planning. IBM could offer hardware, software, training, security, networking, and services that pulled all of these things together.

Rather than promoting any particular product or becoming obsessed, like Microsoft, with content, IBM concentrated on figuring out how to make the Internet useful to customers. One of its first decisions was to abandon its own browser ("a consumer thing that isn't really us," said Wladawsky-Berger). Soon afterward, in 1996, it shed its Prodigy on-line service.

The New Strategy Is Announced

As part of IBM's efforts to strengthen its position in the world of networked desktop computing, IBM had purchased Lotus Development in June 1995. IBM wanted Lotus Notes for its powerful communications capabilities in a networked world.

Lou Gerstner was ready to articulate his vision of network-centric computing on November 13, 1995, at the Comdex trade show.

We've come to understand that client/server is, in fact, not a full-blown phase of computing. It's really the leading edge of what will

be the next phase: network-centric computing. There are a lot of forces propelling us to this phase.

As part of its effort in networked computing, IBM was betting heavily on another software technology that it did not invent: Sun Microsystems's much-heralded programming language, Java, the ideal language for a networked world in which connected computers often run incompatible operating systems. A program written in Java can potentially run on any of them, from the largest mainframe to the smallest palmtop computer.

Gerstner acknowledged toward the end of 1995 that IBM was betting much of its future on the network-centric world. "So I hope you get the idea that we're taking network-centric computing very seriously at IBM. I'd say we're betting much of our future on it."

Meeting for three hours with Wall Street analysts and major investors in New York, Gerstner, in March 1996, declared that the company's traditional strengths would make it a power in the new era of network computing:

The industry is coming back our way. It's coming. It's coming back to our sweet spot. Everything you have been reading and hearing about the Internet plays to our strengths.

In the future, Gerstner added, IBM planned to tailor more and more network-based services to the needs of specific industries. One example: a network for three major health care providers covering eight states, including Colorado, Ohio, and Montana, that would link doctors, patients, and hospitals. Among other tasks, the network would automate paperwork and make records available as patients move between hospitals.

As Fundamental As the Light Bulb

With those high hopes for IBM's main strategy, Gerstner told IBM shareholders at the annual meeting on April 30, 1996, that he felt the shift to network computing was profound indeed:

I truly believe it will reshape the world as fundamentally as the invention of the printing press, the light bulb or manned flight. It

will reshape every business and institution in the world. It will affect—it's already affecting—each and every one of us . . .

But the most important driver of the shift to network computing isn't technology. The main driver of this shift is grounded in the priorities of our customers all over the globe. Nearly all of them are focused on increased speed to market, faster product development, providing better customer service, reducing cost, opening new markets.

He noted again that network computing was central to IBM:

For a company of IBM's size and breadth, it's hard to define a single strategy that embraces all our products, services and people. Yet, because network computing is so all-embracing, it has emerged as IBM's integrating strategy. It's the trail we're following—blazing—to get back on top. Now comes the hard part—implementing . . .

On September 5, 1996, IBM became the first major company to introduce a network computer, the IBM Network Station, a new kind of desktop device that provided access to networked applications and processing power while dramatically reducing the cost of desktop computing. Gerstner was enthusiastic about the new product and about the excitement exhibited among IBM customers for the whole concept of network computing. On November 11, 1996, the IBM Network Computer Division was formed.

Exactly what is network computing? Gerstner explained that it's a new model of computing based on networks, most notably the Internet. It is not simply linking computers together so they can talk to each other—IBM had been doing that for a long time. Rather, network computing is a large change in *how* computing is used and *where* it takes place:

It changes where computing takes place because it shifts most of the work—the processing, the data, the applications—from desktop machines to computers, called "servers," laboring behind the scenes in the network. This saves customers a lot of money because they don't have to replace desktop computers and desktop software every time a new upgrade comes along. All of that can be done once, on the server. This also gives our business customers greater control of their critical business data because the information is no longer distributed—sometimes haphazardly—over hundreds or thousands of individual PCs. . . .

We're adapting and enabling every hardware and software product in our portfolio for the "Net." Today, all our server platforms, from PC servers to supercomputers, are Web servers and offer price/performance competitive with any in the industry. Together with Tivoli [the software firm IBM purchased] we're enabling multi-platform systems management across the corporate infrastructure and out to the Web. All our key software products, for example, databases and transaction systems—are Web-enabled.

IBM's Lotus team continues to innovate and extend its lead in groupware, Gerstner concluded. More important, Notes and Domino have become the platform of choice for building Internet applications. (Domino is a network-centric Web server software that helps companies manage Notes for Internet collaboration.)

Network computing would pose a great challenge to IBM, he believed . . .

The network increasingly is becoming the place where transactions occur, where communication takes place, where business is conducted, where students are taught, where citizens are served by their governments.

As this happens, Gerstner believed, there would be tremendous demand for several things at which IBM excelled. Technology was one thing. Networks were by definition complex, requiring large processors, great amounts of storage capacity, large-sized databases, powerful transaction processing software, and comprehensive systems management. As transactions across networks increased, demand for IBM products would as well.

A More Confident Lou Gerstner

In 1997, a more confident Lou Gerstner began to implement the new strategic vision for IBM. Gerstner wanted to lead big companies into the new networked world. The plan called for IBM to devise the technology strategies for large companies; to construct and run their systems; and eventually to become the architect and clearinghouse for corporate computing. IBM would tie together companies—even whole industries—with the goal of using as much IBM hardware and software as possible.

Analysts agreed with Gerstner. Network computing definitely played to many of IBM's strengths. According to Laura Conigliaro, "The networked systems world that IBM has embraced is a palette for some of IBM's greatest skillsets... and today's IBM is in a better position to capitalize on it."

In effect, Gerstner wanted to take IBM back to the good old days when it was the information technology company for corporate America. The rise of the Internet had made that possible. With the arrival of the networked world, IBM appeared to be well positioned to become an indispensable factor in that new world.

IBM's goal was to refocus nearly everything it did to aiding customers do network-centric business. The key to IBM's strategy was concentrating on three solutions: E-commerce payment systems, supply-chain services and software, and customer-relationship solutions, including business intelligence and call-center technologies. IBM was realizing some of the benefits of E-business. The company noted that in 1997 it sold 100,000 network computers.

Gerstner believed that IBM was in a great position to exploit the switch to networking computing:

We know something about leadership. But when the industry moved away from many of the things that made us successful, some of us questioned what we stood for, and wondered if customers valued what we brought to the marketplace.

The reason that IBM has turned things around, he explained, was that

We're also catching a break with the shift to networks as the new model of computing. Once you understand what's required to make the networked world real for customers, you see that the

industry is coming back to our enduring strengths—enterprise computing and integrated solutions.

But it was still early—far too early—to tell whether Lou Gerstner had hit pay dirt. He certainly thought he had and wasted no time in communicating that to IBM and the rest of the world. He was bristling with confidence that IBM was going to lead the world in networked computing. Would he succeed? Gerstner knew the stakes were high and a great deal was riding on the outcome. After all, Gerstner was gearing the entire company up for the coming revolution in networked computing. He knew he had better be right.

Chapter 27

———◆———

Is the World Ready for Network Computers?

"There isn't a part of a CEO's agenda today that it isn't touched by the network. And this is right in front of us. It's right in the strengths of IBM."

*I*N FEBRUARY 1998 Gerstner acknowledged that the networked world still had very little relevance for people running large institutions because it was usually described as having to do largely with e-mail and on-line entertainment services, the AOL phenomenon, and the rivalry among the various search engines for customers. It was all, as he put it, "inside baseball," all sort of consumer-oriented, and CEOs still did not understand how networks could help their businesses. Still, he felt that IBM was defining the whole world of networking properly and was confident that CEOs would soon gain some understanding of the new phenomenon:

> **The minute you make the translation and say, "Wait a minute, networking skills, networking capabilities, as defined the way IBM sees them, become enormous assets in supplying chain management and in reducing your cycle time by having your suppliers operate as a virtual part of your enterprises," and the CEOs light**

up immediately. And if you say to them, "Think about what you can do, if you're a pharmaceutical company that we work with, to put all of your researchers on a knowledge-sharing basis around the world using Lotus Notes, and your ability to get pharmacological information together globally in real-time fashion," well, then the CEO says, "My God, that's what I'm trying to do; I'm trying to get my pharmaceutical agents approved sooner, and it's worth millions of dollars every day that I do that."

Translating the concepts of networking technologies and networking solutions into the priorities of the CEO were, he said, relatively easy when IBM executives sat down and talked about it in terms that other CEOs could understand:

I had the CEO of one of the largest manufacturing companies in the world, a European company, European-based—a global company—here last week, and he is a far-sighted executive, and he understands that his ability to communicate rapidly and consistently around the world and to share knowledge—engineering information, customer information, supply chain information, and even the kinds of information that one would argue create cultural dimensions of your organization—to be able to do that very, very rapidly and very consistently is a huge advantage for him. He knew he wanted to do that. And so we were talking about what we've done with Lotus Notes in IBM to achieve that kind of horizontal knowledge sharing across an enterprise for competitive advantage.

In February 1998, Gerstner observed that customers will no longer want to purchase just one device, like the PC, to access information. All kinds of devices will be developed; some will look like a PC, some will be network computers. Network computers will be a major improvement over PCs, because they will cost less; will be easier to manage; and will bring more applications and more data to the user than the PC:

I think we are ahead of everybody because I think we are not speaking about this as a simple box that replaces another box. In order to make network computing work and pay off for our cus-

tomers, it's really a system and a network statement, not a client statement. So we are building the capabilities to manage these devices through a server, to make them effective, to deal with the encryption and security issues, the network reliability issues. Those are the things that IBM—in other words, this is not coming from the PC space. It's a funny thing. You say network computers are simple PCs. They are. But in order to make them work, you got to manage them from a server space, and that's where I think there's no doubt that we are the leading company in terms of having built reliable, secure server products.

For all of Gerstner's enthusiasm over network computers, sales of the product were surprisingly bleak. Dataquest estimated that only 144,000 network computers had been sold in 1997, well below the original 400,000 forecast. But IBM had not done too badly. By April 1998, it had shipped 100,000 network computers to 3,000 customers. IBM's success stemmed from being one of the first to offer network computers running either Windows or Java programs. Yet, with only 20 percent gross margins, network computers were not great profit producers.

And by June 1998 it appeared that E-commerce was not the catalyst Gerstner had predicted two years earlier when he had stated that the Internet would spark demand for IBM's mainframes and large storage systems. In the eyes of some, Sun Computers had gained the advantage over IBM in network computing.

Despite Lou Gerstner's efforts to be consistent—to set a vision, and not violate it—information technology managers were confused about what he was trying to do, according to a July 1998 Forrester Research report called "IBM's Internet Opportunity." When asked if IBM's strategy was clear to them, half said no. An official from a commercial bank said, "The company is so big that it is riddled with confusion and mixed messages. One day, IBM is praising client/server, but then it turns around and promotes mainframes the next day. What is going on?" Different people have different views of IBM's strategy: "IBM's strategy is to be a solutions provider—to get beyond the individual hardware or services and become the total solution." That was how one employee from an electrical equipment company described IBM's strategic vision. Another employee at a commercial bank noted: "IBM's strategy is to push mainframes and sell them as a solution to everything." Those in the survey who thought that IBM's strategy was clear were then asked, what is its strategy? Some 30 percent said it was to be a service company; 26 percent, to push E-business; 17 percent, to be a total-solution provider; 13 percent, to prolong the mainframe; 9 percent, to make money; and 5 percent had other (unexplained) answers.

In October 1998, Gerstner made a rare television appearance during which he talked at length about the opportunities networked computing and E-business provided to IBM. The interviewer asked him what was IBM's largest opportunity:

> **To bring our customers to this networked world, to show them and deliver to them the enormous promises it has of reaching out to new customers, increasing their globalization, through the network, improving cycle times, supply chain management. There isn't a part of a CEO's agenda today that isn't touched by the network. And this is right in front of us. It's right in the strengths of IBM. The networked world goes to our strengths. That's the biggest opportunity we have and it's really what's beginning to drive our growth.**

Gerstner has said for a long time that the Internet is not about browsing, it was not about a replacement for the post office or a replacement for the telephone (via chat groups). It was not about a consumer looking up weather reports around the world. It was about vocational activities, about almost every kind of imaginable transaction in the world that is going to move to an electronic interface: physician to patient, schools to students, governments to citizens:

> **It's not going to replace physical transactions but it's going to augment them in an enormous way. So business is going to happen over the network and we've been building over the last three years the capabilities you need to really do serious transactions over the Net. Not again browsers. They're important. It's nice. It's like having a front door. But you need the whole rest of the house if you're going to have a suitable living quarters and that requires very complex, very sophisticated technology and that's IBM's strategy to deliver to our customers.**

Lou Gerstner was not discouraged. He had decreed that network-centric computing would be IBM's vision, and he had no intention of veering from that new vision. He had staked a significant share of IBM's resources and personnel on networking, the Internet and E-commerce. And it seemed clear that he had every intention of remaining in the race for the long haul. He was confident that eventually the computer industry would shift gears once again—and ride the bandwagon of a network-centric world.

Chapter 28

———•———

Edging Toward
Double-Digit Growth

*"We've got to gain market share.... None of us at IBM
is here, certainly not me, because we want to work
on a perpetual turnaround. We're finished with
the turnaround."*

THE CYNICS CONTINUED to question Lou
Gerstner's ability to achieve meaningful growth at IBM. Yet when
1998 rolled around, he was able to demonstrate to them that the company was indeed expanding at a healthy clip. Throughout the year,
IBM had been getting good play in the press. As Lehman Brothers analysts wrote in May 1998:

> **IBM remains the largest company within the computer industry
> and has shown a solid financial recovery in recent years. The com-
> pany has strong positions in several key growth markets, includ-
> ing services, software, servers, E-business solutions, PC, and the
> Internet. IBM is now utilizing its large R&D spending to develop
> leadership positions in many of the markets it serves.**
>
> **IBM, with 1997 revenues of $78.5 billion, remains by far the
> largest technology provider within the computer industry. Even if**

> **the company was broken into components, the hardware ($36 billion), services ($19 billion), and software ($13 billion) areas would all be the largest companies in the world for their respective categories.**

All this despite the company posting what seemed like quite ordinary, lackluster results for the first quarter of 1998. Earnings per share declined 9 percent from first-quarter 1997 to $1.06. Revenue rose a meager 1.8 percent to $17.62 billion. But things were not as bad as they seemed. Excluding a dismal decline in PC sales, revenue would have increased more than 7 percent. On a constant currency basis, this would have translated to an increase of 11 percent.

Also, the composition of revenue has changed significantly since the early 1990s. Almost 60 percent of sales were now nonhardware-related, thereby reducing the volatility of IBM's top line.

Other hardware sales, excluding PCs, had a very good showing in that first quarter. AS 400 and its associated OS 400 middleware host-based software sales saw an increase in the low double digits. The hardware component alone grew in the high single digits. RS 6000 server sales grew about 14 percent and were expected to maintain that level for the rest of this year.

Software revenue grew only 2 percent that quarter. Excluding currency fluctuations, the number was closer to 7 percent. Host-based software, which represented about 70 percent of software sales, showed a respectable 5 percent growth rate, while the faster-growing distributed software products from Lotus and Tivoli grew only 11 percent. Software sales represented only about 17 percent of total sales, similar to 1997.

On February 2, in an annual employee pep talk, Gerstner addressed IBM's 270,000 workers via television:

> **We've got to gain market share. This is the year we've got to make it happen. None of us at IBM is here, certainly not me, because we want to work on a perpetual turnaround. We're finished with the turnaround.**

Proving its credentials in large systems once again, IBM envisioned a number of projects that might emerge from the most famous chess match in history. In April 1998, the company announced a new computer—the RS 6000 SP—that was five times more powerful than the IBM computer that beat Gary Kasparov, capable of analyzing 1 billion chess moves per second. In the twelve months since Deep Blue's extraordinary triumph, IBM started working with the Department of Energy to build an SP supercomputer that will be the fastest in history—handling 1 trillion calculations per second. The agency planned to use it to simulate nuclear reactions, and thereby eliminate the need for live weapons tests. IBM also began using "deep computing" (with powerful computers like Deep Blue) so that pharmaceutical firms could imitate chemical reactions, knocking off years of drug research and development. Another application described as data mining would sift through huge amounts of information to find patterns and relationships that had never been detected.

In an interview in THINK in 1998, Gerstner said IBM had to go on the offensive. An interviewer noted that he had described IBM's last five years as playing defense and the next five years as the time when it gets to play offense. What would that feel like?

> **It's going to be fun. We're going to enjoy it more. You can already see it. There's an excitement, a looseness, a freedom of action, a collegial camaraderie, a sense of winning, of sharing in each other's victories—just feeling good about the company and what we're doing with each other. You saw it with some of the things that came out of our technical community last year—Deep Blue, the copper chip, some things in storage. People started to get excited and say, "Hey, IBM R&D is really coming back." . . .**
>
> **When you start to perform well, career opportunities expand, the security of a future in IBM gets stronger, and there's the opportunity to increase financial rewards—whether in variable pay, or stock repurchase, or stock options. All of that adds to people's feeling of well-being.**

Optimism for the Analysts

It was an ebullient Lou Gerstner who appeared before financial analysts in May 1998, telling them that he firmly believed that IBM could grow as fast as its smaller rivals. He was confident that the exceptional growth in computer services would help IBM achieve double-digit top-line growth. He had previously warned Wall Street to expect growth no higher than 8 or 9 percent for the last few years.

Revenue from IBM's services business jumped 21.6 percent in 1997 and services now accounted for 25 percent of the company's revenue and employed one-third of its workforce.

Gerstner said outsourcing revenue was growing 30 percent annually, with overseas sales soaring. In 1996, IBM closed twenty-seven deals worth over $100 million each, twenty-one of which were in the United States. In 1997, fourteen out of twenty-four deals were outside the United States. In 1998, the first five out of seven deals came from overseas.

It was clear that as of June 1998, Gerstner had turned IBM around—at least partially. IBM's mainframes were still a disappointment. IBM's midrange servers, selling for $100,000 to $1 million, had sold $6 billion in 1997, a paltry 1 percent increase over 1996. Mainframe revenues had dropped from $10 billion in 1992 to $5 billion by May 1998 (but the dropoff was to some extent misleading, IBM officials claimed, noting that IBM had cut prices, accounting for the diminished revenues).

Personal computers had come back but not as strongly as Gerstner had hoped ($15 billion in sales in 1997, up 5 percent). Several of IBM's products, although cash cows, were competing in undoubtedly mature markets. Even when it announced relatively weak first-quarter figures, the company had won back respect on Wall Street.

IBM relied heavily on clever financial engineering. Since 1995, it has spent $20 billion on share repurchases—a period during which operating profits have been more or less flat. IBM said that the buyback effort was due to its desire not to hoard more cash than the business needed. But critics wondered why a technology company couldn't exploit either its R&D spending or identify a few acquisitions with high-growth prospects. Costs were cut, but Gerstner acknowledged that too many IBM employees still valued "face-time" and meetings that produced little in the way of results. Critics argued that without Global Services, IBM's financial picture would be much worse; but that same argument could be applied to the largest business of any conglomerate. Critics also wondered why IBM continued in the PC business when other PC makers seemed to be beating IBM in that cut-throat arena. Gerstner contended that, even with these weaknesses,

IBM as a whole was worth more than its parts, that by leveraging aspects of IBM, the company was able to provide better, more integrated solutions to customers.

A New IBM

Still, there was no doubt about the emergence of a new IBM. The media was beginning to give Gerstner credit for transforming IBM. Here was *Business Week*'s lead in its June 1, 1998, story:

For five years, Gerstner has been masterminding one of the most remarkable revivals in corporate history. Double-digit earnings growth, a laser focus on costs, and one of the industry's most aggressive beads on electronic commerce. For the first time in years, pockets of the company are excelling. In 1997, Gerstner turned up the heat on high-tech services, a $19.3 billion business that grew 22 percent. Chips and disk-drive operations racked up sales at a 20 percent clip. And software acquisitions, such as Lotus Development Corp and Tivoli Systems Inc. are paying off big time.

And that same month, *The Economist* noted:

Today, thanks to an extraordinary mixture of luck and the intuition of a new boss who had previously run a biscuit maker—Lou Gerstner, hired from RJR Nabisco in 1993—Big Blue is back as a force to be reckoned with. Both IBM's profits and its share price have recovered; and after nearly a decade of job cuts, it has been rehiring. Although the scar tissue is still livid in places, there is a tangible sense of renewed confidence. Young IBMers walk with a spring in their step, while older hands can scarcely believe the extent to which their company's fortunes have turned around. Even more remarkable is the way rivals in the computing industry who were preparing to dance on IBM's grave a little while ago are now falling over themselves to imitate its business model.

But the turnaround was not total by any means. Gerstner knew that there had been slippage in personal computers, servers, storage systems, and, sadly—for this had always been IBM's bread and butter product—mainframes. IBM ended 1997 with nearly 64 percent—a staggering $50 billion—of its business flat to down. It was the same story in the first quarter of 1998.

Overall, IBM's revenues rose a mere 3.4 percent in 1997 and a tiny 1.8 percent in the first quarter for 1998. (Gerstner argues that IBM's growth was in fact 8.5 percent when adjusted for currency fluctuations overseas. Since IBM does 55 percent of its business overseas, Gerstner feels that it is only fair to measure the company's growth by factoring in currency fluctuations around the world.)

Perhaps more depressing than IBM's meager 3.4 percent growth was this reality: Compaq Computer, Sun Microsystems, Cisco Systems, HP, and Microsoft were growing four to seventeen times faster! (In April 1999 Compaq suffered a comeuppance when a first-quarter profit shortfall caused its stock to plummet 24 percent in one week; soon thereafter, CEO Eckhard Pfeiffer and Chief Financial Officer Earl Mason were ousted by cofounder and chairman Ben Rosen, who replaced Pfeiffer temporarily.)

One additional reality stung IBM: Microsoft was now the world's largest software provider, having edged past IBM with $13.1 billion in software sales during 1997 versus $12.8 billion for IBM. In the $6.6 billion database-software market, Oracle slipped past IBM in 1997 as well to become top in that field. Oracle's database revenue jumped 20 percent, to $1.82 billion, while IBM's grew 8 percent, to $1.8 billion.

IBM was on the brink of losing its leadership in hardware as well. When Compaq completed its $9 billion merger with Digital Equipment, their combined hardware operations was $34 billion, significantly larger than IBM's $26 billion, a figure that was essentially flat from 1997.

Lou Gerstner has shown that it was possible for a company of IBM's size to grow at a high single-digit pace on a constant currency basis even with the presence of older declining businesses. But that does not tell the whole story. When one examines the company up close, the full picture emerges: half the company was growing at a rate in the mid-teens while half was not growing at all.

The semiconductor business under Gerstner has been one of IBM's big successes. IBM's sales were up 17 percent when the rest of the worldwide semiconductor sales did not fare as well. People were convinced that IBM could not compete in the semiconductor business; it was too fast-paced. But IBM was first to come out with copper technology and IBM was considered by the summer of 1998 the leader in semi-conductor process technology.

Only in the services field has there been spectacular growth within IBM. Services as of May 1998 accounted for 28 percent of revenue and soon would constitute one third of revenue. Some analysts were predicting that one day services might account for half of IBM's revenues.

The hardware business remained flat and well under peak revenues of 1990. This had to do in large measure with the shrinkage in the mainframe business. Still, Gerstner told the analysts of IBM's thriving component-hardware unit, which sells hard-disk drives and chips to other computer firms; that business grew 22 percent in 1997 to $5.6 billion, aided to some extent by technological breakthroughs such as "giant magneto-resistive" hard drives, which sharply expand the storage capacity of disks.

Gerstner, in his talk to analysts, singled out the software division for special praise. While the division's revenue was up only 4 percent in 1997, to $12.8 billion, Gerstner said he was truly pleased that software had emerged as a major business for IBM. Critics of Gerstner say that while IBM's distributed-software business (products such as Lotus Notes that run on a variety of platforms) have been growing fast (about 11 percent in 1997), some 70 percent of its total software sales were still proprietary products, mostly for its S 390 and AS 400 host computers. This suggested that mainframes were still the driver for most of IBM's revenues; yet mainframe revenues were in decline.

IBM's collective family of clients and servers accounted (in June 1998) for 25 percent of revenues—about the same as its services division. The worst part of IBM's hardware business was PCs, due in large measure to intense price competition.

Meanwhile, as of the spring of 1998, IBM seemed stuck at the mid- to high single-digit growth level. IBM's fear: If revenues didn't grow, earnings would suffer because there was only so much more financial engineering that it could do to help its stock (stock buybacks and adjusting tax categories). In May 1998 IBM was growing at 6 to 7 percent, while segments of the computer industry were growing at as much as 30 to 100 percent. Gerstner, some analysts felt, should have been producing double-digit growth figures. IBM's revenue increased 3.4 percent in 1997, down from 5.6 percent in 1996 and well off the 12 percent growth of 1995.

Heading for a Good Year?

It was hard to imagine that IBM could wind up with a good year based upon second-quarter figures for 1998. Revenues were off 0.3 percent, although most analysts had expected sales to grow by at least 3 percent. Using IBM's "constant currency" measure, sales would have risen 4 percent; but even that figure was far less impressive than the growth rates produced by other companies, which made no currency adjustments at all: Microsoft, 26 percent increase; Sun Microsystems, 13 percent; Compaq, 7 percent; EMC, 33 percent.

The good news was that the software business grew by 5 percent and services shot up 22 percent. Hardware sales, however, dropped 13 percent over the quarter a year earlier, largely due to a slump in the PC business when an inventory glut led to price cutting. Mainframe revenues were flat compared to the quarter a year before.

IBM's earnings rose just a measly 0.4 percent.

Third-quarter results for 1998 showed the biggest growth spurt in some time. Revenues reached $20.1 billion that quarter, an increase of 8 percent—11 percent at constant currency rates. Third-quarter net earnings totaled $1.5 billion, compared with $1.4 billion in 1997's third quarter. Gerstner seemed quite pleased:

As our results indicate, our business accelerated significantly in the third quarter. We showed strong revenue and earnings growth and substantial improvement across nearly all parts of our product line. In short, we executed well on the strength of our broad portfolio of businesses.

He was especially encouraged by across-the-board revenue growth in IBM's server group, by ongoing strength in its services and software businesses, and by good improvement in its PC unit:

While IBM is entering the fourth quarter with some real momentum, we are facing a number of significant short-term issues, including an uncertain global economic environment, ongoing weakness in some parts of Asia and Latin America, and continued price pressures in semiconductors.

Over the longer term, though, we believe we are exceptionally well positioned as we move toward the next millennium. It's clear that customers increasingly are embracing our technology strategies as they seek highly integrated products and services to solve their business problems. We are committed to providing these solutions while maintaining our focus on delivering consistent financial results.

Revenues for the nine months ended September 30, 1998, came to $56.5 billion, an increase of 3 percent (7 percent at constant currency) compared with $54.8 billion as of September 30, 1997.

Soon after the third-quarter figures were released, Gerstner, appearing on a television program, noted:

Our business is strong across the board in the last quarter. Strong in hardware, software was strong, PCs returned from a very difficult first half; the microelectronics, semiconductor business continues to be difficult. The PC business has remained relatively strong all year; Manufacturers were reducing inventories during the first half; customers were still buying them; but we were not selling PCs into the dealers; the market was strong.

Gerstner's newfound optimism might have seemed out of place. After all, IBM had suffered through a fairly mediocre first half of 1998. But the second half of the year had proven much better for the company. Gerstner might have breathed a little easier, but he could not, for he knew that growth remained the most important benchmark as IBM approached the millennium. And IBM's growth was still not living up to Wall Street's expectations.

Part

VIII

On the Future

———◆———

"As we look ahead to the next
millennium, I don't think there's
any longer a question about the
profound power of this [IT]
technology. In an incredible
short span of time, it has
developed to the point where we
can talk about it in the context of
any of the other great
technologies that have
transformed the world."

———◆———

Chapter 29

When You Think You're Done, You're in Trouble

"We believe very strongly that the age-old levers of competition—labor, capital and land—are being supplemented by knowledge, and that the most successful companies in the future will be those that learn how to exploit knowledge."

WHERE DOES Lou Gerstner think the computer industry will go? What does the future hold for the industry and IBM? In what direction will his company move in the next five years? In the next decade?

The computer industry was bound to change, to grow larger. And what an incredible industry it has become:

- In 1998 more PCs were sold annually worldwide than either televisions or cars.
- Computers had diminished in size, but grown in power.
- The typical car held twenty to thirty microprocessors—far more computing power than had been inside the computers in the landing craft that took the first astronauts to the moon.

And the world was beginning to shift over to the products the computer industry offered:

- In 1997 there were five times more e-mail messages sent than the number of pieces of paper mail delivered worldwide—2.7 trillion e-mails. Moreover, the power of computers has risen while prices of those computers have dropped.
- In the mid-1970s, when the first supercomputers appeared, they could do "only" 100 million calculations per second. And they cost $1 million a piece. By 1998, the average laptop was twice as fast as those supercomputers and cost under $3,000.

The downward trend in the cost of data storage was equally as impressive. In the early 1980s, the standard unit of computer storage—1 megabyte (1 million bytes of information)—cost about $100. Today's megabyte: 10 cents; in two years it will cost only 2 cents.

A Trillion-Dollar Industry

Lou Gerstner was confident that the pace of advances in technology would only accelerate in the future. Microprocessors, storage, communications, memory, and the other products of the computer industry were bound to get faster, smaller, and cheaper.

He saw two trends that he deemed to be important signposts of how the future computing industry will look. The first is what he called "deep computing," which combines superfast processing with sophisticated analytical software. One key area where deep computing was already being applied was simulation: the replacement of physical things with digital things in order to replicate the reality of the real world inside a computer system. The first important steps in this new field were being taken: early in 1998 the U.S. Department of Energy asked IBM to construct a huge supercomputer that would simulate nuclear weapons so that it would no longer be necessary to detonate *real* nuclear weapons for testing purposes.

Data mining is a second kind of deep computing that will be used increasingly in the future. It is what people call business intelligence, the ability to "look" at large amounts of information and detect relationships and trends that were hitherto unfathomable. For example, banks are already beginning to look at spending patterns and other demographics that will suggest which customers will be the most profitable. To uncover hidden indicators of disease, health care firms are using data mining to analyze millions of patient records in the hope of making people healthier and reducing costs in the $100 billion-a-year health industry. One American company saved itself $38 million on a $400,000 investment in data mining technology: it uncovered fraudulent billing practices of a physician who was sending in weekly bills for a procedure that was only rarely performed in actual practice. One other more humorous discovery resulted from data mining: one retail chain determined that new fathers—for whatever reason—often purchase disposable baby diapers and beer at the same time. The chain decided never to discount the two items on the same day!

In 1996, Gerstner talked about the future of the computer industry:

Our industry is about to crack the trillion-dollar mark. We see the industry growing by about $400 billion to $1.2 trillion in the next four years. About half of that growth—$200 billion—will be driven by network computing. And the majority of that growth will be in solutions and services.

He believed that the potential for the Internet was huge, going on to say:

By the year 2000, 75 percent of the investments in Web software will be made for intranet applications. . . . The E-commerce business model is harder to describe, and the pay-off is harder to predict. But the potential is enormous. Some people say Web-based electronic commerce volumes will exceed $300 billion within five years. (It was only $8 billion in 1997.) And I think that is a very reasonable number. But people still ask, "Is there real money to be made on the Internet?" Yes. Yes there is. And the evidence grows every day.

Elsewhere, Gerstner spoke about the impact the Internet would have in the next few years:

Universal connectivity, driven primarily by the phenomenon of the Internet. The power of information technology is moving out

to touch hundreds of millions, perhaps a billion people by the year 2000.

Our notion of libraries will be up-ended when people can access the content found in books via the Internet 24 hours a day, 7 days a week, directly from their homes and schools. Telemedecine will allow your physician here in Atlanta to consult via the network with a specialist in Massachusetts or Tokyo, and they can simultaneously view the same X-rays and CAT scans. "Distance learning" makes the same quality education that is available in affluent suburban schools available in the forgotten enclaves of inner cities.

Use Knowledge to Adapt Quickly

Lou Gerstner predicted that success will come only to those corporations that learn how to use knowledge, not just technology:

We believe very strongly that the age-old levers of competition—labor, capital and land—are being supplemented by knowledge, and that the most successful companies in the future will be those that learn how to exploit knowledge—knowledge about customer behavior, markets, economies, technology—faster and more effectively than their competitors. They will use knowledge to adapt quickly—seizing opportunities and improving products and services, of course, but just as important, renewing the way they define themselves, think and operate.

The rise of a globally connected world is changing everything. It's rewriting the basic assumptions of business, the economy—and global society—and the new text reads like an IBM play book. If IBM didn't exist—if we had disintegrated it five years ago—somebody would have to recreate us to lead this new era. (That's just what some of our competitors are trying to do.)

On another occasion, he raised important questions that will have to be addressed regarding the Internet in the future:

Today [1997] there are about 50 million people with Internet access. That will soon be 100 million. Then hundreds and hundreds of millions. . . . What will they [customers] want to do? What will they value? Most importantly, what will they be willing to pay for?

We believe the answer is: most if not all the things they do today. Buy and sell. Bank. Access entertainment. Pay bills. Get an education. Renew a driver's license. Maybe go to a shareholders meeting.

In 1998, Gerstner noted that there was no longer a question about the power of technology. It now could be ranked with the other great technologies that have transformed the world:

We're watching the emergence of something much bigger than a new model of computing or even a new channel for human inter-action. Information technology—and specifically networked tech-nology—represents the most powerful tool we've ever had for change. It's a new engine for real economic growth, a new medium that will redefine the nature of relationships among gov-ernments, among institutions and businesses of all kinds—and the people they serve now, and might serve tomorrow.

It was as if Lou Gerstner knew he was riding on a wave, and the wave would only bring bigger and better things for IBM.

Yet, when he cast an eye at the future, he knew that he could not auto-matically depend upon the nascent network society to recast IBM as the computer industry's leader. He could be deeply satisfied—and there was every indication that he *was*—that he had engineered the greatest turn-around in corporate history. In his first five years he had eradicated the company's losses and put the company on to a new growth path; he had brought the company's expenses in line and launched an aggressive ini-tiative to stake out IBM in the electronic commerce field. Several of IBM's businesses were unmitigated success stories: services as of 1998 was growing at a 21.4 percent clip, with revenues of $23.4 billion—up from $19.3 billion a year earlier. Software was showing decent gains, growing at 5.4 percent in 1998, with revenues of $13.5 billion—an increase over its $12.8 billion performance of a year earlier. The acquisi-tions of Lotus Development and Tivoli Systems were providing substan-tial payoffs. And finally, the component business (chips and disk drives) was growing nicely ($5.6 billion in 1997; $6.6 billion in 1998).

But Gerstner knew a darker truth as well, or at least he should have: He had done little to turn around several other businesses such as personal computers, servers, storage systems, and mainframes. In one of the most hard-to-swallow statistics, roughly half of IBM's businesses—$40 billion—were down at the end of 1998.

How was IBM positioned for the future? Which of its product lines would do well? How was Lou Gerstner hoping to keep IBM growing?

It seemed clear that IBM could remain a strategic vendor for the computer needs of large companies, but not if it remained wedded to its hardware focus and legacy products. Hanging on to the past was simply not a recipe for growth. Gerstner has been banking on getting consistent annual double-digit growth rates by dominating the market for Internet business solutions and creating software that spurred Internet-oriented services—but to succeed, he will have to take the courageous step of winding down large segments of IBM's slow-growth hardware business.

Lou Gerstner was of course counting on computer services to remain a major source of growth for IBM. "I have never seen a better growth business than [information technology] services," he noted. But he was not putting all of his growth eggs in one basket. He also wanted to expand business in collaborative software, PC servers, and hardware components. In May 1998, he was bullish about IBM's component-hardware business. And he was pleased with the progress of the software business (although its revenues had been up only 4 percent in 1997, to $12.8 billion, it was showing consistent growth: in 1998, it grew 5.4 percent, to $13.5 billion). It was Gerstner's hope that IBM could become the main supplier of E-commerce software and services as well as the manufacturer of technology to construct Net-ready information appliances.

Pinning his hopes on these growth-potential businesses, Gerstner predicted in May 1998 to financial analysts that there would be strong demand for computer services and components, so Wall Street could look for double-digit revenue growth from IBM over the next several years.

Just Getting Started

In October 1998 Lou Gerstner sounded as if he were just getting started in the job. He now had a pretty good grasp of what had gone wrong with the company in the past. And he was determined not to repeat any of those mistakes. After running IBM for five and a half years, he was quite certain that there was much more he could do to improve the company. And, though some people thought he had completed his task at IBM, he was in no rush to leave.

My belief is that all large successful companies run the risk of trying to codify their success. When you try to codify your success you become internal, you become preoccupied with what's going on inside. So the first thing we did was that. We just said we're going to drive this company from the outside in. And we energized an incredibly talented group of people who were here and were waiting for the leadership that would bring the company back in again.

"Are you done?" asked the interviewer.

No. We're never done. That's my point. That's what happens to large successful companies. They think they're done, so it's time to write the book, write the manual, write the procedures guide, let's go codify everything, including what you wear. No, you're never done. You're never done. And when you think you're done, you're in trouble.

In October 1998, he was predicting that IBM's growth would be between 8 to 11 percent for the year, and 8 to 10 percent for 1999. Those kind of lofty predictions seemed unrealistic to analysts unless IBM was prepared to take some drastic steps.

Analysts at Forrester Research, for instance, believed that IBM would have to alter its future direction, because Gerstner was able to get only mediocre growth out of most of his businesses. The main source for new growth, they believed, would come from the Internet. IBM could, they predicted, leverage the Internet to drive its revenues beyond $100 billion by the year 2001.

They forecast that IBM's Global Services would grow from $19.3 billion to $50.7 billion by 2001; that the software business would grow from $12.8 billion to $15.1 billion in 2001; that hardware would drop drastically from $25.8 billion to only $12 billion by 2001; and that IBM's other businesses, which brought in $20.6 billion in 1997, would bring in slightly more by 2001: $22.3 billion. But their prediction that IBM could reach $100.1 billion in revenues by 2001 assumed that the computer giant would get out of the desktop PC business.

That IBM should heed the Forrester proposals was borne out by the company's 1998 financials. While for the first time IBM's revenues topped the $80 billion mark ($81.7 billion to be exact), it had turned in a rather mediocre 4 percent growth figure, half of what Lou Gerstner predicted. Its earnings for 1998 had shown no great leap forward, as the company had an income of $6.3 billion—only $200 million more than the previous year.

While Gerstner seemed overjoyed with IBM's fourth-quarter results for 1998, Wall Street clearly was disturbed by Big Blue's overall annual results for 1998. The day after the company announced its 1998 figures, IBM's stock plummeted 17¼ a share, closing at 179¾ on January 22, 1999.

IBM's fourth-quarter results for 1998 showed a profit of $2.3 billion on revenues of $25.1 billion. In the same quarter a year earlier, IBM had come in with earnings of $2.1 billion on $23.7 billion in revenue. The impressive fourth-quarter results for 1998 were due in large measure, Gerstner indicated, to strong showings in global services and software. Fully 60 percent of IBM's gross profits came from those two divisions. IBM's service revenue grew 20 percent to $7.1 billion compared to the same quarter a year ago; software revenue rose 9 percent to $4.1 billion, aided greatly by the 5 million Lotus Notes users added in the 1998 fourth quarter, raising the total number of users to 34 million.

A Look at the Gerstner Years

Although he had ended 1998 with less than stellar annual results, Lou Gerstner knew that he had accomplished far more for IBM during his six years at the helm than had been originally predicted. Back in March 1993, when he was chosen to take over IBM, the cynics—and there was no shortage of them—simply assumed that Gerstner had been hired solely to assure that IBM's dismemberment would go off without a hitch. He was not expected to put the company back together again; simply to make sure that its fall would be as painless as possible. There had been little or no expectation that he might actually turn the company around and propel it to new heights. Not Lou Gerstner, the man everyone called an outsider; the man who knew more about candy bars than computers. Sure, he had done well in running other businesses before, and sure, he seemed a true professional business-turnaround artist; but none of the other companies in which he had been involved could match IBM's size or financial woes.

To Gerstner's good fortune, he came into the IBM job with few people truly believing that he could work a miracle. To be sure, everyone *wanted* him to perform one. No one wanted to see IBM fall apart. But few would have blamed Lou Gerstner for trying and doing no better than John Akers. No one would have blamed him for failing. So almost any improvement that Gerstner made to the ailing computer giant would have made him look like a genius.

Starting off slowly, trying to learn the ropes first before making major decisions, Gerstner seemed a major disappointment to many. True, he was not expected to turn the company around, he was probably going to fail, but the people on Wall Street were still dying to know what was going on in his head, what plans he had to *try* to save the company. When Gerstner suggested to analysts that he really possessed no grand vision for the company, he only served to reinforce their original fears that he was not up to the job. Rather than reshape IBM, he seemed to be doing little else besides presiding over the old IBM.

But then slowly but surely, Gerstner began the turnaround in earnest. He made his most important decision fairly soon after taking over: he would keep the company whole and not let the dismemberment, already in progress, move forward. Gerstner understood better than almost anyone else at the time (he certainly had his critics on this issue) that whatever small chance he had of turning the company around depended entirely on whether there *was* a whole company! To allow IBM to be split up was, in his eyes, tantamount to signing its death certificate. Gerstner had no desire to play the role of coroner—or liquidator.

He was ready to play the role of tinkerer. He wanted no wholesale revolutions at IBM. There was plenty of good at the company. The trick, he felt, was to get employees to start executing—start performing better. Tinkering inevitably meant, in the case of the overly bureaucratic, overweight IBM, wielding an ax. This was the unpleasant part, and Gerstner decided to get through with it as quickly as possible. He also vowed that he would never put the company through such unpleasantness a second time. And he lived up to that commitment.

Next, he took a hard look at IBM's product line, giving special attention to the company's vaunted mainframe division. He made a crucial decision: contrary to those who insisted that mainframes were on their way out, and therefore that IBM was better off concentrating on personal computers and other nonmainframe business, Gerstner opted to make mainframes a main focus for IBM. Many thought he was nuts. But he understood—again, better than most—that IBM needed to give a fresh emphasis to mainframes in order to convince customers that Big Blue was the best place to do one-stop computer shopping. It was not enough to manufacture almost everything else in the computer industry—and de-emphasize mainframes. If customers were going to look to IBM for computer solutions to business issues, IBM had to make sure that it remained a major factor in mainframes.

As he moved to refocus the company around mainframes, Gerstner refused to give up on the personal computer segment of the company, a division that had gone through a withering storm of fierce competition during the 1980s and early 1990s. Again, Gerstner wanted customers to feel that IBM was the *only* place to shop—and therefore it had to make sure its personal computer division was viable.

In time, Gerstner came to appreciate that IBM had a great thing going for it in its burgeoning service component. Other large companies around the United States were discovering the same phenomenon—that as their manufacturing divisions were running into more and more competition, there was a growing amount of business to be won in the service realm. The secret was not to abandon manufacturing. To win over service contracts, a company like IBM had to continue to demonstrate that it *could* manufacture all the products that would be used to fulfill those contracts.

Tinkering with the company's bureaucracy, sprucing up IBM's product lines, none of this would matter, Gerstner knew, if he could not get his employees to pay more attention to customer needs. It was no longer enough—as many at IBM thought it was for decades—to guide the customer through the computer thicket, or, more bluntly, to tell the customer what IBM products to buy. That had worked quite well in the old days when customers knew little about the computer world and *wanted* the guidance, *wanted* to be told what to buy. Customers were smarter now, and Gerstner's great insight was to understand just how smart they were. He understood that customers were smart enough to determine on their own what kind of computer products they wanted. But he also realized—and this represented one of his keenest insights—that potential customers would still need IBM's guidance on how to use computers to solve their various business problems. So he required of his sales force that it not push products down customers' throats, but rather work with them to come up with creative solutions in the running of their businesses.

Lou Gerstner avoided thinking of long-term visions. In the early phases of running IBM, he preferred to deal with the here and now, with making the company more efficient, with getting employees to perform better, with improving the way products got to market. But he eventually turned to the changes occurring within the computer industry, focusing on how IBM could position itself to take maximum advantage of those changes. He sensed, quite correctly, that the industry was moving with meteoric speed into the Internet age, and that it was incumbent upon IBM to become the one company that everyone would turn to for their Internet needs. When people thought of the new network-centric world, he wanted them to think of IBM. In some cases, as with Lotus Notes, he was having great success. Whether in fact Big Blue would become the main address for people with Internet needs remained an unanswered question, but Gerstner was devoting an increasing amount of IBM's resources to achieve that goal.

Don't Give Up

We have focused on Lou Gerstner's six years at IBM not simply to celebrate the performance of one man who had some bright ideas, applied them, and in the course of time, turned around one of America's great business icons. We have focused on Gerstner for another reason: the business strategies that he has employed can be applied to many other businesses. Those businesses need not be in their death throes, as IBM was. They could simply yearn for better financial performance.

We have focused on a number of key Gerstner business strategies that, taken together, give a sense of how he has pulled IBM out of its quagmire. But the overriding message of the Lou Gerstner turnaround story is this: Don't give up. Too many people at IBM, dating back to the mid-1980s, simply abandoned all hope for Big Blue's recovery. They began to coast, and as a result, so did the company. When Gerstner took over IBM, he could have gone into neutral and let the company continue to drift (and in the early months, some feared that was precisely what he was doing). But he had a deep faith in the company, a faith that was based on the many years he had watched IBM from the sidelines. He also had great self-confidence, and felt that he knew, more or less, how to turn companies around. He knew that what was needed was not just brain power but courage; not just broad-based leadership skills but the ability to communicate and win people over.

Performing Miracles

In his six years at the helm, a relatively short time for someone to put a large company like IBM back on its feet, Gerstner performed a number of miracles:

Miracle number one: Bringing an end to the staggering financial losses IBM was suffering

Miracle number two: Reshaping the company into a manageable, efficient entity, one that had a chance of becoming profitable

Miracle number three: Actually turning Big Blue into a profit-making machine once again

One miracle still eludes Gerstner, the miracle of strong top-line growth. To be sure, IBM has grown since Gerstner took over. In 1993, the company's revenues were $64.5 billion. A mere five years later, Gerstner had boosted those revenues to $81.7 billion, a highly respectable figure by most standards. But that $80 billion-plus figure did little to disguise the indelible fact that too much of IBM was not growing at all, too many of the company's product lines were in no better shape than on the eve of Gerstner's arrival. By putting his eggs in the service basket, admittedly a shrewd move, Gerstner could point to a certain growth, but one only had to look at the rather mediocre annual growth rates for 1997 (3.4 percent) and for 1998 (4 percent) to appreciate the fix that Gerstner was in.

Little had been expected of him when he took over IBM in April 1993. But six years later, a great deal was expected. The analysts tended to forget about the good that Lou Gerstner had done for IBM; they thought mostly about the next quarter, and the quarter after that. They certainly had little reason to dwell on the past. But Lou Gerstner did. And he rarely missed an opportunity to remind audiences of what he had accomplished: much more than getting rid of the dark suits and white shirts (though he had done that too); much more than shortening IBM's infamous meetings (though the length of meetings had been cut back sharply); much more than ending the days when the computer industry had looked upon IBM with disdain (though now most computer firms had growing respect for Big Blue).

Having achieved so much and solved virtually all of IBM's once-life-threatening problems, Gerstner has redefined what constitutes success at IBM. Six years ago, cynics asked: How much longer does IBM have before its inevitable collapse? In 1999, with the turnaround an ongoing reality, those pundits asked a different question: When will Gerstner produce impressive, consistent, year-after-year growth at IBM? While that remains the key question facing the computer giant as it approaches the new millennium, Gerstner silenced some of his critics on April 22, 1999, when IBM announced its first quarter results that far exceeded Wall Street estimates: Thanks to a 17 percent surge in hardware sales, a 19 percent hike in services, and a 10 percent rise in software, Big Blue's revenues soared 17 percent while earnings skyrocketed 42 percent, sending IBM stock soaring 23 points, closing April 22 at 194 and 7/8. It was IBM's best first quarter ever in revenue, earnings, and earnings per share. The company's surprisingly strong results sent the Dow Jones Industrials racing to another record high of 10,727.18. The heady first quarter results gave Gerstner renewed confidence that he could bring off that consistent double-digit growth that Wall Street was clamoring for. If the IBM chief could show that first quarter 1999 was no fluke, if he could turn in consistently great results in the coming year or two, he would once again provide a miracle for Big Blue.

Epilogue

THE PHOTOGRAPH of Lou Gerstner on the second page of the 1998 Annual Report shows him with a big smile, hands extended, the very picture of a business leader who has accomplished much and has a good deal of optimism about the future. As he moves into the spring of 1999, Gerstner is indeed feeling good. He has just sealed one of the most important deals of his six-year tenure—this one in early March with Dell Computer Corporation, which has agreed to purchase $16 billion of equipment from IBM under a seven-year arrangement that also called for the companies to jointly develop new computer technology. It marks IBM's largest deal yet and it has been done with one of its most aggressive rivals. Dell promises to buy such IBM equipment as disk drives, flat-panel displays, and memory chips to put into its computers. No wonder Gerstner is smiling: IBM is getting a guaranteed source of sales over the next few years—a partial answer to those critics who feel that IBM is not growing rapidly enough.

A few weeks later, Gerstner's letter to shareholders appears inside the 1998 Annual Report. It is a letter that is bristling with hope for IBM's future, in marked contrast to the gloomy few months that preceded Gerstner's start at the company a mere six springs earlier.

In that letter, he suggests that the greatest measure of IBM's progress had been its market capitalization, which has grown by $69 billion in 1998 thanks to a 76 percent leap in the company's share price (making for $146 billion of market cap growth since 1993).

Gerstner writes that he believes 1999 will be markedly different from his previous years at IBM's helm:

What makes 1999 different . . . is that a historic shift—something IBM began talking about three years ago—is taking hold, and it's reshaping everything: how we work, how we shop, how we interact with our governments, how we learn, what we do at home. Every day it becomes more certain that the Internet will take its place alongside the other great transformational technologies that first challenged, and then fundamentally changed, the way things are done in the world.

Reminding everyone that IBM had been arguing that the Net was about mainstream business, not browsing, about conducting real commerce, not simply accessing content, Gerstner asserts that while the gurus had once thought Big Blue "uncool" for such thoughts, "this position is feeling a lot less lonely." E-business could reach $600 billion in the next few years, and IBM hopes to capture a large segment of that new business, he states.

What will make 1999 unique, he predicts, will be the shakeup that will ensue as people begin to grasp what the arrival of this networked economy means. New leaders will arise, old ones will disappear. And competitors—whom Gerstner calls "something.com"—will materialize out of nowhere. IBM, he believes, is uniquely qualified, structured, and situated to take advantage of all this change.

He then puts forward five principles on which he believes the new leaders will have to focus on in the next two years:

The Internet isn't just creating new businesses. It's creating new business models.

The greatest competitive advantage in the information technology industry is no longer technology.

The PC era is over.

We're only at the beginning—more is coming.

The Year 2000 problem is important and it's being addressed. But a lot of work remains to be done—fast.

With the Internet creating new business models, with every business and institution now having the chance to rethink what it does, IBM is in a strong position to help, he argues, especially through the company's solutions business.

If the greatest competitive advantage in the IT industry is no longer technology, then what is it? Gerstner argues first of all that technology is changing far too speedily for a company to build a sustainable competitive advantage on that basis alone. Then he adds . . .

> **More and more, the winning edge comes from how you help customers use technology—to steal a march on their competitors, to implement entirely new business models. That means creating integrated solutions that draw on the full range of products and, increasingly, services.**

And, Gerstner insists, IBM is well positioned to win a disproportionate share of the growth in the information technology services business. IBM Global Services has grown in eight years from a $4 billion to a $24 billion business—at an average annual growth rate of 20 percent. Gerstner is clearly proud of that accomplishment.

Contending that the PC era is over, Gerstner suggests that the PC's reign as the driver of customer buying decisions and the primary platform for application development has come to an end. It has been replaced by the network. This is good news for IBM.

As he summarizes IBM's year, Gerstner says that he feels that IBM is at a key inflection point in the company's history:

> **Given what we have accomplished over the past six years, it would have been natural for IBMers to indulge themselves in well-deserved pride at having turned the ship around, or comfort in resuming a familiar role and stature. When I came to IBM in 1993, frankly, my fondest wish was for the company to return to its former position of leadership.**
>
> **More and more, however, my colleagues are preoccupied not with our achievements of the recent past, but with the vast prospects opening before us. . . .**
>
> **This is something I never dreamed of six years ago. Spurred by the extraordinary adventure of building a networked world, this large and storied enterprise now believes that its best years lie ahead of it—that its past, and that of the information technology industry as a whole, were just a preamble.**

For all of his glowing optimism, for all of Lou Gerstner's conviction that IBM was riding a wave that would keep it atop the IT business for years to come, he still has challenges ahead of him, he still has to convince his critics that IBM is more dynamo than dinosaur, more a growth engine than a sputtering old icon. Lou Gerstner knows that he still has time to silence the critics, but he does not have that much more time. He has saved Big Blue. Now he looks forward to rebuilding it into the institution that Tom Watson Sr. had made famous. That remains his biggest task.

Acknowledgments

Few American companies are as intriguing as IBM. For decades it stood at the top of the computer industry, the model for all American corporate life. It was seemingly indestructible. And yet, during the 1980s and early 1990s, it went into a dangerous tailspin and the very future of the enterprise appeared in doubt. Then, as I have recounted in these pages, the company enjoyed a surprising upturn. Much had been written about the rise of IBM and a certain amount about its near-perilous fall. But at the time I decided to look at the company, no one had examined the last six years as it was going through its shocking revival. And no one had chronicled the business strategies of the man who led that revival, IBM chairman and CEO Louis V. Gerstner Jr. The editors at McGraw-Hill, with whom I have worked previously on a number of books on American business personalities, agreed that Gerstner's leadership lessons and turnaround tactics were worth exploring.

In researching the book, I was able to obtain a modest degree of cooperation from IBM. Requests to interview Gerstner were refused on the grounds that he was too busy to see those who were writing books about IBM. He did, however, authorize his public relations staff to turn over ample amounts of material to me about the company and to answer my questions, which were plentiful. I made use as well of Gerstner's interviews with the media, his speeches, and some valuable internal memos. I supplemented this part of the research by holding interviews with a whole array of IBM consultants and financial analysts who devote most of their waking hours to monitoring Lou Gerstner and his company. I made a special point of interviewing those who knew Gerstner personally and, at the same time, could offer a broad perspective on IBM's ups and downs.

IBM put me into the capable hands of Tara Sexton, the company's director of corporate media relations. I wish to thank her for all the time she took in helping me to make this book as accurate as possible.

In many ways *Saving Big Blue* was a team effort, with the other member of the team being my editor, Jeffrey Krames. It was his insight at the outset that it was the right time to do a book on Lou Gerstner and IBM, and he played a major role in crafting the structure and format of this book. I want to thank Jeff not just for the chance to work with him on this book, but for our entire fifteen years of teamwork. I also want to thank McGraw-Hill's Philip R. Ruppel, Vice President and Group Publisher, Business and General Reference, and my agent, Chris Calhoun, at Sterling Lord Literistic.

I save my biggest thanks for my immediate family, my wife Elli, my children, Miriam, Shimi, Adam, and Rachel, and my grandchildren Edo and Maya. They make my book writing possible—and enjoyable.

Endnotes

Deep Blue to Mr. Kasparov: Checkmate!

4   "It's great what you've done...," *The New York Times,* May 8, 1997.

Chapter I

16   "rarefied WASP world with few...," "Deep Blue's Deep Pockets," *Forbes,* June 19, 1997.

19   "IBM executives were not allowed to...," Lucy Baney, interview, May 15, 1998.

20   "Both revolutions transformed the way...," IBM History, www.ibm.com.

22   "Software was looked upon as...," Sam Albert, interview, May 8, 1998.

23   "We've gone from being perhaps...," John Akers, quoted in "America's Most Admired Corporations," *Fortune,* January 19, 1987.

23   "giant pools of peanut butter...," "Dinosaurs?", *Fortune,* May 3 1993.

24   "It seemed like you had to...," Philip Baker, interview, July 23, 1998.

24   "It was sacrosanct to...," Sam Albert, interview, May 8, 1998.

25   "and it just so happened...," Philip Baker, interview, July 23, 1998.

25   "Akers recognized that...," Dan Mandresh, interview, May 20, 1998.

25   "You didn't innovate...," (anonymous source).

Chapter 2

28   "The senior people knew what was going on...," Gideon Gartner, interview, August 15, 1998.

29   "this unreasonable anxiety about...," Philip Baker, interview, July 23, 1998.

29   "It troubled me greatly...," Carl Conti, interview, July 9, 1998.

29   "Corporate welfare was a...," Ibid.

31   "IBM was on the verge...," Laura Conigliaro, interview, May 14, 1998.

31   "The fact that we're losing share makes me goddamn mad...," "Better Days in the Life of a Global Giant," *Business Week,* June 17, 1991.

32 "IBM had the image of motherhood...," Peter Thonis, interview, August 25, 1998.

32 "I didn't acknowledge the curses...," Ibid.

33 "We expect these more independent...," John Akers, IBM press release, December 5, 1991.

Chapter 3

37 "It's fair to say some...," "IBM After Akers," *Business Week*, February 8, 1993.

38 "is 35 years old...," "Bossidy on IBM's Ideal Boss," *Fortune*, April 5, 1993.

40 "convinced me that a great...," "I'm Going to Let the Problems Come to Me," *Business Week*, April 12, 1993.

40 "Lou was tougher than...," "He's Smart, He's Not Nice. He's Saving Big Blue...." Reprinted from the April 14, 1997, issue of FORTUNE by special permission; copyright 1997, Time Inc.

40 "Apparently, IBM gets a lot...," Ibid.

40 "He began to convince me...," *The New York Times*, March 27, 1993.

41 "a technical genius to run...," Jim Cannavino, interview, August 19, 1998.

41 "I've never been a person...," Ibid.

Chapter 4

43 "From the first time we got...," "He's Smart, He's Not Nice. He's Saving Big Blue...," *Fortune*, April 14, 1997.

44 "Back it up." Ibid.

44 "McKinsey had a culture...," "The McKinsey Mystique," *Business Week*, September 20, 1993.

45 "I love beating...," Lou Gerstner, interview, *Contact*, August-September 1985.

45 "This is a violation...," "He's Smart, He's Not Nice. He's Saving Big Blue...," *Fortune*, April 14, 1997.

46 "If you're looking for...," "Current Biography," Profile of Lou Gerstner, June 1991, p. 35.

47 "hardest job in America...," "Faith in a Stranger," *Business Week*, April 5, 1993.

47 "I came on board a $17 billion...," "Managing: Does the CEO Really Matter?" *Fortune*, April 22, 1991.

47 "This was a company...," Ibid.

48 "When I got here...," Ibid.

Chapter 5

53 "The most avidly watched...," *The New York Times*, March 27, 1993.

53 "a certain amount of fear...," Rawleigh Warner Jr., quoted in "Industry: Can This Man Save IBM?" *Fortune*, April 19, 1993.

53 "may be the toughest...," quoted on National Public Radio, March 26, 1993.

54 "The challenge they've laid...," Ibid.

55   "I think it's risky to bring...," "Faith in a Stranger," *Business Week,* April 5, 1993.

55   "People here were hoping...," Ibid.

56   "This is going to take...," *The New York Times,* March 27, 1993.

58   "There was a lot...," Lucy Baney, interview, May 15, 1998.

59   "Some of you were hurt...," Lou Gerstner, memo to IBM employees, April 6, 1993.

60   "The message of the nineties...," "Poised for Leadership," *THINK,* no. 1, 1998.

60   "we can say to customers...," "Lou Gerstner's First 30 Days," *Fortune,* May 31, 1993.

Chapter 6

62   "He just went right...," Sam Albert, interview, May 8, 1998.

62   "Being the six-hundred-pound gorilla...," Steve Milunovitch, interview, July 25, 1998.

63   "IBM stock no longer provides...," *The New York Times,* April 27, 1993.

63   "There are two or three $10 billion...," *The Washington Post,* July 3, 1993.

64   "Competitors are coming after my...," "Lou Gerstner's First 30 Days," *Fortune,* May 31, 1993.

66   "IBM had taken...," Jim Cannavino, interview, August 19, 1998.

68   "I have reached the firm conclusion...," Lou Gerstner, memo to employees, September 13, 1993.

Chapter 7

73   "Our first task was to attack...," Lou Gerstner, speech to shareholders, Dallas, Texas, April 29, 1997.

74   "a blowout quarter, really on track...," *The New York Times,* April 22, 1994.

74   "nothing to write home about...," Ibid.

74   "Barring the unforeseen...," Lou Gerstner, speech to shareholders, Toronto, Canada, April 25, 1994.

75   "So far, the Gerstner game plan...," *The New York Times,* June 26, 1994.

75   "Look, this is a three-step...," Ibid.

76   "I think it's fair to say...," Lou Gerstner, letter to shareholders, Annual Report, 1994.

Chapter 8

81   "what wasn't clear was what...," Lou Gerstner, speech to shareholders, Dallas, Texas, April 29, 1997.

81   "just a theory...," *The New York Times,* June 26, 1994.

81   "When I agreed to take this job...," "Blue Is the Color," *The Economist,* June 6, 1998.

82   "I don't think getting the economics...," "Lou Gerstner's First 30 Days," *Fortune,* May 31, 1993.

82   "You and I want to make IBM...," Lou Gerstner, memo to employees, July 27, 1993.

83   "In summary, the changes outlined...," Lou Gerstner, memo to employees, September 13, 1993.

83   "Gerstner put an end to the breakup...," George D. Elling and Lous R. Miscioscia, Lehman Brothers report, May 8, 1997.

83   "Perhaps the key, and yet...," Robert Djurdjevic, newsletter, Annex Research, August 22, 1996.

84   "I have followed the company...," J. Gerald Simmons, letter to editor, *Fortune*, January 24, 1994.

84   "When I arrived in the spring...," Lou Gerstner, quoted in "It's Time to Execute," *Software*, July 1997.

85   "The decision meant we had a lot...,"

86   Ibid. "When I joined IBM..." (anonymous source).

Chapter 9

90   "We were a billion dollar...," Jim Cannavino, interview, August 19, 1998.

90   "Our culture was very congenial...," Sam Palmisano, quoted in "He's Smart, He's Not Nice. He's Saving Big Blue...," *Fortune*, April 14, 1997.

91   John Kao, Lou Gerstner, case no. 485–176. Boston: Harvard Business School, 1985, p. 9. Copyright © 1985 by the President and Fellows of Harvard College; all rights reserved.

92   "You look at the creative...," Ibid., p. 4.

92   "In one of the divisions...," Ibid., p. 3.

93   "In our strategic planning...," Ibid., p. 2.

93   "If the CEO isn't living...," Ibid., p. 3.

93   "It finally became clear...," Ibid., p. 2.

94   "I'm almost not trying to understand...," "Lou Gerstner's First 30 Days," *Fortune*, May 31, 1993.

94   "I do not think...," "Road Map for the Revolution," *Think Twice*, December 1993.

94   "I haven't reached a conclusion...," "Lou Gerstner's First 30 Days," *Fortune*, May 31, 1993.

95   "We have been...," "A Rough Year for Superstar CEOs," *Business Week*, April 4, 1994.

Chapter 10

97   "I'm talking about the *old* old...," "Poised for Leadership," *THINK*, no. 1, 1998.

98   "[The problem] was more the attitudes...," "We Won't Stop...Until We Find Our Way Back," *Business Week*, May 1, 1995.

98   "We have a geographic reach...," Ibid.

99   "It has to be—if you want...," "Poised for Leadership," *THINK*, no. 1, 1998.

101   "You can't have politicians...," "Can this Man Save IBM?" *Fortune*, April 19, 1993.

102   "It was a little spooky for...," "He's Smart, He's Not Nice. He's Saving Big Blue...," *Fortune*, April 14, 1997.

103 "Gerstner's Guerrillas...," "Road Map for the Revolution," *Think Twice,* December, 1993.
103 "Committed to the long-term success...," Ibid.
106 "IBM's new headquarters at Armonk...," "Blue Is the Color," *The Economist,* June 6, 1998.

Chapter 11

110 Kao, Lou Gerstner, Harvard Business School case 485–176, p. 4.
110 "We must have a clear sense...," "Road Map for the Revolution," *Think Twice,* December, 1993.
111 "I've got to immerse myself...," "I'm Going to Let the Problems Come to Me," *Business Week,* April 12, 1993.
111 "I have no idea how best to...," Ibid.
111 "I haven't spent any time...," "Lou Gerstner's First 30 Days," *Fortune,* May 31, 1993.
111 "Besides, I really do want to disabuse...," "I'm Going to Let the Problems Come to Me," *Business Week,* April 12, 1993.
112 "I do not want to undertake...," "At IBM, More of the Same—Only Better?" *Business Week,* July 26, 1993.
112 "Oh, no, no, no...," "Interview with Lou Gerstner," *U.S. News & World Report,* December 19, 1997.
113 "There's been a lot of speculation...," "A Work in Progress."
113 "eight principles...," "Road Map for the Revolution," *Think Twice,* December, 1993.
114 "You must understand I am...," *The Washington Post,* March 25, 1994.
115 "He's thinking like a businessman...," "Gerstner's 1st Year at IBM: Observers Rate Him a B-Plus," *Gannett News Service,* March 21, 1994.
116 "Our results on expense reduction...," "Is He Too Cautious to Save IBM?" *Fortune,* October 3, 1994.

Chapter 12

118 "Execution is not going to meetings...," *THINK,* 1996.
119 "Our customers know...," "Road Map for the Revolution," *Think Twice,* December, 1993.
119 "In any transformation...," "It's Time to Execute," *Software,* July 1997.
120 "Sam, if we do that and miss...," "He's Smart, He's Not Nice. He's Saving Big Blue...," *Fortune,* April 14, 1997.
121 "Ten months is not a...," Ibid.
121 "I would argue that...," *USA Today,* December 4, 1996.
121 "I make calls...," Frank Dzubeck, interview, May 18, 1998.
121 "I don't understand...," "He's Smart, He's Not Nice. He's Saving Big Blue...," *Fortune,* April 14, 1997.
121 "Three years ago, when I...," Lou Gerstner, speech to shareholders, Atlanta, Georgia, April 30, 1996.
122 "The single biggest challenge at IBM...," Lou Gerstner, interview, CNBC, October 22, 1998.

Chapter 13

125 Kao, Lou Gerstner, Harvard Business School case 485–176, pp. 4–5.
126 "I am trying to avoid...," Ibid.
126 "In the past...," Jim Cannavino, interview, August 19, 1998.
127 "I don't want a feel-good...," Peter Thonis, interview, June 3, 1998.
127 "There's no question that...," "He's Smart, He's Not Nice. He's Saving Big Blue...," *Fortune,* April 14, 1997.
127 "I'm tough-minded...," Ibid.
128 "Having done this three times...," Ibid.
129 "My surveys indicate that...," "Poised for Leadership," *THINK,* no. 1, 1998.
129 "I don't view the role...," "Can This Man Save IBM?" *Fortune,* April 19, 1993.

Chapter 14

132 Kao, Lou Gerstner, Harvard Business School case 485–176, p. 1.
133 "Each business had to be...," Jim Cannavino, interview, August 19, 1998.
134 "When I joined IBM...," Lou Gerstner, speech, Working Mothers 10th Anniversary Reception, New York City, September 11, 1995.
136 "We have clear accountability...," "The Man Who's Rebooting IBM's PC Business," *Business Week,* July 24, 1995.
137 "What's really important is the...," "Poised for Leadership," *THINK,* no. 1, 1998.

Chapter 15

139 "Leadership isn't a popularity...," "Dear Colleague," *THINK,* no. 1, 1997.
140 "Lou wants to be in the very...," "He's Smart, He's Not Nice. He's Saving Big Blue...," *Fortune,* April 14, 1997.
142 "Before Lou came along...," Peter Thonis, interview, June 3, 1998.
142 "When it came to the prior...," Ibid.
142 "You only had...," Ibid.
143 "He liked the notion of getting...," Ibid.

Chapter 16

152 "I've spent ten years of my life...," "Gerstner at the Gates," *Business Week,* April 21, 1997.

Chapter 17

157 "a tightly-coiled package...," "Is He Too Cautious to Save IBM?" *Fortune,* October 3, 1994.
157 "A fleshy, impeccably groomed...," Ibid.
158 "You're not getting inside...," "He's Smart, He's Not Nice. He's Saving Big Blue...," *Fortune,* April 14, 1997.
159 "I had won almost...," Ibid.
161 "A workaholic is someone who wants...," "Current Biography," profile of Lou Gerstner, June 1991.

161　"I don't want to get too ...," *USA Today,* December 4, 1996.
162　"Once I have a feeling ...," Ibid.
162　"The idea of going ...," Ibid.

Chapter 18

166　"I had access to all executives ...," John D. Loewenberg, quoted in "The Few, the True, the Blue," *Business Week,* May 30, 1994.
168　"I was basically the first ...," "Interview with Lou Gerstner," *U.S. News & World Report,* December 19, 1997.
168　"I want to take ...," "How IBM Became a Growth Company Again," *Business Week,* December 9, 1996.
169　"My view is that the company ...," Louis Gerstner, quoted in "Déjà Blue," *Industry Week,* November 17, 1997.
169　"we need to spend a whole ...," "Lou Gerstner's First 30 Days," *Fortune,* May 31, 1993.
170　Kao, Lou Gerstner, Harvard Business School case 485–176, p. 2.
170　"We don't rely on our ...," "Road Map for the Revolution," *Think Twice,* December, 1993.
170　Kao, Lou Gerstner, Harvard Business School case 485–176, p. 3.
172　"I talk to CEOs every week ...," "déjà Blue," *Industry Week,* November 17, 1997.
172　"I won't listen ...," George Colony, interview, August 19 1998.
172　"when I arrived here ...," *Dallas Morning News,* August 30, 1996.
172　"We have focused this company ...," Lou Gerstner, interview, CBNC, October 22, 1998.

Chapter 19

177　"I don't know what ...," "Is He Too Cautious to Save IBM?" *Fortune,* October 10, 1994.
178　"The kind of clients we have ...," *The Independent,* September 13, 1994.
179　"But it will not happen ...," Lou Gerstner, letter to shareholders, Annual Report, 1994.
180　"It gives him tremendous power ...," George Colony, interview, August 19, 1998.
180　"His thoughts revolved around ...," Jim Cannavino, interview, August 19, 1998.
181　"I came here with a view ...," "How IBM Became a Growth Company Again," *Business Week,* December 9, 1996.
182　"we focus on what I believe ...," Lou Gerstner, speech to Gartner Symposium, Orlando, Florida, October 9, 1996.
184　"[There are] tens of thousands ...," "Interview with Lou Gerstner," *U.S. News & World Report,* December 19, 1997.

Chapter 20

189　"IBM and you all deserve ...," "Return of the Dinosaurs," *Business Week,* August 1, 1994.
190　"When I arrived at IBM ...," Lou Gerstner, conference call to customers, March 4, 1996.

190   "People are talking about...," *Gannett,* June 9, 1998.
191   "We had a reputation of being...," "IBM Is Back," *Fortune,* November 11, 1996.
191   "We have a reliable supply...," Ibid.
191   "Our traditional businesses...," Lou Gerstner, speech to shareholders, Dallas, Texas, April 29, 1997.
192   "The problem is: Gerstner is not...," Jon Oltsik, interview, August 19, 1998.
193   "It requires a whole change...," "IBM's Road Map," *Information Week,* February 9, 1998.
193   "E-business moves the agenda...," Ibid.
194   "When the time comes where...," Ibid.

Chapter 21

197   Kao, Lou Gerstner, Harvard Business School case 485–176, p. 1.
198   "We must move with less...," "Road Map for the Revolution," *Think Twice,* December, 1993.
198   "Entrepreneurial companies are oriented...," "Ibid.
198   Kao, Lou Gerstner, Harvard Business School case 485–176, p. 5.
199   "If I left American Express tomorrow...," Ibid., p. 8.
201   "I remember going to early...," "Ibid., p. 2.
201   "The biggest threat to...," Ibid., p. 9
202   "We act in a way that is...," "Road Map for the Revolution," *Think Twice,* December, 1993.
202   "We only have to tell...," Ibid.
203   "Productivity simply means returning...," Ibid.
203   "We want—and we will demand...," Ibid.
203   Kao, Lou Gerstner, Harvard Business School case 485–176, p. 1.
203   "too often our personal...," "Road Map for the Revolution," *Think Twice,* December, 1993.

Chapter 22

206   "Gerstner has shown that...," "Companies: Throughout a Charmed Corporate Career...," *Time,* August 9, 1993.
207   "Lou's charter is...," "At IBM, the Great Shrink-Down May Be Over," *Business Week,* September 25, 1995.
208   "I told them that soon...," *USA Today,* December 4, 1996.
210   "The predominant focus of...," "Big Blue Is Betting on Big Iron Again," *Fortune,* April 29, 1996.
211   "If you go back and read...," *The Washington Post,* December 15, 1996.

Chapter 23

213   "There is no place to hide...," "He's Smart, He's Not Nice. He's Saving Big Blue...," *Fortune,* April 14, 1997.
214   "When I got here...," Ibid.
218   "In 1993 many of...," George D. Elling and Louis R. Miscioscia, Lehman Brothers report, May 8, 1997.

218   "Gerstner is succeeding in his...," Laua Conigliaro, Goldman, Sachs report, May 13, 1997, p. 2.
219   "Even IBM's once stuffy...," "50 Top Leaders of the Information Age," *Vanity Fair,* October 1997.
220   "I've been here four years working seven days a week...," "On Arrogance, When to Quit, and Chitchat," *Fortune,* April 14, 1997.
220   "First, the job...," Lou Gerstner, letter to shareholders, IBM Annual Report, 1995.

Chapter 24

227   "Services grew to become...," Lou Gerstner, letter to shareholders, Annual Report, 1995.
228   "Services now are our second...," Lou Gerstner, conference call to customers, March 4, 1996.
229   "the fastest-growing part...," Lou Gerstner, speech to shareholders, Dallas, Texas, April 29, 1997.
229   "If previously, IBM had been mostly a collection...," Laura Conigliaro, Goldman, Sachs report, May 13, 1997, p. 5.
230   "The main driver of solutions is...," Steve Milunovich, interview, July 25, 1998.
231   "There are a lot of people...," *The Wall Street Journal,* May 14, 1998.

Chapter 25

236   "Solutions require more than...," Lou Gerstner, letter to shareholders, Annual Report, 1996.
237   "The No. 1 thing that will...," *USA Today,* December 4, 1996.
239   "Our customers are not...," July 1997, "It's Time to Execute," *Software,* July 1997.
239   "Perhaps one of Lou...," Laura Conigliaro, Goldman, Sachs report, May 13, 1997, p. 1.
239   "One of the key things...," Andrew Neff, interview, May 5, 1998.

Chapter 26

241   "Almost immediately there was...," Lou Gerstner, letter to shareholders, Annual Report, 1995.
242   "There is no question...," "Lou Gerstner on Catching the Third Wave," *Business Week,* October 30, 1995.
244   "a sense of elation," "Blue Is the Color," *The Economist,* June 6, 1998.
245   "I truly believe it will reshape...," Lou Gerstner, speech to shareholders, Atlanta, Georgia, April 30, 1996.
246   "It changes where computing...," Lou Gerstner, letter to shareholders, Annual Report, 1995.
247   "The network increasingly...," Lou Gerstner, speech to stockholders, Atlanta, Georgia, April 30, 1996.

248 "The networked systems world...," Laura Conigliaro, Goldman, Sachs report, May 13, 1997, p. 2.

248 "We know something about leadership...," "Dear Colleague," letter from Lou Gerstner, 1997, *THINK,* no. 1, 1997.

Chapter 27

251 "The minute you make the translation...," interview with Lou Gerstner, *US News & World Report,* December 19, 1997.

252 "I think we are ahead of everybody...," Ibid.

253 "The company is so big...," Jon Oltsik, Carol D. Howe, Waverly Deutsch, and Carrie Endries, "IBM's Internet Opportunity," Forrester Research, July 1998.

254 "To bring our customers to this...," Lou Gerstner, interview, CNBC, October 22, 1998.

Chapter 28

259 "It's going to be fun...," "Poised for Leadership," *THINK,* no. 1, 1998.

261 "For five years...," "IBM: Back to Double-Digit Growth?" *Business Week,* June 1, 1998.

261 "Today, thanks to an...," "Blue Is the Color," *The Economist,* June 6, 1998.

265 "Our business is strong across...," Lou Gerstner, interview, CNBC, October 22, 1998.

Chapter 29

271 "Our industry is about to crack...," Lou Gerstner, letter to shareholders, Annual Report, 1996.

271 "universal connectivity, driven primarily...," Lou Gerstner, speech to shareholders, Atlanta, Georgia, April 30, 1996.

272 "We believe very strongly...," Lou Gerstner, letter to shareholders, Annual Report, 1997.

272 "Today there are about 50 million people...," Lou Gerstner, speech to shareholders, Dallas, Texas, April 29, 1997.

273 "We're watching the emergence...," Lou Gerstner, speech to CeBIT '98, Hanover, Germany, March 18, 1998.

274 "I have never seen a better growth...," "IBM: Back to Double-Digit Growth?" *Business Week,* June 1, 1998.

275 "My belief is that all large...," Lou Gerstner, interview, CNBC, October 22, 1998.

Epilogue

284 "What makes 1999 different...," Lou Gerstner, letter to shareholders, Annual Report, 1998.

284 "uncool," Ibid.

284 "this position...," Ibid.

285 "More and more, the winning edge...," Ibid.

285 "Given what we have accomplished...," Ibid

Index